# THE ED GEIN CHRONICLES

By

Scott E. Bowser

# Copyright © 2023 Scott Bowser

All rights reserved. This book or any portion thereof may not be reproduced or used in any manner whatsoever without express written permission of the publisher except for the use of brief quotations in a book review.

**ISBN 979-8-218-32811-5**

A special thank you to Lori and DeeDee from the Waushara County Historical Society and Museum for their help in creating this book.

# INDEX

**PREFACE** ............................................................................................. 5

**CHAPTER 1: The Gein Family** ......................................................... 6

    George Phillip Gein ........................................................................ 8

    Augusta Gein ................................................................................. 10

    Henry Gein ..................................................................................... 12

    Ed Gein .......................................................................................... 14

**CHAPTER 2: Bodies Dug Up** ............................................................ 24

    Grace Beggs .................................................................................. 26

    Elsie Sparks .................................................................................. 28

    Karen Marie Bergstrom: ................................................................ 30

    Mabel Cornelia Everson: ............................................................... 32

    Eleanor M. Adams ........................................................................ 34

    Ursula J. Calanan ......................................................................... 36

    Lola E. Foster ............................................................................... 38

    Harriet A. Sherman ....................................................................... 40

    Alzaida B. Abbott ......................................................................... 42

**CHAPTER 3: Murdered Victims** ....................................................... 43

    Mary Hogan ................................................................................... 45

    Bernice C. Worden ........................................................................ 47

**CHAPTER 4: Ed Gein In The News** ................................................. 48

**CHAPTER 5: Ed Gein Timeline** ....................................................... 236

**Final Thoughts** ................................................................................. 242

# PREFACE

The enduring tale of Ed Gein has left an indelible mark on popular culture, evident in its frequent appearances in movies, music, and literature. Gein's grim narrative found its way onto the silver screen through adaptations like "Deranged" (1974), "In the Light of the Moon" (2000, later retitled "Ed Gein" for the U.S. market), and "Ed Gein: The Butcher of Plainfield" (2007). His influence is particularly pronounced in the creation of fictional characters, with iconic serial killers such as Norman Bates (Psycho), Leatherface (The Texas Chainsaw Massacre), and Buffalo Bill (The Silence of the Lambs) drawing inspiration from Gein.

For many years, Ed Gein loomed as a boogeyman in the American psyche. Even today, his crimes echo as a chilling reminder of the nightmarish consequences that can arise from a distorted childhood.

During countless hours of interrogation, Ed Gein exhibited no signs of remorse or emotion. His discussions about the murders and grave-robbing escapades were delivered with unsettling matter-of-factness, occasionally even laced with a disturbing cheerfulness. It became evident that he possessed no grasp of the enormity of his crimes.

# CHAPTER 1

## The Gein Family

# George Gein

## August 4th, 1873 – April 1st, 1940

**George Gein Dies** 1946

George Gein, 66, was born Aug. 4, 1873, and passed away April 1, 1940.

His mother and father and little sister preceded him in death. They were gone to town and he was staying at home because of the high water, as it was raising in the Mississippi river. The father, mother and little sister never returned, leaving him an orphan boy. This flood occurred in Vernon county, Wiconsin, years ago.

On December 14, 1899, Mr. Gein was united in marriage to Augusta Wilemina Lehrke.

He lived in La Crosse until 1914, then going to Plainfield. He had lived here since.

He was a member of the Immanuel Lutheran church at La Crosse.

He is survived by his wife, and two sons, Henry and Edward.

Funeral services were held at the Goult funeral home Thursday afternoon, with the Rev. Wendell Bennetts, pastor of the Methodist church, officiating. Interment was made in the Plainfield cemetery.

# George Phillip Gein

George Gein, born on August 4th, 1873, in Bergen, Wisconsin, played a pivotal role in the life of Ed Gein, shaping his family's narrative. Originally known as George Gee, his early years were marked by tragedy when his parents and sister succumbed to a devastating flooding accident, leaving him an orphan. Seeking solace, he found refuge with his uncle Leonhardt from his maternal side, an event that would influence his character in years to come.

In a symbolic move, George later adopted the surname "Gein," perhaps signifying a break from his past and the beginning of a new chapter. His life took a significant turn when he crossed paths with Augusta Wilhelmine Lehrke. Their union on December 4th, 1899, at the Chaseburg Vernon County Lutheran Church, marked the establishment of a new family.

Setting up their residence at 1931 Wood Street in La Crosse, Wisconsin, George and Augusta embarked on the journey of parenthood. Their first child, Henry, arrived on January 17th, 1902, prompting a move to 612 Gould Street in La Crosse.

However, George's life was not without its struggles. Employed as a Tanner at the Davis, Medary, and Platz Tannery in La Crosse, he battled with alcoholism. His excessive drinking became a source of turmoil within the family, leading to both verbal and physical abuse directed at Augusta and their sons.

As the years passed, George's health deteriorated, with his dependence on alcohol contributing to his demise on April 1st, 1940. His story is not just a backdrop to Ed Gein's infamous legacy but a testament to the complex interplay of personal struggles, family dynamics, and the enduring impact of early-life trauma.

# Augusta Gein

## July 21, 1878 – December 29th, 1945

**OBITUARY**

**AUGUSTA GEIN 1945**

Augusta Willamina Lehrke was born on July 21, 1878, at a home on 3d street in La Crosse, Wis. and was a daughter of Fred and Amalgo Lehrke.

The Lehrkes, with Augusta and an older brother, moved to a farm near Chaseburg, Wis., and Augusta lived at home until graduating from school, then worked at Chaseburg and LaCrosse, Wis., until the sickness of her mother called her home as her older sister was married and Augusta was the oldest girl left in the family. Her older brother was working out West at the time. Augusta cared for her mother for about 3 years before she passed away, Feb. 1, 1897, at the age of 50 years, 7 months and 4 days. Augusta cared for her father, brother and sisters, until she met and married George D. Gein and with her husband, moved to La Crosse, where Henry and Edward were born. Augusta was called home by the sickness of her father, who died in 1903.

From LaCrosse the Geins moved to Juneau, Wis., staying on a farm for a year. They came to the town of Plainfield thirty years ago. George Gein passed away April 1, 1940, and three years later Augusta suffered a stroke on the left side of her body, from which she never fully recovered. May 16, 1944, Henry Gein passed away, leaving his mother and brother alone. On Dec. 22, 1945, Augusta suffered a light stroke on the right side of her face. She appeared to be recovering nicely at her home, but passed away at the Wild Rose hospital Dec. 29th at the age of 67 years, 5 months and 8 days. She leaves to mourn her death, her son Edward, and three brothers and 3 sisters. An older brother and an older sister preceded her in death.

# Augusta Gein

Augusta Wilhelmine Lehrke, born on July 21st, 1878, in La Crosse, Wisconsin, emerged as a central figure in the Gein family saga. Raised on a farm near Chaseburg, Wisconsin, she developed her musical skills, mastering the accordion in her leisure moments. Augusta, who hailed from German parents, was bilingual, and proficient in both German and English. Her upbringing was firmly rooted in the tenets of a robust Lutheran household.

The trajectory of Augusta's life took a significant turn when she married George Gein on December 4th, 1899. Their union marked the beginning of a family that would be marked by both triumphs and tragedies. The arrival of their first son, Henry, on January 17th, 1902, was followed by the birth of Edward on August 27th, 1906.

In 1909, the couple acquired the former Schultz Grocery store, transforming it into A. Gein Mercantile, situated at 914 Caledonia Street in La Crosse, Wisconsin. Notably, Augusta maintained ownership of the store due to George's struggles with alcohol and financial irresponsibility.

A fervent Lutheran, Augusta held strong convictions about the perceived immorality of the world. She fervently preached against alcohol consumption and propagated the belief that all women, except herself, were inherently sinful, portraying them as instruments of the devil. Augusta's daily routine included reading graphic verses from the Old Testament to her sons, and delving into themes of death, murder, and divine retribution.

The family faced a turning point in late 1944 when Augusta suffered a debilitating stroke triggered by the death of her son Henry. Ed, now tasked with caring for his ailing mother, took on new responsibilities. Augusta's health further deteriorated, and on December 29th, 1945, she succumbed to complications from a subsequent stroke, passing away at the Wild Rose Hospital in Wild Rose, Wisconsin.

Augusta's life, filled with deeply rooted convictions and the formidable challenges she confronted, provides a poignant backdrop to the complex narrative of the Gein family.

# Henry Gein

## January 17th, 1902 – May 16th, 1944

## Rites Today For Man Who Died in Roche-a-Cri Fire

Plainfield, Wis.—Funeral services were held here this afternoon for Henry Gein, 42, town of Plainfield farmer who died of a heart attack while trying to protect his farm from the ravages of a grass and brush fire.

Mr. Gein, who lived on a farm in the Roche-a-Cri community with his brother Edward and with their mother, Mrs. George Gein, was burning over their marsh Tuesday when the fire escaped control and required the emergency help of a crew of voluntary fire fighters.

At day's end, with the fire under control, the men returned to their homes when it was discovered that Henry Gein had not come in with the others.

A searching party, with lanterns and flashlights, searched the burned over area and in the evening, several hours after the search began, found the dead body of Mr. Gein, lying face down. Apparently the man had been dead for some time when he was found, and it appeared that death was result of a heart attack, since he had not been burned or otherwise injured.

The services this afternoon will be at Goult funeral parlors in Plainfield, the Rev. Wisner, new Baptist minister at Plainfield, officiating. Burial will be in Plainfield cemetery.

Mr. Gein is survived by his mother and brother. He had lived all his life in the Plainfield community and was unmarried.

# Henry Gein

Henry Gein, born on January 17th, 1902, in La Crosse, Wisconsin, played a significant role as the elder brother to Edward Gein.

The Gein brothers, Henry and Ed, faced a challenging upbringing under their mother Augusta, who, despite their efforts, was seldom pleased with them. Augusta's abusive behavior and belief in their inevitable failure, much like their father George, created a strained environment. Throughout their teens and early adulthood, the brothers maintained a solitary existence on their farmstead, finding solace only in each other's company.

After the death of their father in 1940, Henry and Ed took on odd jobs to support the family farm and their mother. During this period, Henry purchased a 40-acre plot of land across from the Gein farm, displaying his commitment to their shared responsibilities. Ed admired Henry, viewing him as a hardworking man with a strong character. However, a shift occurred in Henry's perspective after their father's death. He rejected Augusta's worldview and initiated a relationship with a widowed woman who had a child, causing tension with Augusta.

Concerned about Ed's unhealthy attachment to their mother, Henry openly criticized Augusta on multiple occasions, a departure that surprised Ed.

Tragedy struck on May 16th, 1944, as both brothers battled a brush fire on Henry's land. During the efforts, Ed lost sight of Henry, and upon extinguishing the fire, Ed reported his brother missing to the police. In a perplexing turn of events, Ed led the search party directly to Henry's lifeless body, lying untouched by the fire, with bruises on his head. Despite suspicions of foul play, authorities dismissed the possibility, listing asphyxiation as the cause of death. Some investigators speculated about Ed's involvement, but no charges were filed.

At 38 years old, Ed found himself alone with his mother. He inherited Henry's 40-acre land, marking a significant shift in the dynamics of the Gein family.

# Ed Gein

## August 26th, 1906 – July 26th, 1984

## Obituaries

### Gein burial

Private burial for Ed Gein, 77, a former Plainfield area resident, took place in the Plainfield Village Cemetery. No services were held. Gasperic Funeral Home, Plainfield, handled arrangements.

Mr. Gein died Thursday morning at Mendota Mental Institute, Madison, of respiratory failure, according to institute officials.

He was born Aug. 26, 1906, in La Crosse, son of the late George and Augusta Gein. He was a farmer. He had been in state mental institutions since his arrest in 1957 for killing a woman.

There are no survivors.

### Wool price set

The support price for 1984 marketings of wool is $1.65 per pound for

# Ed Gein

Edward Theodore Gein, born on August 27th, 1906, at 11:00 pm in the Gein household at 912 Gould Street in La Crosse, Wisconsin, came into the world under the care of midwife Kathryn A. Kemp at the age of 24.

In 1913, at the tender age of seven, Ed and his family relocated to a cattle farm in Camp Douglas, Wisconsin. A year later, at eight, Augusta, Ed's mother, decided to move the family once again, this time to Plainfield, Wisconsin. Augusta's purchase of a 195-acre farm at N5691 Second Avenue marked a symbolic departure from the perceived immorality of the city and its inhabitants.

Ed and his brother Henry attended Roche-A-Cri Grade School, a tiny one-room building with only 12 students. Ed, often engaged in farm chores, struggled with an effeminate demeanor that made him a target for bullies. His odd mannerisms, like random laughter, and his mother Augusta's discouragement of friendships exacerbated his social challenges. Despite this, Ed excelled academically, particularly in reading. He also developed musical talents, playing the violin and mouth organ. However, at the age of 14, Ed dropped out of school after completing eighth grade.

The year 1940 marked the death of Ed's father, George, at the age of 66, succumbing to a heart attack and pneumonic fluid in his lungs. Ed was 34 years old, and Henry, his brother, was 39 at the time.

In 1942, Ed faced the possibility of leaving the farm for the first time when he was eligible for the draft. However, a growth over his left eye led to his rejection of military service due to impaired vision.

May 16th, 1944, brought tragedy as Ed's brother Henry passed away while both were fighting a brush fire on Henry's land. Although suspicions arose regarding Ed's involvement, no concrete evidence was found. With Henry gone, Ed found himself alone with his mother Augusta.

Late in 1944, Augusta suffered a debilitating stroke triggered by Henry's death, and Ed took on the responsibility of caring for her. On December 29th, 1945, Augusta suffered another stroke and passed away in a hospital in Wild Rose, Wisconsin. Now truly alone after losing his best friend,

Ed remained on the farm, sustaining himself through odd jobs. He boarded up rooms that once belonged to his mother, including the entire upstairs, the downstairs parlor, and the living room, leaving them untouched.

At 39 years old, Ed Gein resides in a small room adjacent to the kitchen, his isolation is intensified by a morbid fascination with death cult magazines, adventure stories, and wartime publications focusing on Nazi crimes. A particular article in Life magazine catches his attention, detailing the horrific actions of Ilse Koch, a Nazi who committed atrocities at Buchenwald Concentration Camp, including creating gruesome items from the skin of prisoners.

In February 1947, eighteen months after Augusta's death, Ed, driven by intense loneliness and peculiar visions, entertains the idea that he can raise the dead through his will. Admitting to attempting to dig up his deceased mother, he finds himself thwarted by her burial in a cement vault.

Seeking morbid solace, Ed starts scanning the obituaries in the local newspaper, The Plainfield Sun, searching for deceased women who remind him of his mother. At 41 years old, around February 4th or 5th, he visited Spirit Land Cemetery. Armed with a piece of re-rod, he tests the caskets of the deceased, discerning between wood and fiberglass. Ed can only access caskets made from wood, prompting him to unearth the body of Grace Beggs and transport it to his home.

On Wednesday, March 29th, 1950, Ed claims his first victim from Plainfield Cemetery, Elsie Sparks. Concurrently, Ed engages in thresher work for Elmo Ueeck, supplementing his income by leasing his land for $10.00 a year, although he feels exploited by those who fail to compensate him adequately.

During this unsettling period, Ed babysits for Lester and Irene Hill's son, Billy, who develops an unexpected friendship despite Lester having bullied Ed in school. The Hill family's residence at N6520 3rd Street in Plainfield becomes a focal point. Notably, on February 6th, 1951, Marie Bergstrom became Ed's third victim, the second from the Plainfield Cemetery.

On Sunday, April 15, 1951, the passing of Mabel Everson at 6:30 pm became a macabre milestone for Ed Gein. At 39 years old, residing in a small room next to the kitchen, Ed's obsession with death cult magazines and wartime stories had taken a dark turn. Mabel Everson's death marked the fourth body that Ed removed from the Plainfield Cemetery. Acknowledging an unsettling guilt, Ed found himself compelled to return to the gravesite, and reburied some of Mabel's body parts just below the surface, a haunting testament to the disturbing path he was on.

Saturday, November 29, 1952, witnessed the passing of Ursula Jane Callanan, leading to yet another grim chapter in Ed's life. At 46 years old, Ed dug up Ursula, making her the sixth body he had disturbed from the tranquility of the Plainfield Cemetery.

In 1953, Ed ventured to Hancock Cemetery in Hancock, Wisconsin, and laid bare the remains of Lola Foster, marking the seventh body in his gruesome collection.

By 1954, Ed's notoriety extended to The Fox Head Bar in Babcock, Wisconsin. Mary Hogan, the bar's owner, a robust and foul-mouthed woman bearing a resemblance to Ed's mother, Augusta, became the unwitting subject of Ed's dark impulses.

On Wednesday, December 8, 1954, after the bar closed its doors, Ed returned to The Fox Head Bar, armed with a .32 caliber pistol. He shot Mary Hogan in the head, killing her instantly. Ed callously loaded Mary's lifeless body into the back of his 1938 Chevy pickup, transporting her remains to his farm. The subsequent investigation revealed a grotesque skin-face mask fashioned from Mary Hogan's face, while the rest of her remains remained unidentified.

The morning of November 15, 1957, dawned with the opening day of the gun deer season. Ed, now well-versed in his morbid rituals, arrived at Worden's Hardware Store located at 110 S. Main Street in Plainfield, Wisconsin. His seemingly routine request for antifreeze for his car would mark a tragic turn of events. Bernice Worden, the store's owner, filled up Ed's jar, unknowingly facilitating her own demise. While Ed inspected a .22 caliber rifle in the gun rack, he seized the opportunity, pulled a .22 caliber bullet from his jacket pocket, loaded it into the rifle, and shot Bernice Worden in the back of the head. At 51 years old, Bernice became the latest victim in Ed's gruesome narrative.

Ed's modus operandi remained consistent. He dragged Bernice's lifeless body to the rear of the store and onto the loading dock before placing her in the back of the Worden Hardware delivery pickup. Driving it to East Road, Ed parked the truck in the pine trees. In a chilling routine, Ed returned to the hardware store, drove his car out to East Road where Worden's truck was parked, loaded Bernice's remains into his trunk, and drove them back home. His disturbing indifference extended to passing by Lars Thompson, who had just shot a deer on Ed's property, without stopping to talk.

The dark saga of Ed Gein continued to unfold, revealing a mind plagued by isolation, morbid curiosity, and an unquenchable thirst for the macabre.

Meanwhile, in Plainfield, Frank Worden, concerned about his mother Bernice's absence, discovered the hardware store closed at an unusual hour. Suspecting something amiss, he entered the store to find a pool of blood on the floor. Alarmed, Frank contacted local Sheriff Arthur Schley immediately. Frank, a Plainfield Deputy Sheriff and Fire Warden, recalled Ed Gein's earlier visit to the store to buy antifreeze and immediately expressed his suspicion that Ed might be involved in his mother's disappearance.

Sheriff Arthur Schley, along with Captain Lloyd Schoephoester from the Green Lake Sheriff Department, headed to Ed Gein's farm to question him about Bernice Worden's disappearance. Their approach was cautious, circling to the back of the property, where they found an open door to the woodshed. Inside, a gruesome scene awaited them—Bernice Worden's decapitated body hung upside down, wrists bound by ropes, and ankles secured with a crossbar. Her torso was eerily dressed out like a deer, indicating a disturbing ritual. Her head, found in a burlap sack, featured nails hammered through each ear, ready to be hung as a trophy. Bernice had been shot with a .22-caliber rifle, and the mutilations occurred post-mortem.

Sheriff Schley promptly issued an all-points bulletin for the arrest of Ed Gein for the murder of Bernice Worden.

Ed Gein, oblivious to the discovery at his farm, was enjoying a pork chop dinner at the home of Lester and Irene Hill on N6520 3rd Street. The commotion in Plainfield reached their ears, prompting Ed and Bobby Hill to investigate. They decided to take a ride to Plainfield in Ed's maroon 1949 Ford sedan. However, as they were about to get into the car, a patrol car pulled in behind them. Around 7:30 pm, Ed was taken into custody by Sheriff Arden Spees and Deputy

Dan Chase, and transported to the Waushara County Jail in Wautoma, Wisconsin. Ed's car sat in Lester Hill's driveway for three days after his arrest, a silent witness to the horrors that would be uncovered

The Wisconsin State Crime Lab was called in to investigate Ed's farm. Searching the house, authorities found:

- Four noses
- Whole human bones and fragments
- Nine masks of human skin
- Bowls made from human skulls
- Ten female heads with tops sawed off
- Human skin covering several chairs and seats
- Mary Hogan's head in a paper bag
- Nine vulvas in a shoe box
- Skulls on his bedposts
- Organs in the refrigerator
- A pair of lips on a drawstring for a window shade
- A belt made from female nipples
- A lampshade made from the skin of a human face
- Found a quantity of formaldehyde and an embalming needle

Under questioning, Ed Gein revealed the horrifying extent of his nocturnal activities. Between 1947 and 1952, he admitted to making approximately 40 visits to three local graveyards, exhuming recently buried bodies while in a "daze-like" state. Strikingly, on about 30 of those occasions, he claimed to snap out of his trance at the cemetery, leaving the graves undisturbed and returning home empty-handed.

However, on other occasions, Ed confessed to digging up the graves of middle-aged women who resembled his deceased mother. Taking the bodies home, he engaged in gruesome practices such as tanning their skins to create macabre paraphernalia. In total, he admitted to robbing nine graves and willingly led investigators to their locations.

After his mother's death, Ed Gein descended further into madness, expressing a desire for a sex change. He began crafting what he termed a "woman suit," an unsettling project aimed at allowing him to pretend to be a female. This practice, described as an "insane transvestite ritual," involved donning the tanned skin of women he had exhumed. Ed insisted that he did not engage in sexual acts with the bodies, claiming, "They smelled too bad." Additionally, during the interrogation, he admitted to the shooting death of Mary Hogan, the tavern owner who had been missing since 1954.

Bobby Hill, a 16-year-old whose parents were friends with Ed Gein, provided chilling corroborating evidence. Hill reported being aware of shrunken heads in Ed's possession. Ed had allegedly described them as relics from the Philippines sent by a cousin who had served in World War II. However, upon police investigation, these heads were determined to be human facial skin carefully peeled from cadavers and repurposed as masks by Ed Gein.

The legal proceedings, however, were not without controversy. Waushara County Sheriff Art Schley faced allegations of physically assaulting Ed Gein during questioning. Gein claimed that Schley had banged his head and face into a brick wall at the jail, leading to the ruling of Gein's initial confession as inadmissible.

In a tragic turn of events, in December 1968, Sheriff Art Schley died of a heart attack at the age of 43, only a month after testifying at Ed Gein's trial. Friends and acquaintances stated that he was traumatized by the horror of Gein's crimes, and the fear of having to testify, especially regarding the alleged assault on Gein, contributed to his early demise. One friend remarked, "He was a victim of Ed Gein as if he had bothered him."

On November 22, 1957, Ed Gein was arraigned on one count of first-degree murder in Waushara County Court, appearing before Judge Boyd Clark. Despite his plea of not guilty by reason of insanity, he was found mentally incompetent for trial. Consequently, Ed Gein was committed to the Central State Hospital for The Criminally Insane, later known as the Dodge Correctional

Institution, a maximum-security facility in Waupun, Wisconsin. Eventually, he was transferred to the Mendota State Hospital in Madison, Wisconsin.

The psychologist and psychiatrist who evaluated Ed on November 23, 1957, concluded that he was suffering from schizophrenia, shedding light on the disturbed mental state that fueled his grotesque actions.

Further disturbing revelations unfolded on November 24, 1957, as the graves of Eleanor Adams and Marie Bergstrom were exhumed. To the horror of investigators, both caskets were found empty. Subsequently, on November 29, 1957, deputies discovered more bones in a 40-foot trench on Ed Gein's farm, unveiling the extent of his macabre activities.

By December 17, 1957, a packet from the Central State Hospital recommended that Ed Gein was insane and should be permanently committed to the institution. On January 6, 1958, a sanity hearing in Wisconsin Rapids declared Ed legally insane, as pronounced by Judge Herbert Bunde. Consequently, Ed was recommitted to the Central State Hospital.

As news of the horrors discovered on Ed Gein's farm spread, reporters from around the world descended upon the small town of Plainfield, Wisconsin. The town, once serene and unremarkable, now found itself thrust into the global spotlight. Ed Gein became an infamous celebrity, his deeds shocking and repulsing the public. Psychologists from various corners of the globe sought to unravel the psyche of this peculiar man, who had become one of the most notorious figures of the 1950s, a symbol of necrophilia, transvestism, and fetishism.

The residents of Plainfield grappled with the invasion of reporters disrupting their daily lives, bombarding them with questions about Ed. Despite their initial shock, many residents eventually became entangled in the mania surrounding Ed Gein, contributing whatever information they could. Plainfield, once an ordinary town, now echoes with the infamous association with Ed Gein. Residents who once knew him only as a slightly peculiar, quiet man with a quirky grin and a strange sense of humor were forced to confront the unsettling truth: the man they thought they knew was, in fact, a murderer who violated the graves of friends and relatives. The facade of normalcy shattered, leaving behind a community forever changed by the horrors of Ed Gein's actions.

After spending a 30-day period in the mental institution, Ed Gein was evaluated as mentally incompetent, rendering him no longer eligible to be tried for first-degree murder. The people of Plainfield expressed their frustration and anger at the court's decision that Ed would not face trial for the death of Bernice Worden. Despite the community's outcry, there was little they could do to influence the court's ruling. Ed was sentenced to the mental institution, and his farm, along with some of his belongings, went up for auction.

On March 20, 1958, at 2:30 am, Ed Gein's farm was mysteriously burned to the ground in what was suspected to be arson. Many eyes turned toward Fire Warden Frank Worden, raising suspicions in the community. When Ed learned of the incident, he seemingly shrugged it off, saying, "Just as well."

On March 30, 1958, the remains from the fire were auctioned off. Notably, Ed's 1949 Maroon Ford Sedan, the vehicle he used to transport the bodies of his victims, was sold for $760 to carnival sideshow operator Bunny Gibbons. The car later became a macabre attraction, charging spectators 25 cents to see it. Ed's blue 1938 Chevy pickup was sold for $215 to Chet Seales of Chet's Wrecker Service.

After spending a decade in the mental institution, the courts deemed Gein competent to stand trial. The proceedings began on Monday, January 22, 1968, to determine his guilt or innocence by reason of insanity for the murder of Bernice Worden. The actual trial commenced on Thursday, November 7, 1968. Seven witnesses, including lab technicians who performed Bernice Worden's autopsy, took the stand. Despite the strong evidence against Gein, one week later, the judge reached a verdict: guilty of first-degree murder. However, due to Gein's insanity at the time of the killing, he was later found not guilty by reason of insanity and acquitted. Subsequently, he was escorted back to the Central State Hospital for The Criminally Insane.

The families of Bernice Worden, Mary Hogan, and those whose graves were raided felt that justice had not been served. Despite their belief that Gein escaped the punishment he deserved, there was no recourse to reverse the court's decision.

Gein would spend the remainder of his life at the mental institution, where he surprisingly found contentment. He got along well with other patients, mostly keeping to himself. Ed enjoyed three square meals a day, having noticeably gained weight since his arrest. An avid reader, he engaged in regular conversations with staff psychologists, participated in occupational therapy like stone polishing and rug making, and even developed an interest in ham radios, using his earnings for inexpensive receivers.

Despite the horrific nature of his crimes, Ed Gein seemed to have found a sense of peace in the confines of the mental institution, living out his days in a manner that, in stark contrast to his past, appeared strangely ordinary.

Despite the horrors he had committed, Ed Gein proved to be an amiable and docile patient during his time at the hospital. Unlike many others, he never required tranquilizing medications to manage his behavior. Other than his disconcerting habit of staring fixedly at nurses and female staff, Ed displayed few outward signs of his mental illness.

On Thursday, June 27th, 1974, at the age of 68, Ed filed a petition with the Waushara County Clerk of Courts, claiming that he had fully recovered from his mental illness and was now competent. However, a judge, after reviewing Ed's petition, ordered a re-examination and ultimately rejected his plea. Ed was returned to the hospital.

In 1978, at 72 years old, Ed was transferred to the Mendota Mental Institute in Madison, Wisconsin. As the years passed, Ed faced the challenges of senility and battled cancer. On Thursday, July 26th, 1984, Ed Gein succumbed to respiratory failure in the geriatric ward at Mendota. At the time of his passing, he was 78 years old.

On Friday, July 27, 1984, at 4 pm, Ed Theodore Gein was laid to rest by Bennie and Betty Petrusky in a blue casket, resting between his mother and brother.

In a macabre turn of events, in 2000, Ed Gein's gravestone was stolen. It wasn't until June 2001 that the gravestone was recovered in Seattle, Washington. Strangely, the gravestone was never reinstated on Ed's grave; instead, it has been stored in the basement of one of the Plainfield Cemetery board members residing in Plover, Wisconsin.

The unsettling legacy of Ed Gein, a man whose actions left an indelible mark on the annals of criminal history, continues to intrigue and disturb to this day.

# CERTIFICATE OF BIRTH.

*To be returned within thirty days to the health officer of the city in which the birth occurs, and in towns and villages to the town or village clerk who will forward at the end of the month to the Register of Deeds of his county.*

1. Full name of child __Edward Gire__
2. Color (a) __white__   3. Sex __male__   4. Name of other issue living (born of same parents) __Harry__
5. Full name of father __George Gire__
6. Occupation of father __Laborer__   7. Full name of mother previous to marriage __Augusta Linker__
8. Hour, day of week, of month, and year of birth __Monday Aug. 27 — 11:30 PM 1906__
9. The place (b) town or township and county in which born __612 Gould St. N. La Crosse Wis__
10. Birthplace of father __America__
11. Birthplace of mother __?__
12. Any other important information __Not any__
    (Presentation.)

_____ (c) Physician, midwife or other person reporting.
Residence __929 M____ St.__

STATE OF WISCONSIN,
County of __La Crosse__ } ss.

I hereby certify, that the above is a true return of the said birth and of the other facts here recorded.

Dated at __La Crosse__, said county, this __16__ day of __Oct__, 1906.

__R. A. Major__
(c) Health Officer, Town or Village Clerk.

Residence __La Crosse Wis.__

NOTE.—(a) State the color so distinctly that the race also may be understood, as white, black, mulatto, Indian, mixed white and Indian, etc.  (b) If city, insert street and number.  (c) Strike out the words not representing the one signing the return. State any important facts in making the return—an illegitimate birth, or still birth should be so specified.

# CHAPTER 2

Bodies Dug Up

# Grace Beggs

## September 21ˢᵗ, 1877 – February 4ᵗʰ, 1947

### Sister of Local Man Dies; Rites Planned Friday

Plainfield—Mrs. Myron W. Beggs, 69, sister of John Taminga, 2230 Lincoln street, died suddenly at 4 o'clock Tuesday afternoon at her home in the town of Pine Grove, Portage county, following a heart attack.

Funeral services will be held at 1:30 Friday afternoon at the Goult Funeral home in Plainfield and at 2 o'clock at the Spiritland school house. Burial will be in the Spiritland cemetery.

She was born September 21, 1877, at Mount Morris, Ill., and in 1881, moved to Hancock where she lived until her marriage March 6, 1903.

Survivors besides her husband and brother, John, include five children, Mrs. Loran Lovejoy, Wild Rose; Bernard, Plainfield; Mrs. Earl Dittburner, Pine Grove; Herbert, Minocqua, and Earl, at home; three other brothers, Jake Taminga, Washington; George Taminga, Plum City, and Arthur Taminga, Hancock; three sisters, Mrs. Ed Ellerman, Star Lake; Mrs. Carl Clark, Della, Ia., and Mrs. Jennie Bishop, Hancock; 10 grandchildren, and one great grandchild.

# Grace Beggs

Grace Beggs was the first body Ed Gein dug up from the Spirit Land Cemetery in Plainfield, Wisconsin. Grace Beggs was born on September 21, 1877, and passed away from a heart attack on February 4th, 1947.

Grace lived at 2230 Lincoln Street in Pinegrove, Wisconsin, and was employed as a housekeeper. She was married to Myron Wyatt Beggs, and they had seven children: five boys and two girls.

Upon her death in 1947, she had 10 grandchildren and was survived by her husband Myron, who died in 1966. She was laid to rest at 2:00 pm on February 9th, 1947.

Elsie Sparks

**JUNE 10TH, 1894 – MARCH 29TH, 1950**

## Funeral on Sunday For Mrs. Bert Sparks

Funeral services will be held at 2:30 Sunday afternoon at the Baptist church in Plainfield for Mrs. Bert Sparks, 55, Route 1, Wisconsin Rapids, who died Thursday morning at Riverview hospital. The Rev. A. Hoskins is to officiate and burial will take place in the Plainfield cemetery. Mrs. Sparks had resided in the Plainfield community prior to moving to this area a few weeks ago.

# Elsie Sparks

Elsie Sparks was the second body Ed Gein dug up. Elsie was born on June 10th, 1894, and passed away on March 29th, 1950.

She was 55 years old at the time of her death. She was married to her husband Bert Sparks. Elsie was survived by her husband Bert who died in 1976. Not a lot is known about her life.

# Karen Marie Bergstrom

## MARCH 4th, 1866 – FEBRUARY 6th, 1951

BERGSTROM,
MRS. KAREN MARIE
1413 Villa St.

Age 84. Passed away Feb. 6 in St. Mary's Hospital. Mrs. Bergstrom was born in Denmark on March 4, 1866, came to the United States 65 years ago and had lived in Plainfield, Wis., before coming to Racine 16 years ago. She was a member of the Church of Atonement of Mygatts Corners and the Danish Sisterhood of Menominee, Michigan. Surviving are three daughters, Mrs. Francis Pfister of Racine, Mrs. Rueben Danielson of Franklin, Minn., and Mrs. Raymond Kelly of Elgin, Ill.; four sons, Leonard and Alfred of Racine, Ernest of Minneapolis and Frederick of Hawthorne, California; 23 grandchildren; 16 great-grandchildren. Funeral services will be held Friday, 10 a. m., in the Maresh Funeral Home, Rev. Jerome Miller officiating. Burial will be in Plainfield, Wis. Friends may call at the Maresh Funeral Home Thursday afternoon and evening.

## Karen Marie Bergstrom:

Marie Bergstrom was the third body Ed Gein dug up. Marie was born on March 4th, 1886, and passed away at the age of 84 on February 6th, 1971. Marie came here from Denmark and moved to Plainfield, where she met her husband, Nels. They later moved to Racine, Wisconsin. Marie and Nels had three daughters, who gave them 23 grandchildren and 16 great-grandchildren.

Marie was a member of the Church of Atonement of Mygatts Corners and the Danish Sisterhood of Menominee Falls, Michigan. She is buried in the Plainfield Cemetery with her husband, Nels, in Plainfield, Wisconsin.

# Mabel C Everson

## June 7th, 1882 – May 15th, 1951

## Mrs. Mabel Everson Dies at Plainfield

**Plainfield**—Mrs. Mabel Everson, 69, died at 6:30 Sunday evening at her home in Plainfield following an illness of heart trouble. She had resided in the area all her life.

Funeral arrangements have not been completed; however, the services will be held at the Assembly of God church in Plainfield with the Rev. Irvin Bowers officiating. Interment is to take place in the Plainfield cemetery.

Mrs. Everson was born in the town of Oasis, Waushara county, on June 7, 1882, the daughter of Mr. and Mrs. Charles Leavitt. She married Oscar Everson in the town of Deerfield on October 13, 1900. Her husband and one daughter preceded her in death.

Surviving are two daughters, Mrs. Charles Harrington, Plainfield, and Mrs. Norman Rehwinkel; two sisters, Mrs. Fred Spees, Wenatchee, Wash., and Mrs. Gertrude Hinc, Plainfield; two brothers, Ira Leavitt, Deerfield, and Bert Leavitt, Staten Island, N. Y., and seven grandchildren.

The body is at the Goult Funeral home.

# Mabel Cornelia Everson:

Mabel Everson was the fourth body that Ed Gein had dug up. Mabel was born on June 7th, 1882. She was married to her husband Oscar, and they had two daughters. They lived on a farm in Plainfield, Wisconsin. She did have seven grandchildren.

Mabel passed away from heart trouble at the age of 69 on April 15th, 1951. She and her husband Oscar are buried together in the Plainfield Cemetery.

# Eleanor M. Adams

## November 27th, 1898 – August 26th, 1951

### Mrs. Floyd Adams, Plainfield, Succumbs

**Plainfield** — Mrs. Floyd Adams, 51, Plainfield, died at 6:15 Sunday morning at the Wisconsin General hospital in Madison. She had been ill the past year.

Funeral services will be held at 2 o'clock Tuesday afternoon at the Goult Funeral home with Dr. Granville Calhoun officiating. Burial is to follow in the Plainfield cemetery.

Mrs. Adams, whose maiden name was Eleanor Rozell, was born at Plainfield on November 27, 1899, the daughter of Mr. and Mrs. Sam H. Rozell, and resided in the community all her life. Her marriage took place in Plainfield on November 19, 1919.

Surviving are her husband; one daughter, Mrs. Barbara Goodwin, and one son, George, both of Plainfield; two sisters, Mrs. Iva Rozell, Friendship, and Mrs. Ralph Wing, Plainfield, and two grandchildren. One son, Junior, died in 1940. Another child died in infancy.

Mrs. Adams was a member of the West Plainfield Homemakers' club and the Plainfield Grange.

# Eleanor M. Adams

Eleanor Adams was the fifth body that Ed Gein dug up. She was born on November 27th, 1899, and was married to her husband, Floyd. Eleanor and Floyd had one daughter and one son. She was a member of the West Plainfield Homemakers Club.

Eleanor passed away on August 26th, 1951, after a year-long illness. She was survived by her husband Floyd and both of her children. Eleanor was buried in the Plainfield Cemetery.

# Ursula J. Calanan (Woodward)

## January 14th, 1877 – November 29th, 1952

### Rites at Plainfield For Former Resident

PLAINFIELD- Funeral services were held Friday afternoon at the Goult Funeral Home for Mrs. Ursula Jane Callanan, 75, who died Nov. 29 at a Los Angeles, Calif., Hospital. The Rev. Asa Hoskins officiated, assisted by the Rev. Lee Clinton of Wisconsin Rapids. Burial was in the Plainfield Cemetery.

Services had been held at Lynwood, Calif., on Tuesday, prior to bringing the body to Plainfield by plane the following day.

Mrs. Callanan was born at Deerfield, Wis., on Jan. 14, 1877, the daughter of Mr. and Mrs. George T. Pierce, moving to Plainfield with her parents at the age of 10. She graduated from the Plainfield High School and taught school at Wild Rose. On Feb. 23, 1889, she married L. T. Woodward and there were six children. Her marriage to M. F. Callanan of Holcombe took place on March 24, 1916, and she resided in Northern Wisconsin about 20 years before going to California.

Survivors include the six children, Mrs. A. C. Hodge, Lynwood, Calif.; H. L. Woodward and Mrs. M. H. Rumpel, Plainfield; Mrs. E. J. Collins, Ladysmith; H. D. Woodward, Forest Grove, Ore., and O. K. Woodward, Wisconsin Rapids; one brother, J. T. Pierce, Canada; two sisters, Mrs. Mary Potter and Mrs. Eva Foote, Portland, Ore., several grandchildren and great-grandchildren.

# Ursula J. Calanan

Ursula was the sixth body Ed Gein dug up. Ursula was born on January 14th, 1877. She was married to her husband Leroy Woodward.

Ursula was a schoolteacher for the Wildwood School District. Ursula and Leroy had several grandchildren and great-grandchildren. Ursula passed away in Los Angeles, California on November 29th, 1952.

# Lola E. Foster

## September 12, 1887 – February 17th, 1953

## Hancock Lady

HANCOCK — Funeral servi for Mrs. Charles Foster, Sr., Hancock, were held at the Ha[r]ton Funeral home Thursday af[ter]noon at 2 o'clock. The Rev. H. Ferris officiated. Burial was m[ade] in the family lot at Hanc[ock] Cemetery. 1953

Mrs. Foster died last Tues[day] morning at 9:20 o'clock at home in Hancock after an ill[ness] of several weeks.

She was born at Strongs Pra[irie] on Sept. 12, 1887, the only chil[d of] Ida and Bradford Robinson. [The] family moved to Hancock w[hen] she was 5-years old and she l[ived] there until her death.

Mrs. Foster was married [to] Charles Foster on Sept. 8, 190[9 at] Hancock.

Surviving are her husband; sons, Norris and Elvin, Hanc[ock] Marion, Coloma, Charles, V[ic]toma, and Alan, Plainfield: daughter, Mrs. Marion Steb[bins] Plainfield, and 10 grandchild[ren].

She was preceded in death [by] two daughters.

# Lola E. Foster

Lola Foster was Ed Gein's seventh body he dug up. Lola was born on September 12th, 1887.

She was married to her husband Charles and lived on a farm in Hancock, Wisconsin. They had five children, three boys and two girls. Lola and Charles had 10 grandchildren.

Lola passed away on February 17th, 1953, after a long illness. She was buried in the Hancock Cemetery and was survived by her husband and children.

# Harriet A Sherman

## May 4th, 1885 – November 22nd, 1955

**Mrs. Addison (Ted) Sherman**

Mrs. Addison (Ted) Sherman, 70, a former resident of the town of Pine Grove, died at her home near Big Flats (Adams county) Tuesday evening.

Funeral services will be held Saturday at 2 p. m. at the Plainfield Baptist church, and burial will follow in the Plainfield cemetery. Rev. Asa Hoskins will officiate at the rites. The body is at the Goult funeral home in Plainfield.

Mrs. Sherman had been in ill health for a number of years, following a stroke.

She was the former Harriet Airabelle Rozell, daughter of the late Mr. and Mrs. Nelson Rozell, and was born near Rozellville (Marathon county) on May 4, 1885.

Her marriage to Mr. Sherman took place Oct. 27, 1901. The couple lived in Pine Grove for many years and then resided in Tomahawk before moving to Big Flats.

Mrs. Sherman is survived by her Harry Hansen and Mrs. Albert Timm, Plainfield, Mrs. Robert Taylor, Brookfield, Mrs. Gale Hall, Bancroft, and Mrs. Jane Rathermal; three sons, Henry, Bancroft, Sylvester, Woodstock, Ill., and Rollie, Richford, and two brothers, Abner Rozell, Hancock and Bert Rozel.

# Harriet A. Sherman

Harriet Sherman was the eighth body dug up by Ed Gein. She was born on May 4th, 1885, and was married to Edison. The couple had ten children—six daughters and four sons. Harriet worked as a housekeeper, and they resided in Big Flats, Wisconsin.

Harriet passed away on November 22nd, 1955, due to a stroke and is buried in the Plainfield Cemetery.

# Alzaida B. Abbott

## March 3rd, 1883 – November 28th, 1956

**Abbott:** Alzaida B. Abbott was born in the town of Almond, Wisconsin, March 3, 1883, and passed to her rest November 28, in the hospital at Pascagoula, Mississippi. Miss Abbott was a nurse, having received her training in our sanitariums in Madison, Wisconsin, and Battle Creek, Michigan. Old friends will remember her work in Wisconsin cities, and in Cleveland, Ohio. She has been living in Ocean Springs, Mississippi since 1926. Those surviving are: one brother, John Abbott; four sisters, Mrs. Isel Petersen, Mrs. Catherine Beggs, Mrs. Rose Knapp, and Mrs. Gladys Richards; nieces, nephews, and a host of friends.

## Alzaida B. Abbott

Alzaida Abbott was the ninth body Ed Gein had dug up. Alzaida was born on March 3rd, 1887. She was employed as a nurse at various sanitariums around the Madison, Wisconsin area. She had one brother and three sisters.

Alzaida passed away at the age of 72 on November 28th, 1956. Not a lot was known about her life.

# CHAPTER 3

Murdered Victims

# Mary Hogan

1901? – December 8th, 1954

# Mary Hogan

Mary Hogan was born Mary Curran in 1901 in Duesenberg, Germany, to Frank and Antonia Curran. It is unknown when Mary came to the United States. Mary married Joseph C. Hogan on October 4, 1920, in Springfield, Illinois. She divorced Joseph on December 23, 1925. Mary married for a second time to Louis Peck on February 17, 1935, and divorced him on October 27, 1939. Mary had a daughter, Christine Medved Selvo, in 1927, who was raised in foster care. Mary worked in the composing room of the Chicago Carton Company located at 4200 Pulaski Road in Chicago from 1920 to 1946. She also worked as a die-cut press feeder at Atlas Box Makers at 5025 W. 65th St. in Chicago from 1946 to 1948. During this time, Mary Hogan lived at 525 Leamington Street in Chicago. Mary moved to Babcock, Wisconsin, in 1949 and bought The Fox Head Bar located at 140 Highway D in Babcock, Wisconsin. Ed Gein frequented Mary's bar, and on December 8, 1954, he walked into The Fox Head Bar after closing and shot Mary with a .32 caliber pistol, taking her life. He loaded Mary into his pickup and took her back to his place. Later that morning, Seymour Lester discovered blood at The Fox Head Bar and called the police. Police never found Mary Hogan until after they searched Ed Gein's farmhouse and found a skin face mask made from Mary Hogan's face.

When the CSI Investigation team entered Ed Gein's home on November 16th, 1957, they removed all the body parts and took them to Madison, Wisconsin. This included all the skin masks and Ed's skin suit he made of women's skin. Also taken was the head of Mary Hogan. In 1962, the judge overseeing the CSI department released all the remains back to Plainfield, Wisconsin, for burial. Without the technology of DNA, the remains were to be put in a mass grave in the Plainfield Cemetery.

# Bernice Worden

## May 9th, 1899 – November 16th, 1957

## Services For Mrs. Worden On Wednesday

Funeral services for Mrs. Bernice Worden, 58, murdered Saturday at Plainfield, will be held Wednesday afternoon at 2 o'clock at the Plainfield Methodist Church, with burial in the village cemetery.

Plainfield business places are expected to close during the services.

Friends may call at the Goult Funeral Home in Plainfield from this evening until the time of the services.

Mrs. Worden, born in Canton, Ill., on May 9, 1899, was a daughter of the late Mr. and Mrs. Frank Conover. She came to the Plainfield area as a girl with her parents, who settled on a farm west of the village.

Her husband, Leon, operated the Worden Hardware and Implement Store in Plainfield until his death in 1931. Since then, his widow had run the store.

Mrs. Worden is survived by a son, Frank, Plainfield; a daughter, Mrs. Donald (Miriam) Walker, Lincoln, Nebr.; four grandchildren; a sister, Mrs. Clifton Johnson, Plainfield, and three brothers, Lloyd Conover, Plainfield, Lester Conover, Almond, and Burl Conover, Aurora, Ill.

She was a member of the Order of the Eastern Star and the American Legion Auxiliary in Plainfield.

# Bernice C. Worden

Bernice Worden was born Bernice Conover on Monday, May 9, 1899, in Canton, Illinois, to Frank and Angus Conover. Bernice's father was part owner of the Worden Hardware Store with partner Leon Worden, Bernice's future husband. Bernice had three brothers: Lester, Burl, and Lloyd, and one sister, Gladys. Bernice and Leon took over the Worden Hardware Store located at 110 S. Main Street in 1931. Before being a hardware store, the building used to be Schultz Garage. Leon and Bernice had one son, Frank Worden, who was born on Monday, November 27, 1922. Frank later lived at 226 Poplar Street in Plainfield, Wisconsin. Leon Worden passed away on Sunday, February 15, 1931, at the age of 40, leaving Bernice to run the store alone. Bernice was a member of the American Legion Auxiliary of Plainfield and was a member of the Grand Chapter of the Wisconsin Order of the Eastern Star out of Wautoma, Wisconsin.

On the morning of November 16, 1957, at around 8:00 am, Ed Gein came into the Worden Hardware Store for some antifreeze. He took the antifreeze out to his car. He returned to the store and asked Bernice if he could see the .22 caliber rifle in the rack. Bernice handed the rifle to Ed, and she went to look out the window, viewing the Shell Station located across the street. Ed pulled a .22 caliber shell out of his pocket, loaded it into the rifle, pointed the rifle at Bernice, and shot her in the back of the head, killing her. Bernice fell to the ground, and Ed dragged Bernice's body to the rear of the store and onto the loading dock. He placed her body into the back of the Worden Hardware delivery pickup and drove it to East Road where he parked it in the pine trees. Ed walked back to the hardware store, where his car was parked. Then Ed drove his car out to East Road where Worden's truck was parked. He then loaded Bernice Worden's lifeless body into his trunk and drove home.

Frank Worden came back from hunting, and when he walked into the store, he noticed a pool of blood on the floor. He saw on the store sales register that Ed Gein had bought antifreeze earlier in the day. Frank informed the police. Bernice's body was found at 2:00 pm that same day hanging from the rafters at Ed Gein's farm. Bernice Worden was killed by Ed Gein on Saturday, November 16th, 1957, at 8:00 am; she was 58 years old.

# CHAPTER 4

## Ed Gein In The News

## Discover $3,000 In Tavern Of Missing Woman

Sheriff Harold S. Thompson disclosed today that a sum of more than $3,000 was discovered in the rear room of Mary's tavern in the town of Pine Grove by officers searching the tavern after the disappearance Dec. 8 of Miss Mary Hogan, operator of the tavern.

Thompson and Vilas O. Waterman, town of Pine Grove supervisor who has been appointed temporary receiver of the property, were counting the money this morning before depositing it in Miss Hogan's account at a local bank. The money was previously counted by state crime laboratory investigators, they said.

Thompson said the money was found in cigar boxes, plastic bags and purses scattered among candy and other supplies in the rear room. Included were coins, ranging from pennies to silver dollars, and several hundred dollars in small bills.

The coins were loose in boxes and wrapped, some in printed wrappers and some in strips of blank paper.

**Bank Deposit**

The sheriff said Miss Hogan had deposited about $1,500 at a local bank about two weeks before her disappearance.

"A considerable sum," is believed to have been taken by the person who apparently murdered Miss Hogan, the sheriff said. Law enforcement officers are convinced Miss Hogan was murdered and her body was taken away by the murderer.

Miss Hogan disappeared sometime between 4:40 and 5:30 p.m. Dec. 8. Seymour Lester, a neighbor, came to the tavern about 5:30 and found the door unlocked, lights turned on and a trail of blood leading from an overturned chair to the door. On the table near the chair an empty coffee cup in a pool of spilled coffee and a novel showed that Miss Hogan was probably sitting at the tafl drinking coffee and reading when she was shot. A used .32 caliber automatic pistol cartridge case was found on the floor.

No trace of the missing woman has since been found.

**Born In Germany**

Attempts to trace her background have revealed that she was born in Germany and came to Portage county about five years ago from Cicero, Ill. She was apparently married twice, the sheriff said, but no relatives have been found.

Friday, Waterman was appointed a temporary receiver by County Judge Levi to conserve Miss Hogan's property pending a conclusion of the case.

MISSING WOMAN — This snapshot, taken sometime in the last few years, shows Miss Mary Hogan, missing town of Pine Grove tavernkeeper, in the door of her tavern. The picture was discovered by authorities searching her effects.

## Claim More Basis For Mindszenty Report

Vienna, Austria —(AP)— Kathpress, a Roman Catholic press service in Austria, today claimed support for its report of last week that Josef Cardinal Mindszenty had been freed. It also spoke of "relief measures . . . practically equal to a discharge."

There has been no confirmation from Budapest, nor at the Vatican.

TAVERN INTERIOR — This view of the interior of the town of Pine Grove tavern from which Miss Mary Hogan vanished Dec. 8 was taken by state crime laboratory investigators called to the scene that night.

# Mary Hogan's Life Story Has Big Gaps

Who was—or is—Mary Hogan? The farther authorities delve into her past, the more mysterious she becomes.

A Mary Curran was born in 1901 at Dusenberg, Germany, to Frank Curran and his wife, the former Antonia Hofbauer.

Mary Curran was married Oct. 4, 1920, at Springfield, Ill., to Joseph Medved, who gave his occupation as miner. She was 19, he was 34. She deserted him March 1, 1922, and he was granted a divorce on Dec. 23, 1925.

Then a blank spot appears in the record, a spot authorities have been unable to fill.

She next appears as Mary Hogan, but no record of the marriage has been found.

Mary Hogan was married Feb. 17, 1935, at Crown Point, Ind., to Louis Peck. Both gave their address as Chicago and she then gave her maiden name as Mary Curran.

Mrs. Peck was granted a divorce, Oct. 27, 1939, at Chicago on grounds of cruelty.

During the time she was married to Peck, however, she was using the name Hogan, and immediately after the divorce, only the name Hogan appears in her records.

Miss Mary Hogan next appears in the town of Pine Grove when she was granted a tavern license in 1949 and opened a tavern on County Trunk D. She disappeared from the tavern Dec. 8 and authorities are convinced she was murdered. No trace of the missing woman has been found since that time.

District Attorney Robert C. Jenkins, in attempting to trace Miss Hogan, learned of her background through old records. Acquaintances who knew her while she lived in Chicago—during her marriage to Peck—have been questioned, but they apparently known little of her background.

German authoritites will be contacted, Jenkins said, and an attempt made to trace relatives through records in Germany.

Miss Hogan owned the tavern and a home behind it, and left a considerable estate. She apparently was paying premiums on an accident insurance policy, but no information on beneficiaries has yet been received.

# Butcher Gein Goes Behind Bars

WAUPUN, Wis.—Two hospital guards flank "Plainfield butcher" Edward Gein, 51, as the bachelor farmer is led behind asylum bars at Wisconsin Central State Hospital for the Criminal Insane. He was committed for a minimum 30 days observation period.

(International Soundphoto.)

# Gein Hinted Car Could Be Buried in Conversation

*Dec 4 1957*

Amid rumors, speculation and "hot tips" there was little actual new evidence uncovered by investigators at the Ed Gein farm during the past few days.

Sheriff Herbert Wanserski of Portage County told the United Press Tuesday that he was checking a "hot tip" on where Gein might have buried additional bodies, but sheriffs and deputies from Waushara, Adams and Portage counties were unable to come up with anything tangible in digging on Monday and Tuesday.

Sheriff Wanserski had also expressed a belief that a skull found late last week was that of either Victor "Bunk" Travis or man hunting with him known only as Ray Burgess. The men disappeared in November of 1952 while hunting near the Gein farm.

However, the State Crime Laboratory determined Monday that the skull was that of a woman 30 to 50 years old. Attorney General Stewart Honeck made the announcement Monday and said the laboratory still believes the skull, and the bones found with it, came from a grave robbery and not slaying.

Honeck said the finding of another skull was "not inconsistent" with information gained during lie detector tests of Gein.

The rumors of finding a buried car and the use of bulldozers on the Gein farm are "completely untrue", according to Waushara County Sheriff Arthur Schley.

Stories circulated on Monday had the car complete with the two missing hunters (Travis and Burgess) unearthed on the farm.

The possibility of there being such a "buried treasure" was not ruled out by the sheriff, however.

The sheriff said that Gein had mentioned in a conversation with a neighbor at the time the men turned up missing that "it would be no trick at all to bury a car in the area".

When the neighbor mentioned that it might be difficult to keep the sides from caving in, Gein noted that it wouldn't be if the sides of the excavation were tapered.

Sheriff Schley also spiked another rumor concerning a conversation Gein had with a renter.

The report was that Gein had told the renter he could not plow over a certain area of the farm, and when the renter did plow over the area, Gein became enraged.

There was no such conversation, the renter told investigators.

Two special investigators have been assigned to the case and are aiding in the search for new evidence. One, a retired FBI agent is seeking information from persons who knew Gein. The other, from the state attorney general's office, is working out of the sheriff's office at Wautoma.

# Officers Tend to Accept His Story as True

## But Investigation of Plainfield Horrors Is Continued; Lie Test Slated at Madison

**By RICHARD C. KIENITZ**
Of The Journal Staff

Plainfield, Wis. — Authorities Tuesday were trying to check Edward Gein's claim that he murdered only Mrs. Bernice Worden and that he got the rest of his grisly collection of human heads and skulls in a series of ghoulish grave robberies.

Waushara county authorities appeared to be convinced by Gein's story.

"Our case is pretty well cleaned up," said Dist. Atty. Earl Kileen. "We have no missing persons in our county. The only thing here is the murder rap."

Neither Kileen nor Sheriff Art Schley would say whether they had checked the cemeteries where Gein said he robbed graves—or that they intended to. They jokingly claimed that they "didn't remember" if they had checked any of the supposedly violated graves Monday.

### No Visitors Allowed

When asked Tuesday morning if he planned to check the cemeteries, Schley looked out a window at snow that was falling. "I wouldn't know about that," he said, implying that it was too nasty outside.

The sheriff did say that the snow and icy roads might prevent him from taking Gein to Madison, where the 51 year old farm recluse was scheduled to undergo a lie detector test at the state crime laboratory.

A news blackout imposed by Schley as soon as the butchered body of Mrs. Worden was found Saturday in a summer kitchen of Gein's ramshackle farm home remains in force. The sheriff refused to let reporters or photographers visit Gein in his jail cell, saying that they would upset Gein and that they hadn't finished talking to the suspect.

### "Very Annoying Fellow"

Kileen added that Gein was "a very annoying fellow to talk to—sometimes he'll want to go into great detail and other times he'll shut up and won't say anything." Kileen explained that Schley feared that the presence of reporters and photographers might frighten Gein into a sustained silence.

Gein was returned to jail after his arraignment Monday in Wautoma on an armed robbery charge. The charge was filed by Kileen to hold Gein until the crime laboratory had completed its investigation.

Gein told County Judge Boyd Clark that he wanted an attorney and could afford to hire one. He selected Atty. William N. Belter of Wautoma, a former assemblyman. Belter said Tuesday that he didn't know whether he would defend Gein. He said he hadn't talked to him yet.

### Bond Set at $10,000

Gein's bond was set at $10,000. Kileen had asked for $5,000 but Schley suggested it be doubled. The armed robbery charge arose from that fact that a cash register containing $41 or $42 was taken from Mrs. Worden's store at the time of the slaying. It was found in Gein's home.

The preliminary hearing on the charge was set for next Monday. However, Kileen said he expected Gein's lawyer (whoever he may be) to ask for a delay.

At Madison, Charles Wilson, director of the state crime laboratory, said that a check of cemeteries wasn't necessary yet.

"There's no sense going out with a pick and shovel to check the graveyards near Plainfield until we have exhausted the possibilities of evidence we already have," Wilson said.

Wilson said that if Gein's grisly collection of human heads, skulls and bones came from graves "there will be

*Turn to page 3, col. 1*

# Single Killing Theory Told

## Officers in Waushara County Think Others Were From Graves

*From page 1, column 8*

traces of embalming fluid and we'll find them."

Wilson also said that detailed physical descriptions of persons who had disappeared in recent years would be checked against what was found in Gein's farm home. He said the department had gathered such descriptions in many cases of disappearing persons.

Gein told authorities that he committed the grave robberies while in a "daze." He was quoted as saying that he committed at least 10 grave robberies from 1944 to 1952 and that each grave was that of a woman.

### He Read Obituaries

He was also quoted as saying he read obituaries in the newspapers and then went out to dig up the new graves. It was reported that some of the grave robberies were at cemeteries near his home.

There have been conflicting reports about what authorities found in Gein's home. Lt. Vern Weber, chief of detectives at La Crosse, said he saw part of the collection in the crime laboratory truck.

He said there were 10 women's heads, some with eyes and some without. He said some were complete with skulls, others were merely skin.

Weber said that all of the heads appeared to be those of women of middle age or older.

Weber said he was told that no full skulls were recovered—"just pieces"—and that other patches of skin had been recovered.

He said he saw with his own eyes a chair with a seat which appeared to be made of human skin, and a knife with a handle that appeared to have a skin covering. He said the chair was a typical kitchen chair which probably once had a rattan seat.

### Inclined to Believe Him

Weber said that the heads were in a very good state of preservation and that they had been found behind chairs and other furniture in Gein's home.

Weber said that he had talked to Gein twice and that he was inclined to believe his story about the grave robberies. He said that Gein said he had wanted to be a doctor in his youth. He said Gein said he had cured the heads in a brine solution.

Weber said that he had asked Gein "strong questions" about rumors of cannibalism.

"That's out," Weber said. "He said he never ate a bit of that stuff and I don't believe he did."

### "He Needs Help"

Weber said that Gein was "a very sincere, very meek fellow—you'd never believe he'd be the kind of guy to do such a thing—you feel like he needs help awful bad."

The La Crosse detective said Gein said that he could feel his grave robbing spells coming on.

"He said he would pray and that sometimes the prayers would snap him out of it. He said he came out of a spell one time while he was digging up a grave and that he stopped."

Weber said that Gein insisted that he hadn't robbed a grave since 1952. "He said maybe his prayers had been answered."

Gein also claims that he was in a spell when he murdered Mrs. Worden, although he admits he must have done it. "He says he only remembers carrying her out of the store—not the killing or the butchering," Weber said.

Mrs. Worden's body was found hanging by the heels and butchered like a hunter would butcher a deer. Her heart was found inside the farm home. One official pointed out that deer hunters customarily saved the heart and that this would lend some credence to Gein's claim that he thought he was dressing a deer at the time.

### Shoes Don't Fit

Weber came to Plainfield to check if Gein had any connection with the violent disappearance of baby-sitter Evelyn Hartley in October, 1953. He said he was inclined to doubt a connection.

Weber said that tennis shoes found after the disappearance and linked to the murder were too large for Gein. "The shoes we found are size 11½; Gein wears about an 8," the detective chief said.

Weber said that Gein was a native of La Crosse but had left there with his parents when he was 7. "He claims he hasn't been back since," Weber said. "He has some relatives here and we're going to check with them."

Chicago police interviewed Gein for almost three hours until 3 a.m. Tuesday, seeking a connection with unsolved Chicago crimes, notably the Judith Anderson slaying. Gein told them that he hadn't ever traveled south of Milwaukee.

Sheriff Roger Reinel and Dist. Atty. Harold A. Eberhard of Jefferson county came here Tuesday to check any connection with the disappearance of Georgia Jean Weckler in 1947.

Authorities are still trying to establish the details of Mrs. Worden's slaying. She was shot in the head with a .22 caliber bullet. Gein claims that he doesn't own a gun of that caliber although two guns of another caliber were found in his home.

Many persons have been wondering how a person as slight as Gein could dig up so many graves and remove bodies without help. Gein claims that he never took a complete body.

Weber said the chair seat made of skin looked like skin from the chest or back of a human. Where Gein got this skin, he never took a complete body and murdered only Mrs. Worden, has not been answered.

Gein has been questioned about the disappearance of Miss Mary Hogan, 54, from her tavern at the near-by town of Pine Grove (Portage county).

Gein said he was at the tavern two days after her disappearance but admitted no other connection with that disappearance.

Funeral services for Mrs. Worden will be held at 2 p.m. Wednesday at the Plainfield Methodist church.

**Accused Butcher Finishes Lie Tests**

Ed Gein, hatless and handcuffed, leaving Wisconsin crime laboratory in Madison between Sheriff Arthur Wchley (left) and Deputy Leon Murty after lie tests yesterday in which he is said to have admitted deaths of two women. [Associated Press Wirephoto]

# Gein's Story As He Told

## Relates Events Of Saturday In D.A.'s Statement

WAUTOMA (AP)—Waushara County Dist. Atty. Earl Kileen has released the following stenographic record of a statement made by Edward Gein Monday afternoon when questioned by county authorities.

(Mr. Kileen first warns him of his constitutional rights and that everything he says will be used against him.)

Kileen: Now you start from the time you went into the Worden Implement Store. Tell us exactly what happened, the best you can recall.

### Took Jug

Gein: When I went into Mrs. Worden's, I took a glass jug for permanent anti-freeze. When I entered the hardware store she came towards me and said, "Do you want a gallon of anti-freeze?" and I said, "No, a half gallon." She got the anti-freeze and pumped it out, and I held the jug for her to pour it in and then she pumped out another quart and I was still holding the jug while she poured that. Then I paid her with a dollar bill. She gave me back one cent because it was 99 cents. This is what I can't say from now on because I don't know just what happened from now on, you see. She glanced out of the window towards the filling station across the street and said, "They are checking deer there." Then she looked towards the west, out of the west and north windows, and said, "There are more people up town than I thought there would be." She might have said something about opening of the season, she might have said that.

Kileen: Do you remember striking her or shooting her?

took the blood from the body put that out—buried it out toilet house where you p out.

Gein: East of the toilet.

Kileen: Do you remember you had the blood in? Was pail, bucket or jar?

Gein: It must have been a pail.

Kileen: What kind of a pail?

Gein: Probably galvanized. Probably a 10-quart pail. One was a 10 qt. and one was a 12 qt.

Kileen: Then you proceeded to dress out the body? You told me that you thought you were dressing out a deer.

### "Only Explanation"

Gein: That is the only explanation that I can think was in my mind.

Kileen: Do you remember if you had the body all dressed before those people came out after.

Gein: You mean the girl and her brother? Yes, it had to be.

Kileen: How about Mr. Uueck?

Gein: He came before; before the girl and her brother came.

Kileen: Before the body was dressed and hung up? On these other ten skulls found in your house (or shrunken heads)—those other ten shrunken heads. You got from a cemetery or cemeteries?

Gein: Yes. (Nods his head.)

Kileen: Did you ever kill anyone else besides Mrs. Worden?

Gein: Not to my knowledge. The only think I am not too sure that I killed her; that is the only thing, because I didn't have any weapons with me or on my property.

### Doesn't Remember

Gein: No. That is what got me; whether I took my anti-freeze out. That is what I can't remember. It is hard for me to say from now on. My memory was a little vague, but I do remember dragging her across the floor. I remember loading her body in the truck; then I drove the truck out on the East road at the intersection where 51 and 73 separate East of Plainfield. I drove the truck up in the pine trees. Then I walked to town and got my car and drove it out there and loaded her body in the back end of the car, and also the cash register. I loaded the cash register in the truck when I put her body in there. Then I drove out to my farm and took the body out of the car and hung it up by its heels in my wood shed.

Kileen: Tell how you took the blood out and buried it. You used the knife you made from the file to cut her up?

### "Daze-Like"

Gein: That is what is as close as I can remember. I was in a regular daze-like, and I can't swear to it.

Kileen: Then you said that you

ON WAY TO COURT

Edward Gein, right, walks from jail in the custody of Sheriff Art Schley on way to court, who admitted killing two women, to be committed to Central State Hospital for the Criminal Insane at Waupun. Circuit Judge Herbert Bunde ordered Gein. (AP Wirephoto)

# Another Skeleton Is Found on Gein Farm

**Plans Insanity Plea**

Gein was accompanied to court by William Belter, 33, local attorney hired Monday by the confessed slayer.

Belter announced that he wished to make a plea of not guilty by reason of insanity to both the murder charge and to a charge of robbery lodged Monday on which Gein had previously been held. Belter said he would waive rights of his client to a preliminary examination on both charges.

This cleared away any necessity for a preliminary hearing on the robbery charge already scheduled for next Monday and left the way open for Gein to be brought at any time selected by authorities before the local Circuit judge, Herbert A. Bunde, of Wisconsin Rapids, Wis.

Kileen said later that Judge Bunde advised county authorities he will set a date "within two weeks" for the arraignment and a likely sanity hearing for Gein.

**Slayer Brought to Court**

Schley reportedly admitted to Wing that the name of Mrs. Adams, who was 51 when she died of a heart ailment in 1951, was on a list obtained by authorities from Gein as names of occupants of graves Gein has dug up and pilfered in the last 10 years.

The conference between Schley and Wing took place about an hour after Gein had been hustled from his county jail cell in handcuffs for arraignment before County Judge Boyd Clark on a charge of first degree murder.

The court hearing was brief. Gein was brought to court on an affidavit by District Atty. Earl F. Kileen, accusing him of the murder of Mrs. Bernice Worden, 58, Plainfield hardware merchant, whose butchered body was found Saturday on Gein's horror farm 7 miles southwest of Plainfield.

Plainfield is a Waushara county village 15 miles northwest of this county seat town.

**Expect No Formal Trial**

No formal trial is expected either by Kileen or the defense attorney. They expect that by reason of the insanity plea Judge Bunde will order a sanity examination as a prerequisite to trial. If Gein is held in such an examination to be incapable of standing trial because of insanity, he would be committed to the state hospital for the criminally insane at Waupun, Wis., to be detained until such time, if ever, that he becomes sane.

Following his talk with Wing, the sheriff spirited

**WHERE GEIN SAYS HE ROBBED GRAVES**

Pat Danna, sexton of the Plainfield cemetery, stands beside the grave of Mrs. Eleanor M. Adams, which was on the list of those which Sheriff Arthur Schley said were admitted to have been robbed by Edward Gein. Mrs. Adams was a sister-in-law of Ralph Wing, Plainfield town board chairman. The two graves in the next row back are those of Gein's parents. District Attorney Kileen has announced that some of the graves will be opened next week to determine if Gein actually did rob the graves. (AP Wirephoto)

## Won't Dig Up Graves, Waushara DA Insists

### 'It Would Just Upset Relatives,' He Says in Refusing Check of Ghoulish Tale

*Journal Staff Correspondence*

**Wautoma, Wis.** — Dist. Atty. Earl F. Kileen said Wednesday that Waushara county would not make any effort to check Edward Gein's story that he got most of his horrible collection of human remains by robbing graves.

"We're not going to dig up any graves," Kileen said. "I want no part in opening graves to prove anything. Just think how the poor relatives would feel."

Kileen repeated his earlier statement that Waushara county had no missing persons cases and that, because of this, a check of the cemeteries supposedly robbed by Gein "isn't necessary."

### "It's Up to Them"

"If other counties want to get court orders to open graves it's up to them," Kileen said, adding that "if the people concerned (the survivors) don't like it, I'll do everything possible to help them stop it."

Kileen has appeared willing to accept Gein's story that he slew only Mrs. Bernice Worden of Plainfield and that the rest of his grisly collection came from a series of ghoulish expeditions.

Revelations Tuesday that one of the heads found in the Gein house was that of a missing woman tavern keeper from Portage county and a charge that Waushara county did have a missing person case, had failed to sway Kileen in his stand.

### "I Want to Help"

Briefly, Kileen thinks that there is a clear cut case against Gein in the murder and butchery of Mrs. Worden.

"If we get a conviction for murder what use is there to stir up anything more?" he asked. "Of course, if other counties want to solve their cases I want to help, but they'll have to get permission (from survivors) to open any graves."

The charge that Waushara county did have a case of a missing person was made Tuesday afternoon in Madison by former Sheriff Leon Murty, one of the lawmen who brought Gein to the state crime laboratory for the lie test. Murty now is a deputy and village marshal at Wild Rose.

Murty, who was sheriff for six years and whose wife was sheriff for two years, told newsmen that a man named Victor (Bunk) Travis disappeared in Waushara county in 1953.

### Gein Reported Burglary

Kileen insisted Wednesday that Travis' disappearance was an Adams county case even though the man reportedly was last seen in a Plainfield tavern. He said Travis resided in Adams county. Local rumor was to the effect that Travis might have been abducted by a Chicago gang.

Murty said at the time of Travis' disappearance he got several calls about fresh graves being found in wooded sections. Murty said he checked the reports and found two freshly dug graves. He said one was empty; the other contained a dead dog.

The ex-sheriff also recalled that Gein two years ago reported a burglary at his house. He said Gein complained that someone had stolen an antique kerosene lamp and that he wanted authorities to check tire tracks and footprints he found in the yard.

### "I Wouldn't Know"

Murty said he went to the house to check the report but that Gein wasn't home. He said he didn't enter the house in Gein's absence. Later, he said, he found Gein working on a road job and talked to him about the case. The buglary never was solved and Murty said he never again had an opportunity to enter the house.

As to the identification of one of the heads as that of another slaying victim and reports that the number of bodies Gein used in making his horrible collection might reach 15, Kileen said, "I wouldn't know about that."

Kileen was reminded that it was reported earlier that Gein committed only 10 grave robberies and that he only took the head and another small piece of the human anatomy when he robbed a grave. It was pointed out that too many articles made of skin were found in Gein's home to substantiate the story that he took only the head and the other small portion of skin—if he did rob graves.

Kileen said this discrepancy had not occurred to him. He said he didn't look too closely at Gein's ghastly collection.

"I don't know where he got them from," he said. "He said he got them from cemeteries."

But asked if he intended to check any graves to see if they actually were robbed, Kileen stuck by his earlier statement that Waushara county—at least—wouldn't.

## Grave-Robbing Claim Attacked

**WAUTOMA, Wis., Nov. 21** (INS)—A cemetery keeper today touched off conjecture that possibly 11 persons were slain by Wisconsin's "mad bachelor."

Pat Danna, sexton of the Plainfield Cemetery near Edward Gein's "horror farm," asserted it was physically impossible for the 140-pound hermit to open a grave singlehandedly.

Danna, who lives at the cemetery, added he either would have noticed anyone prowling the grounds or detected disarray of the soil on a fresh grave.

Mounting skepticism among townspeople brought talk of carrying complaints against the trend of the current investigation to Gov. Vernon Thomson or Wisconsin Attorney General Stuart Honeck.

Danna said a grave is carefully mounded and carpeted with sod. He added:

"All of this would have to be spaded up, and all the dirt around the casket removed, before anybody could get to the body.

"Then the casket, itself, is closed with screws. Also, most caskets are enclosed in wooden boxes. Many of them are in concrete vaults.

"You can't tell me one man could get to the body in a night—and cover things back up so I wouldn't have noticed it."

### Officials Co-operative

Belter said that he encountered no opposition from authorities when he told them he wanted to tour the Gein home. He said he merely stated that he was the defense attorney and officials arranged for the tour.

He said he understood that officials had resisted others' attempts to see the house because they were "trying to keep out curiosity seekers and people who had no business there."

## District Attorney Got 'a Spanking' From Honeck's Office on Gein Information

*Journal Madison Bureau*

**Madison, Wis.** — The news blackout which has confused the details surrounding Edward Gein's butchery of a Plainfield widow and the macabre collection of human heads, skulls and skin found in his charnel house threatens to become blacker.

Dist. Atty. Earl Kileen of Waushara county, who has given the press the bulk of the few facts that have been available, said Tuesday afternoon that he had been given "a spanking" by the office of Atty. Gen. Honeck.

He said he was advised to withhold facts which might inflame the public and thus deprive Gein of his right to a fair trial.

### Will Follow Advice

Kileen indicated that he intended to follow the advice but added: "The only things I have divulged are what everybody knew anyway—there aren't any more facts left."

Honeck confirmed Wednesday that William Platz of his office had warned Kileen not to release any information which would tend to "inflame potential jurors."

"With the widespread statements being made — some ill founded, contradictory and groundless on things that are supposed to have happened—people might reach conclusions which would affect their ability to sit as jurors," Honeck said.

### Refers to Babich Case

Honeck said that both the United States and Wisconsin supreme courts had condemned the practice of releasing information which might tend to inflame the populace. He referred to the Milton Babich murder case as one in which the state supreme court made such a statement.

"In some places, confessed murderers are walking the streets, turned loose on the grounds that they couldn't get a fair trial," Honeck said. "That's what we're trying to avoid in this case."

The attorney general said that the news blackout was "the farthest thing from our minds." But he conceded that the advice to withhold information would apply until Gein was brought to trial.

### "Will Know Whole Story"

"I think the public will know the whole story at the proper time," Honeck said.

Of Sheriff Art Schley, who has released almost no information on the case, Honeck said that he was "apparently doing his job" and said that Schley's refusal to co-operate with the press was not an indication that he was not performing his duties as a sheriff.

Schley, only 32, was appointed by Gov. Thomson, Oct. 1, to fill a vacancy caused by the resignation of Sheriff Edward Jester because of illness in his family. Schley had been employed by the Waushara county highway department.

Thomson was in Green Bay Wednesday and could not be reached for comment.

## Rundown Farmhouse Was Murder Factory

### Occupant, 51, Lived Alone for 20 Years on Isolated Land Left Unworked

By RICHARD C. KIENITZ
Of The Journal Staff

Plainfield, Wis.—The weatherworn Waushara county farmhouse of Ed Gein, where the eviscerated body of a Plainfield widow and parts of other human bodies have been found, is a rundown two story, once white frame building where the 51 year old bachelor has lived alone for more than 20 years.

It is six miles southwest of here, a mile west of county trunk KK, and about three-quarters of a mile east of the Adams-Waushara county line.

The house is set back about 75 feet on the southwest intersection of two dirt town roads. The nearest neighbor is between an eighth and a quarter of a mile away.

Gein has about 160 acres on his farm, but apparently it has not been farmed in a number of years.

### Many in Soil Bank

This is a sandy area, mostly wide open grassy fields, interlaced with small woodlots and clumps of pine. Many of the farms in the vicinity are under the long range soil bank, with farmers receiving government checks to cover what would have been crop income before they joined the conservation program.

The farmhouse, once painted white, is now spotted with daubs of white paint apparently applied by Gein in recent years. It is an L shaped house of possibly eight rooms, four on each floor, but deputies say that only two had been occupied in recent years.

These are a kitchen and an adjoining bedroom on the first floor—these and a summer kitchen built onto the house where the body of the Plainfield widow, Mrs. Bernice Worden, 58, was found Saturday night hanging by its heels.

From the outside, the second floor appears to be unoccupied and largely empty. Stacked furniture can be seen in some of the first floor rooms and rotted curtains on the windows. Authorities will not permit reporters to approach closer than 20 feet of the house.

### No Known Relatives

Neighbors say that Gein has no known relatives and that apparently the other rooms of the house have not been changed since Gein's mother died in the 1930's. His father, George, had died a short time earlier. Gein lived with a brother for a while until the brother died of a heart attack after fighting a woods fire.

There is a large tangled bush in front of the house about 10 feet high. There are two porches, overhangs with wooden supports over broken concrete floors.

A small barn stands behind the house, also a machine shed—once a pig shed—another small building and an outhouse. All are so weatherworn that paint can hardly be distinguished.

No machinery stands in the yard; some old rusted machinery, nothing modern, stands in the barn and machine shed. No car was visible to reporters, but neighbors said Gein owned a 1950 or 1951 Ford.

### Reporters Gathering

Plainfield, where reporters from distant cities are beginning to gather, is a small village of about 700 population, 30 miles southeast of Wisconsin Rapids on highway 73 and 30 miles south of Stevens Point on highway 51.

Mrs. Worden's hardware store stands on the main intersection. Across the street is the Union State bank. Near by is the office of the Plainfield Sun, a weekly newspaper, which is fast becoming the headquarters of the corps of invading reporters.

## Grave Findings Touch Off Mass Exodus of Press

The findings on opening two graves in the Plainfield cemetery Monday morning has cleared the air on the truth of at least some of confessed murderer Ed Gein's story.

In the two graves opened, no body was found in the grave of Mrs. Eleanore Adams and only a few bones on the casket of the other, that of Mrs. Mabel Everson.

Both Sheriff Arthur Schley and District Attorney Earl Kileen have stated that no more graves will be opened unless relatives of persons on the Gein list request that it be done.

Whether or not other graves will be opened will also depend on the findings of the state crime laboratory and what their investigators deem necessary.

The state attorney general's office has assumed some of the responsibility in the case and have been directed by the governor to examine facts as to whether Gein might have committed other crimes.

Gein was taken to the state hospital at Waupun for 30 days of mental observation Saturday by Sheriff Schley and Deputy Arnold Fritz.

The findings at Plainfield Monday touched off a mass exodus of reporters and photographers from the area and as of Wednesday morning Sheriff Schley, who has been pursued by the press since the first news of the murder broke, stated that there were only a few Chicago reporters still in the city.

The sheriff told the Argus Wednesday morning that reporters had been kept from the Plainfield cemetery as a protection to the relatives of deceased persons whose graves Gein has said that he entered.

He said that one photographer attempted to take pictures from a top a ladder at the edge of the cemetery and others were taken from an airplane hovering over the scene.

## Killer Enters Insanity Plea in 'Butchery'

### Confesses to Murder of Mary Hogan Also; Claims He Burned Most of Body

Journal Staff Correspondence

Wautoma, Wis.—Slayer Edward Gein Thursday pleaded insanity to a first degree murder charge.

He was arraigned in Waushara county court and immediately pleas of not guilty and not guilty by reason of insanity were entered by his attorney, William Belter.

The charge said that Gein "did on the 16th day of November, 1957, at the village of Plainfield in said county (Waushara) feloniously and with intent to kill, murder Bernice Worden, a human being, contrary to section 940.01 of the Wisconsin statutes against the peace and dignity of the state of Wisconsin."

Schley said deputies turned up frozen ground at five places on Gein's farm Tuesday and found no trace of human remains. The Waushara County sheriff said Wanserski has been giving information to the press "before he knows what the hell he is talking about."

Meanwhile there were these developments:

Atty. Gen. Stewart Honeck said at Madison he will continue his investigation into the case. He said technicians from the state Crime Lab are to pay another visit to the farm, but did not elaborate on it.

Superintendent Dr. Edward Schubert of the Central State Hospital at Waupun said Gein has the "freedom" of a maximum security at the mental institution where he is undergoing a 30-day examination to determine if he's sane. If found sane, he must stand trial for his two admitted killings. If found insane, he may never leave the hospital. Schubert said Gein spends much of his time alone and that the examination will be completed on schedule.

# Publicity's Spotlight Enjoyed by Wautoma

## Sheriff Schley, Weary of Whole Gein Case, Slams Door on Interview at Jail

By ROBERT W. WELLS
Of The Journal Staff

Wautoma, Wis.—The glare of a national spotlight that has focused on this community and its still smaller neighbor, Plainfield, since the Ed Gein murder case began less than a week ago, has produced a mixed reaction among the townsfolk here.

Some are profoundly weary of the whole affair. Others, including the residents who have experienced for the first time the heady sensation of seeing themselves quoted in print, are rather enjoying it. To most of those not directly affected, the case has brought the not unpleasant feeling that they are bystanders at an event which the whole nation and parts of the rest of the world are watching.

### 30 Newsmen Here

More than 30 newsmen and photographers from 20 papers, magazines and news syndicates are in this county seat. Watching them roam the downtown streets in packs, keeping a wary eye on each other, townsfolk are tempted to believe that the number is even larger. Brock's motel, east of town, has been nearly full with the visitors all week, and local restaurants have also welcomed the increased business in a season when things are usually pretty slow in Wautoma.

Sheriff Art Schley, on the other hand, would doubtless be happy if he never saw another reporter. A newcomer to his job, faced with the most bizarre murder case in the state's history, Schley has a full time staff of exactly two deputies and an annual budget of a mere $11,500.

He and his wife and three daughters live in the front half of the county jail building. Gein is housed all by himself in the back. A couple of other prisoners were released promptly for good behavior when Gein arrived, and Schley is hoping he won't have to arrest anyone else until he gets Gein off his hands.

### Clamor for Interview

Thursday afternoon and well into the evening, from a dozen to more than two dozen newsmen were packed like sardines into the sheriff's small front reception room. They were clamoring for an interview with the prisoner, which his attorney, William Belter, had agreed to try to arrange.

For most of the afternoon, no one would tell the morose reporters even as simple a matter as where the sheriff was. The newsmen exchanged with each other their dark suspicions that Schley had spirited Gein away to point out in secret the burial places of some of the bones that are still missing. It finally developed, however, that the sheriff was in the jail basement helping repair the hot water pipes.

Belter couldn't reach Schley either for some time. Anyway, the defense attorney is also justice of the peace, so he was hearing game law violations.

But at last, a good eight hours after the newsmen had begun their vigil, Belter got Gein to agree to see six reporters, who would pool the information they got with the others.

### Six Are Chosen

The six chosen by Belter were from the three principal wire services, plus Time magazine, The Milwaukee Journal and the Oshkosh Daily Northwestern. The Chicago Tribune man put up a bitter beef at being excluded, but finally subsided. The six chosen went outside to the jail entrance with Belter, followed closely by a jostling mob of their colleagues, who hoped for a chance to eavesdrop.

Schley, it has been observed, is generally easy to get along with on a man to man basis. But crowds—especially crowds of reporters and photographers—seem to make him nervous. When he saw the mob of newsmen rushing around the jailhouse toward him, he immediately shouted that no more than three could go inside. This brought new cries of anguish and increased the confusion.

Belter, besieged on all sides, finally ruled that the Associated Press, the United Press and Time magazine would get the nod, which brought on a strong protest from International News Service. As the argument waxed heavy, Schley waxed wroth. He slammed the jail door, swore a few times and called the whole affair off. So the day's long wait was wasted.

### Cleaner Than Home

Of all the people most concerned with the case, perhaps the least inconvenienced so far is Gein. The little man, it is true, must spend his time in jail. But the Washara county jail, whatever its shortcomings, is far cleaner and less cluttered than his farm home. The food is better than the canned beans he used to warm on his pot bellied stove. And for the first time in Eddie Gein's life, people are paying attention to him.

A week ago there wasn't a person in the entire world who would have gone far out of his way to have a word with the little handy man with the twisted smile. But Thursday night, when the jail door clanged shut on the representatives of the nation's press and Schley stormed back into his living quarters, the cries of disappointment that went up over being unable to hear a few syllables from Gein's own lips were as heart rending as they were ironic.

Jail doors waited to open for slayer Ed Gein after his arraignment at Wautoma Thursday. Waushara county Sheriff Art Schley led Gein back to a cell after Gein had pleaded not guilty by reason of insanity in the Worden murder.

—United Press Telephoto

# Ran Tavern a Few Miles From Scene

## Embalming Indicated but Proprietor Had Never Been Seen Since Robbery

By WILLARD R. SMITH
Of The Journal Staff

Madison, Wis. — One of the women's heads in Edward Gein's ghastly collection was identified Tuesday afternoon as that of Miss Mary Hogan, 54, who disappeared in December, 1954.

"We've got a head and face that is her's (Miss Hogan's) without question," Sheriff Herbert Wanserski of Portage county told newsmen as he waited for Gein to undergo a lie test at the state crime laboratory here.

Wanserski said the head in question actually only was facial skin and hair peeled back from the skull. But he said it was that of Miss Hogan.

Gein has claimed that the butchered only Mrs. Bernice Worden of Plainfield (Waushara county) and that he got the rest of his grisly collection by robbing graves.

### Doubts Grave Theft

Miss Hogan disappeared from her tavern in the town of Pine Grove some time Dec. 8, 1954. Blood was found splattered through the tavern and a .32 caliber cartridge was found on the floor of the barroom. At the time, authorities said they believed the woman was shot and taken away in a truck seen in the neighborhood. The truck was identified as a 1951 green Dodge pickup truck.

The tavern was about 10 miles from Gein's home near Plainfield.

Wanserski said the face and hair identified as Miss Hogan's smelled of embalming fluid, "but remember, she disappeared and never was seen again—she wasn't buried."

"He (Gein) never robbed a grave in his life," Wanserski said bitterly.

Wanserski and Dist. Atty. John J. Haka of Portage county came here in a car following the car in which Gein rode with Sheriff Art Schley of Waushara county, Deputy Leon Murty and Alan Wilimovski of the crime laboratory.

### "Divided Jurisdiction"

Wanserski was asked by newsmen if the Gein case cut across county lines. He said: "Yes, definitely." It was then that he revealed the identification of Miss Hogan's head.

The Portage county sheriff also said he had strong doubt that Gein ever lived in the farm home where the butchered body of Mrs. Worden and at least 10 heads were found.

He said that there was too much undisturbed dust in the areas of the home where Gein supposedly lived to support that idea. "You couldn't walk by without knocking the dust off," he said.

"Last spring—I think it was April—Ed came around and wanted to know if we'd like to trade our house for his farm," Mrs. Foster said. "We have only an acre or so of land here and we thought the idea was worth considering, so he went out to look his place over."

"We looked into all the rooms except the front bedroom and one room right off what I suppose was originally the dining

—Journal Staff
Bob Hill

room but that Ed used for a bedroom and living room. He had the door closed to that one room. He said it was just an old pantry and was filled with junk.

"No, we didn't see anything to make us suspicious. The place was awfully dirty and full of stuff piled all over the floor. It was pretty dark, too. He had those old dirty curtains at the windows, so we couldn't see much. Anyway, we weren't looking for chairs made from human skin or anything like that.

### She Joked About Heads

"We were looking at the plaster and the things you look at if you're thinking about trading houses. Naturally, we didn't look for anything like the things they say they found. If I came to your house, would I be looking at the chairs to see if they were made from human hide?

"The kids have always said the Gein place was haunted, and they've brought back stories about him having shrunken heads there. So when we were upstairs in his house, I kidded Ed about it — people were always kidding Ed that way."

"We moved on down the stairs, my husband and me talking about how hard it would be to bring electricity into the house, and I thought Ed gave me another funny look. But I decided it was because he was embarrassed, the house being so dirty and all."

### "Always Kidding Gein"

"People were always kidding Gein about things like that," said Norris Diggles, a neighbor of the Fosters and Hills.

"He was a little peculiar," Doris Diggles, Norris' wife, added. "Like the time Mary Hogan disappeared over at Pine Grove. People would kid Ed about it and he'd say, sure, he did it. Whenever there was any crime anywhere Ed would confess to it. Everybody thought it was a big joke."

"That's right," Mrs. Foster agreed. "He's admitted to us he did away with Mary Hogan. We'd kid him about it, like everybody did, and he'd say, 'Yes, I went and got her in my little pickup truck and took her home.' And then he'd grin. Of course, nobody believed him. Not then."

Last Saturday evening, Gein came to the home of Mr. and Mrs. Lester Hill, Bob's parents, and ate his usual hearty supper —in this case pork chops and boiled potatoes. This was after Mrs. Bernice Worden, the widow who ran the local hardware store, had disappeared, but before her body had been found in the summer kitchen attached to Gein's house.

### Son-in-Law Bears News

Jim Vroman, the Hills' son-in-law, came home with the news of Mrs. Worden's disappearance.

"Ed just stood there and listened," Mrs. Hill said. "He didn't act any different than he ever did. He ate a good meal. I remember, when somebody passed the bread, he said that reminded him, he'd got to get a loaf of bread before he went home."

"I even kidded him about Mrs. Worden's disappearing. I said, 'Ed, how come every time somebody gets banged on the head and hauled away you're always around?' And he just grinned the way he always did and said, 'Oh, that was easy.'"

Mrs. Foster said that her 11 year old, Linda, was very fond of Gein, who would hold her on his lap and buy her bubble gum.

### "Did Nothing Wrong"

"He never did anything wrong. But still I knew he was not quite right, and parents do worry. One reason we bought our television set was to discourage Linda from playing with Ed."

"But the kids all liked him. He'd play ball with the kids. Once, when my husband, Don, was away at an auction to buy a tractor, I wanted to go see what was keeping him so long. Ed was around, so I asked him to baby sit with Howard. I told him to help himself to the peaches. He baby sat and ate peaches and watched the television until I came home."

"When he used to come to my house to get water," Mrs. Diggles said, "I'd always lock my door. I'd laugh at myself for doing it—he was just a harmless goof, we thought—but still I'd lock it."

### Talked About Politics

"There are lots of funny people in the world," Mrs. Foster said. "You can't go worrying about all of them. You could talk about politics or something with him, and he'd make sense."

"A lot of people thought he didn't know very much," Mrs. Hill said. "But he knew a lot."

"He could talk on any subject you wanted to talk about," her husband agreed.

"He was always talking about detective stories," Bob Hill said. "But he could talk about flying saucers or anything—he seemed to be well read on most everything."

### "He Wasn't Stupid"

"He wasn't stupid," the elder Hill added. "He could talk as well as you can. Of course, you expect an old bachelor living alone like that to be a little peculiar. But he wasn't stupid."

"I thought I knew him pretty well," Bob Hill said. "I went to shows with him. When I couldn't get the car to go to a basketball game, he'd take me. Once he took my uncle to the hospital."

"He was a very accommodating man," Hill agreed. "He'd go out of his way to do you a favor."

Mr. and Mrs. Norris Diggles

ent...
12-1-57

## Discovery of Skeleton Adds to Gein Mystery

The two obtained permission from Lars Thomsen, owner of the the farm across the road from Gein, to hunt his woods for squirrels. Travis left his 18 year old bride of a few weeks, telling her and his mother that he would return in a few hours.

Travis and Burgess appeared at a Plainfield tavern later in the day and left, saying they intended to return to the Thomsen farm for some more hunting.

In the tavern, Burgess said he had $4,000 in cash with him at the time.

His driver's license carried the address of the Carlton hotel, Milwaukee, but investigators later said the hotel had no record of him. The license number of his car, recorded by Thomsen when he gave the men permission to hunt, was issued in the name of a man who had been dead two years.

Digging was suspended in the garbage trench area at about 3:40 p.m. and the 15 officers in the digging party transferred their operations to a site about 600 yards southwest of the Gein farm home. One of the officers said that this site had never been dug up previously in the Gein investigation.

### Trench Is T Shaped

Saturday, Cummings said, two more pieces of bone were found in the immediate area of the hole dug Friday. They then enlarged the trench until it was in the shape of a T, about 10 yards on the east-west crossbar and 20 yards to the north.

The Saturday digging started at about 11:30 a.m. and the new bones were found about noon. The diggers also found about 15 glass jars with covers and a bottle with a cap. There was liquid in some, but most of them were empty.

The first digging site was on a 40 acre hayfield north of the road that forms the boundary of Gein's main farm. Another road that forms the west boundary of this field is on the Adams county line.

### No New Leads

The second digging site was south of the east-west road.

Sheriff Schley said that Friday morning, he and Sheriff Frank Serles and Dist. Atty. Donald L. Hollman of Adams county and several deputies covered Gein's 160 acre farm on foot, seeking the car that Travis and Burgess were in when they went hunting. Schley said it had never been recovered.

Both Schley and Wanserski say that they have no new leads at the moment.

## Missing Person Probe Revives Travis Mystery

Waushara County law enforcement agencies and the district attorney's office are primarily interested in one thing presently regarding the Ed Gein case. That is proving conclusively, with all possible evidence, that he is responsible for the death of Mrs Bernice Worden.

The identifying of the remains of 9 other skulls found on the Gein farm will be left to the State Crime Laboratory and to officials of other counties who have missing persons on record.

The investigation will be carried further, however, only if it is definitely proven that the bodies were not taken from various cemeteries as Gein states is the case.

In addition to the Mary Hougan case, which the local authorities were involved in to a more or less minor degree since the tavern was located in Pine Grove Township in Portage County, there is one other area "missing person" case that received considerable publicity at the time.

The latter involved the disappearance of Victor "Bunk" Travis who disappeared from a Plainfield tavern on Nov. 1, 1952.

The story, which appeared in The Argus issue of December 3, 1952 read as follows:

"The search for Victor "Bunk" Travis, Adams County man who mysteriously disappeared Nov. 1 with a stranger after leaving Mac's Bar in Plainfield, reached into Waushara County this week with Sheriff Leon Murty checking movements of the men before they were last seen.

"Travis formerly lived in Waushara County, west of Hancock. For some time, however, he lived about four miles south and east of Big Flats tavern and store on state highway 13.

"His disappearance has raised many questions:

"What has happened to Travis?

"Who was the stranger in whose company Travis was last seen about 7 p.m., Nov. 1?

"Why would he leave his pretty young bride of two months without telling her, or his mother, that he didn't expect to be back within a few hours?

"These questions are stirring the imaginations of the natives in sparsely settled Adams County, a county that has thousands of acres of wilderness. A wilderness that is seldom traversed except in limited fashion during deer hunting season. It is wild country that could hide violence for years and perhaps never give up its secret."

The final appearance of Travis and the stranger was at the Plainfield bar (they had been visiting other bars in the area over a period of about a week)

In their last visit to Plainfield they were reported to have stayed at the bar about three hours. They left saying they were going to return to the Lars Thomsen farm in the Town of Plainfield to hunt. Neither of the two men has been seen since.

# Skull Dug Up at Gein Farm Studied as Clue to Lost Man

**But Officials Do Not Know if It Is Male**

## State Crime Experts Remain of Opinion That Only Women Are Involved

Plainfield, Wis. — Officers from three counties were uncertain Saturday whether parts of a skeleton including a skull with a gold tooth, were those of a mysterious stranger who disappeared five years ago while hunting with an acquaintance near the home of confessed killer-ghoul Ed Gein.

The skeleton was unearthed Friday by deputies from Portage county who were digging in a long trench which served as a garbage pit on the Gein farm. Deputies from Waushara and Adams counties later joined in the digging.

Gein has admitted slaying two women and robbing nine graves. Both slayings and the grave robberies involved women. Authorities were unable to say late Saturday night whether the skeleton discovered Friday was that of a woman or a man.

Atty. Gen. Stewart Honeck said at Madison that state crime laboratory technicians were "still of the opinion that Gein's act—both disturbances of graves and murder — do not involve male victims."

### Other Bodies Possible

The attorney general was placed in over-all charge of the investigation by Gov. Thomson last Monday. He said the finding of an additional skeleton on the farm in Waushara county was "not inconsistent" with information obtained from Gein during lie detector tests at the crime laboratory.

And, Honeck said, searchers may unearth portions of two more bodies, in addition to the skeleton uncovered in a garbage pit by Sheriff Herbert Wanserski of Portage county Friday.

However, Honeck declared that state technicians still thought that this skeleton—and perhaps two more—were among those taken from cemeteries in the area.

Honeck said he had sent former FBI special agent James Poster and another special investigator to Plainfield.

"We may come up with something more," Honeck said.

The investigator, Milo Ottow, was in Plainfield Saturday and took the bones found Friday back to Madison for the state crime laboratory to check.

### Total Now 14

Honeck said that the discovery of the new skeletal parts raised the number of human beings whose remains had been found in the case to a tentative total of 14.

Previously, the total had been given as 11 — including two women Gein has admitted murdering and nine other bodies Gein claims to have taken from graves. No. 12, Honeck said, would be the skull and bones found Friday by Portage county officers. Nos. 13 and 14, Honeck said, were "two more possibilities which must be confirmed by further polygraph tests" after mental tests of Gein were completed.

Honeck said that he had been informed by Sheriff Arthur Schley of Waushara county that the bones found Friday included a complete skull and identifiable teeth, but not enough bones to form a complete body.

Schley said that the bones were scattered, indicating that they were not buried as a complete body. He said that there were no ribs or chest bones and that one foot was not found.

Deputies said that they found chunks of material which appeared to be flesh and looked like stiffened rawhide. The digging also produced a three by five inch piece of denim with a brass button and part of a seam.

*Victor Travis*

### "Just About Satisfied"

The sensational new development came as authorities in Waushara county, where Gein lived, expressed themselves as "just about satisfied" with the 51 year old bachelor's story that he had killed and butchered two women, but that parts of an undetermined number of bodies found in his home had been dug out of new graves.

So far, Gein has named nine graves, although state crime laboratory officials indicated that "there might be more than nine" bodies involved in Gein's grisly collection of human heads and other remains.

Gein was arrested just two weeks ago Saturday after the mutilated body of 58 year old Mrs. Bernice Worden was found hanging by the heels in his woodshed. A week ago, Gein was committed to central state hospital for the criminally insane to determine whether he was sane enough to stand trial for first degree murder in the Worden case.

He also has admitted similarly slaying Mrs. Mary Hogan, 54 year old Portage county tavern operator, in 1954.

But he insisted the other human remains came from cemeteries.

### Two Caskets Empty

The case quieted down last week when Dist. Atty. Earl Kileen of Waushara county presided over opening of two graves selected at random from Gein's list, and found both caskets empty.

However, Wanserski and his officers continued to search the weed grown and now snow covered farmstead six miles southwest of Plainfield.

Friday, Wanserski said, he and Deputy George Cummings decided to dig into a trench about a quarter mile from the house after neighbors said they occasionally had seen Gein "burying garbage" there.

After an hour's digging at one end of the 40 foot trench, Wanserski said, the two men uncovered a skeleton, including a complete skull with a prominent gold tooth.

Serles said Saturday that that coincided with the description of a man known to authorities only as Ray Burgess, who went hunting with Victor (Bunk) Travis, 43, of Friendship, on a farm across the road from the Gein place on Nov. 1, 1952.

Neither man ever was seen again.

### Met in Tavern

At the time of the Travis disappearance, investigators found that he had met the man known as Burgess in a near-by Big Flats tavern about a week before the hunting trip. Burgess had attracted considerable attention with his gold tooth and his willingness to scatter $100 bills on the bar to "buy drinks for the house."

# Gein Tells Why He Killed: Wanted to Be a Woman

## Blames Murders, Grave Raids On Desire to Change Sex

MADISON, Wis.—A quiet, lonely farmer with a vacant stare has revealed in horrifying detail how he robbed graves, killed and butchered because of his desire to be a woman.

Ed Gein, 51, "the butcher of Plainfield," told his story to investigators at the Wisconsin state crime laboratory here.

In a lie test given him at the laboratory, Gein admitted killing Mrs. Mary Hogan in her saloon Dec. 8, 1954. He also confessed killing Mrs. Bernice Worden, of Plainfield, last Saturday.

Charles Wilson, head of the crime laboratory, said Gein took the test with "a sort of detachment."

* * *

BUT GEIN'S minute accounting of his ghoulish career came in the long interrogation which preceded the brief polygraph test.

He traced the beginnings of his wish to change sex back to his intense devotion to his mother Augusta — whom he lovingly nursed through two strokes before her death in 1945.

Left alone in his secluded farm, the mousey-looking bachelor bought anatomical text books. He said he thought of operating on himself to change himself into a woman, but later abandoned the idea.

* * *

EVENTUALLY, he began to make moonlight excursions to graveyards to exhume the bodies of women whose obituary notices he had read in local papers.

He had said he was compelled to do this by some "thrill-like urge."

Gein told how he cut up the cadavers at his farm, keeping only the heads, skin and a few other parts. The rest he burned in his kitchen stove.

From the skin he made belts, a drum and, with the torso of one woman, a vest.

He stripped the faces from their skulls and preserved the resulting "masks" by rubbing them with oil and keeping them in cold storage.

* * *

FROM TIME to time, he said, he would put on a mask, the vest and the other woman's parts and would walk alone about his junk-littered house.

Gein said he killed Mrs. Hogan in her Portage County saloon after he had noticed a strong resemblance between her and his mother.

He said he shot her with a .32 caliber pistol and took her body back to his farm in his truck.

There he strung up her body in a shed which his father had formerly used as a pig slaughterhouse and butchered it.

* * *

HE SAID he shot Mrs. Worden with a .22 caliber rifle he suddenly picked up while he was in her hardware store.

Gein said he had often watched her and went to the store last Saturday after he had learned that her son Frank would be deer hunting that day.

He said he loaded Mrs. Worden's body into her trunk and returned to the store for the cash register. Gein, a handyman, said he was fascinated by the mechanics of the device.

* * *

HE DROVE his cargo out of town and returned for his own car. Later, he transferred both the body and the cash register to the car and drove to his farm.

In the slaughter shed, Gein said he carved the body with a knife he made from a file.

He said he interrupted his work occasionally to tinker with his car and the cash register.

## None Surprised At Report in Gein Case

WAUTOMA — Central State Hospital's report on the mental condition of Edward Gein came as a surprise to no one in this county seat town that was shaken by the deeds of the little Plainfield area recluse and handyman.

The medical report that Gein was "not competent to stand trial" surprised William Belter, his attorney, least of all; Belter had pleaded the confessed murderer of two women and molester of graves not guilty by reason of insanity and his own medical experts reported last week that the Plainfield man was insane.

The official findings from the Central State Hospital were revealed Monday by Circuit Judge Herbert A. Bunde at Wisconsin Rapids. Bunde, whose circuit includes Waushara County, committed Gein to the hospital for the criminally insane Nov. 22, less than a week after the butchered body of Mrs. Bernice Worden of Plainfield was found in Gein's debris filled "house of horrors."

Belter, commenting on the hospital report, said this morning that he would await a decision by Judge Bunde on a date for the hearing on the hospital report. Belter indicated a "tentative" date has been set but declined to reveal it, as the judge had announced he would call the formal sanity hearing "at a time and place to be designated later." Judge Bunde told Belter, however, that he would call the hearing on a date "agreeable to all parties."

### Another Report

There were indications, Belter said, that Atty. Gen. Stewart Honeck, who has been placed in charge of the investigation, might bring in a third medical report on Gein's condition. It was considered likely that all medical reports would agree that Gein is unable to stand trial, but in the event Honeck's experts believe Gein sane then there would be a chance for formal arguments at the hearing.

In the event all medical experts agree that Gein is incompetent to stand trial, the sanity hearing is apt to be a mere formality, with Judge Bunde recommitting the confessed murderer back to Central State Hospital for an indefinite period.

At any rate, Gein will be brought back to Wautoma for the sanity hearing before Judge Bunde. Whether he will be asked to speak in the courtroom, Belter indicated, is a matter of speculation. But for the official record, the report of the hospital will be made orally and Judge Bunde will then decide on a course of action.

# Thinks Skull Loot of Grave

## Attorney General Believes Latest Gein Find Came From Cemetery

MADISON—(AP) — Atty. Gen. Stewart Honeck reiterated Sunday the State Crime Laboratory feels analysis would show that a skull unearthed on Edward Gein's farm Friday came from a grave robbery and not a slaying.

Atty. Gen. Stewart Honeck said today that the State Crime Laboratory is trying to determine whether the skull was that of a man or woman and whether it came from a grave robbery or a slaying. Honeck said that a report may be given to him by the Laboratory later today.

State authorities have said they believe Gein's killing and grave robbery involved only women victims.

Sheriffs Herb Wanserski of Portage County and Frank Serles of Adams County have speculated the latest find represents the remains of one of two hunters missing since 1952.

### Molar Doesn't Match

Wanserski and Serles said Sunday that a gold molar found in the skull apparently does not match the dental work of either missing man.

However Wanserski said there was one deep cavity among the front teeth of the skull, indicating a cold-capped tooth might once have occupied the space.

Wanserski and a deputy dug up the skull in a garbage pit on the Gein farm Friday.

He and Serles have speculated the skull might be that of 43-year-old Victor Travis of Friendship, in Adams County, or his companion, a man known only as Ray Burgess.

The skull's gold crown was far back in the mouth.

### Gold Tooth Prominent

Burgess' gold tooth was prominent. The sight of it still is remembered in a tavern where he spent money generously the day he and Travis vanished.

Wanserski said Travis' brother told him Victor had no gold teeth.

The finding of the skull spurred speculation about the location of the hunters' auto which also disappeared. Serles said he was not overlooking the possibility that the auto might be buried in the sandy soil on Gein's farm.

## GIVES STATEMENT

A long statement which Edward Gein (bottom photo) made to Dist. Atty. Earl F. Kileen concerning the slaying of a Plainfield widow was read to reporters (top photo) by Mrs. Arthur Judge, secretary for the district attorney, Monday. The small anteroom to the district attorney's office was filled with reporters and cameramen covering what has been described as one of the grisliest slayings in the history of the United States. In the statement, Gein confessed to the butchering of Mrs. Bernice Worden, 58, a storekeeper from whom he bought anti-freeze Saturday morning, just before she disappeared from her store. (Daily

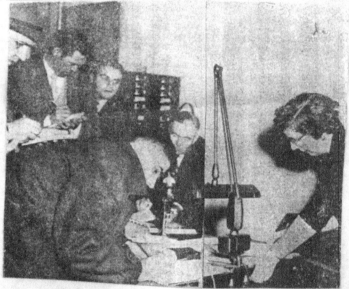

## Honeck Gets OK for Role At Gein Trial

MADISON — Gov. Thomson authorized Wisconsin's attorney general Wednesday to take part in the prosecution of Edward Gein of Plainfield if Gein is found sane enough to stand trial for murder.

Atty. Gen. Honeck had asked the governor earlier Wednesday for the authority after Dist. Atty. Earl Kileen of Waushara County requested the attorney general's participation.

Honeck pointed out that the state has participated in eight murder trials since 1942.

Gein is in the third week of a 30-day mental observation at Central State Hospital where psychiatrists seek to determine whether he is fit to stand trial.

The 51-year-old bachelor is charged with first degree murder in the slaying of Mrs. Bernice Worden, 58-year-old Plainfield widow whose mutilated body was found hanging in a shed at Gein's farm house the night of Nov. 16.

Gein has admitted slaying Mrs. Worden and Mrs. Mary Hogan of Bancroft, who disappeared in 1954, and robbing the graves of at least nine other women.

## UW to Help in Gein Case

### Experts Will Check Skull to Determine What Sex It Is

Madison, Wis. — Atty. Gen. Stewart Honeck said Monday that bones found on the Ed Gein farm in Waushara county Friday and Saturday were being turned over to University of Wisconsin experts to determine if they belonged to a man or woman.

Gein, a 51 year old bachelor, has confessed killing two women and robbing the graves of others. State authorities believe that only women were involved, possibly 14.

However, there was speculation that the new found bones might be those of a mysterious Ray Burgess who disappeared Nov. 1, 1952, while hunting on a farm next to Gein's. The skull dug up Friday along with other bones had a gold crowned tooth, far back in the mouth.

"Those who remember Burgess said his gold tooth was easily seen when he laughed," Sheriff Frank Serles of Adams county said Sunday. "Possibly, if he laughed, it could be visible in the back of his mouth. I can't say for sure. This makes you wonder what that farmhouse really holds."

Burgess and a companion, Victor (Bunk) Travis, 43, of Friendship, disappeared at the same time. Even their car has never been found.

Sheriff Herbert Wanserski of Portage county, who dug up the skeleton Friday, said that Travis had no gold teeth according to a brother.

Wanserski added that, although the gold molar in the skull did not match the dental work of either man, there was a deep cavity among of the front teeth of the skull, indicating that a crowned tooth might have occupied that space.

"This is a mixed up affair," Wanserski added. "I think this will take quite a while to figure out."

### No Time Element

Honeck said that there was no rush to check the skull because the crime laboratory was confident that only women were involved. Assuming that no time element is involved because the bodies are all from graves, he said that it was thought best to question Gein again on the matter.

Gein is now in the central state hospital for the criminally insane at Waupun, undergoing 30 day tests to determine if he is sane enough to stand trial for murder.

Sunday, Honeck conferred with crime laboratory officials, his staff investigator Milo Ottow, and former FBI special investigator James B. Poster. Poster went to Plainfield Monday to gather information to be used in formulating the state's case in the event Gein comes to trial. He will interrogate officials and Gein's neighbors.

Honeck said that there would be no more digging at the farm unless new leads were found.

Ottow was at the farm southwest of Plainfield Saturday and brought back the new bones dug up. There were not enough for a complete skeleton.

### House Under Guard

A strict security guard is still being maintained at the Gein farm to keep out curious people. The United Press reported that Sunday morning, Gein's attorney, William Belter, Wautoma, was even refused admittance when he drove out to look at the garbage pit from which Wanserski dug up the bones Friday.

Belter said he was making plans to have a private psychiatrist examine Gein, who is charged with the murder of Mrs. Bernice Worden, 58, a Plainfield storekeeper. Portage county authorities have not yet filed any charges in the death of Mrs. Mary Hogan, 54, a tavern operator near Bancroft, whose murder Gein has also admitted.

Sheriff Wanserski said that Monday he planned to question more of Gein's neighbors to see if there were any other places Gein might have buried refuse. He said he also planned to question a person who called him Sunday night and was very excited about some information he had but would not give it over the telephone.

## Honeck Urges State Pay Bulk Of Probe Costs

MADISON (UP) — Atty. Gen. Stewart Honeck recommended Friday that the state pay its share and that of the counties for the continuation of the state Crime Lab's investigation of evidence in the Ed Gein murder case.

Honeck made his recommendation to Gov. Vernon W. Thomson after conferring with Crime Lab Director Charles Wilson.

The state shares Crime Lab costs equally with counties that request the lab's services. But, the five counties involved now have most or all of the findings they required and might ask that the tests stop.

Wilson said he wants to continue investigating the "massive" evidence in the case until it has been established, beyond a reasonable doubt that "there were no more murder victims."

### Confessed Two Killings

Gein, 51-year-old Plainfield handy man, has confessed the murder and mutilation of two women, but claims the remnants of other bodies found at his farm home were dug up from graveyards.

The investigation at the laboratory would stop soon if the counties had the information they needed and the state refused to pay for continuing.

Wilson said "it may take weeks, months and even years" to complete tests on all the material in the Gein case. "The lab worked 15 months on the Evelyn Hartley case and there is much more evidence to contend with in this one."

Honeck, chairman of the State Crime Lab Control Board, said murder is the concern of all counties.

### Five To Share Cost

If the state takes over costs of the investigation from here on, the individual counties will be billed for 50 per cent of the work done for them. Counties that will share in the bill are Waushara, Portage, La Crosse, Jefferson and Adams.

Wilson and Honeck had no estimate of the costs for the investigation so far. Crime lab services cost $9.55 an hour for each of the nine technicians on the job. Wilson's salary and other administrative costs are paid by the state.

Work done for the counties in the latest 12-month period cost a total of $47,000 for them and an equal amount for the state. The more populous counties paid the greatest share because of their greater volume and some counties had no expense. Milwaukee County paid the largest amount, $11,682.

Monday, December 2, 1957

## Gein Hinted Car Could Be Buried in Conversation

*Dec 9, 1957*

Amid rumors, speculation and "hot tips" there was little actual new evidence uncovered by investigators at the Ed Gein farm during the past few days.

Sheriff Herbert Wanserski of Portage County told the United Press Tuesday that he was checking a "hot tip" on where Gein might have buried additional bodies, but sheriffs and deputies from Waushara, Adams and Portage counties were unable to come up with anything tangible in digging on Monday and Tuesday.

Sheriff Wanserski had also expressed a belief that a skull found late last week was that of either Victor "Bunk" Travis or man hunting with him known only as Ray Burgess. The men disappeared in November of 1952 while hunting near the Gein farm.

However, the State Crime Laboratory determined Monday that the skull was that of a woman 30 to 50 years old. Attorney General Stewart Honeck made the announcement Monday and said the laboratory still believes the skull, and the bones found with it, came from a grave robbery and not slaying.

Honeck said the finding of another skull was "not inconsistent" with information gained during lie detector tests of Gein.

The rumors of finding a buried car and the use of bulldozers on the Gein farm are "completely untrue", according to Waushara County Sheriff Arthur Schley.

Stories circulated on Monday had the car complete with the two missing hunters (Travis and Burgess) unearthed on the farm.

The possibility of there being such a "buried treasure was not ruled out by the sheriff, however.

The sheriff said that Gein had mentioned in a conversation with a neighbor at the time the men turned up missing that "it would be no trick at all to bury a car in the area".

When the neighbor mentioned that it might be difficult to keep the sides from caving in, Gein noted that it wouldn't be if the sides of the excavation were tapered.

Sheriff Schley also spiked another rumor concerning a conversation Gein had with a renter.

The report was that Gein had told the renter he could not plow over a certain area of the farm, and when the renter did plow over the area, Gein became enraged.

There was no such conversation, the renter told investigators.

Two special investigators have been assigned to the case and are aiding in the search for new evidence. One, a retired FBI agent is seeking information from persons who knew Gein. The other, from the state attorney general's office, is working out of the sheriff's office at Wautoma.

## Gein Returned To Waupun for Indefinite Stay

*Jan 8, 1958*

What may well be the final chapter in the Ed Gein case was written Monday with a sanity hearing in the court of Judge Herbert Bunde at Wisconsin Rapids.

Gein was taken to Wisconsin Rapids early Monday morning by Sheriff Art Schley and deputies Arnold Fritz, Arthur Schwandt and "Buck" Batterman.

Judge Bunde heard testimony from three psychiatrists, who all agreed that he was medically insane, but only two of the three thought he was also legally insane and unable to stand trial.

On the findings of the three and other testimony, the judge ruled that the confessed slayer was legally insane and ordered him committed to central state hospital for the criminally insane at Waupun for an indeterminate term.

The judge commented, "I think it is adequate to say that he will never be at liberty again".

Shortly after 8 p.m. Monday night, Gein was delivered to the state hospital by county authorities.

And unless something unforeseen occurs, there he will stay until the end of his life.

## Lured to Graves by Moon—Farmer

Special to The Chicago American.

MADISON, Wis., Nov. 20—Edward Gein, hermit farmer who confessed butchering a woman neighbor, said last night he believes he robbed graves "by the light of a full moon."

The 51-year-old bachelor, who remained on his 190-acre farm near Plainfield after the deaths of his mother and brother, told Earl F. Kileen, district attorney, he had opened graves in at least two cemeteries. Ten skulls were found scattered around Gein's delapidated frame house, and he said all the skulls belonged to women.

Kileen said Gein has pointed out one grave in the Plainfield Cemetery from which he removed the head of a 60-year-old woman who died in 1949.

Kileen said Gein told him he began opening graves in the Plainfield area "about 1949 and quit it about three years ago."

Gein told the prosecutor he was "interested only in the bodies of women," Kileen said. He added:

"He said he opened the graves at night, removed the heads and other parts of the bodies, then refilled the graves.

"He said he always was in a daze while robbing the graves, but thought he had dug by the light of a full moon."

Kileen said Gein admitted he "always went to fresh graves after reading about burials of women in the papers." Kileen added:

"I am interested only in prosecuting this man for the murder of Mrs. Worden of Plainfield. The grave-robbing penalty is a term of one to three years. To press that charge would necessitate the opening of graves, and I want no part of that. Think how the poor relatives would feel."

Kileen said a woman neighbor who has known Gein all her life told him she "would not be surprised if one of the 10 skulls was his mother's, or that another was that of his brother."

The neighbor told the prosecutor that the mother, Augusta, a widow who died in 1945, ruled her sons with an iron hand. The elder brother, Henry, died in 1944, apparently after a heart attack that followed exertion at a brush fire, which Edward helped him extinguish. Henry was planning to marry at the time, Kileen said.

Kileen said other neighbors have told how Mrs. Gein frequently lectured her sons about the "dangers of meeting up with women who curl their hair or wear corsets."

Plainfield residents have described the Geins as very clannish people "who never attended church but often were heard mouthing references to God and the Bible."

# Detectives Uncover Gein's Grisly Life

BY MICHAEL R. GARRETT

Two Chicago detectives spent two and one-half hours questioning Edward Gein, the "butcher" of Plainfield, Wis.

Sgt. Edward Cagney and Detective George Lundt, of the special investigation unit, declared Gein is a "queer duck—like nothing we have ever seen before."

This is the story Gein told the detectives:

He likes women, but had little to do with them. He never kissed one in his life. He got a thrill from robbing graves which he did only under an urge—and under a full moon.

Cagney and Lundt said he is obviously lying when he talks of blacking out, and he answers only what is already known.

## OPENED 40 GRAVES

The detectives said they asked him the following questions:

Q—How many graves did you open up and rob?

A—I opened up 40 graves, but most of the time I would hear someone tell me "don't do it."

Q—Did you do something or take something from each of the 40 graves?

A—About 30 times I heard someone tell me "don't do it," and I wouldn't. I would close the graves and leave.

Q—What did you take from the graves you robbed?

A—I would cut off the head and other parts of the body and take them with me.

Q—Did you do this during the day or at night?

A—Only at night—when the moon was full.

Detectives Cagney and Lundt suggested he might have read about cannibalism, or saw movies suggesting grave robbing or head shrinking, and Gein replied:

"You know, you may have something there."

Sgt. Cagney asked him:

"Why did you rob graves during a full moon—where did you ever hear about that?"

## THRILL FROM GRAVE

His reply:

"I had an aunt who used to work in an insane asylum, and she once told me that whenever there was a full moon they (the inmates) would go wild."

He said whenever he would open a grave he would get a "thrill" out of it. On occasions the urge overcame him and he would cut off the head from the body.

In each case, whether he would rob the grave or not, he would always replace the earth and leave the grave orderly—as he found it.

Gein said he read the death notices and whenever he would get an urge he would select the grave of a recent burial, always a female. He added:

"But I would always black out in the cemetery."

## EVADING SOMETHING

The detectives said:

"He's evading something he won't talk about. If it was up to me, I would turn the farm upside down—it might turn up the bodies of women and girls whose disappearance never were solved.

"I can't say he is responsible for all these crimes, but I sure would pursue the possibility."

Cagney and Lundt said they switched the questioning to his association with women.

Q—Did you ever have a sweetheart?

A—I went with a girl up here a few times, but I quit her because of the way she treated her mother. I also took one or two girls to a movie a few times, but I never made love to them or kissed them.

Cagney and Lundt said Gein insisted he has never been further south than Milwaukee. He went there during World War II for his induction, but he was rejected for poor eyesight and because he was in farm work.

The detectives had gone to Wisconsin to question Gain and find out if he might have knowledge of three unsolved major crimes here—the triple murders in Robinson Woods, the Grimes sisters deaths and the Judith Mae Andersen torso murder. They returned from the trip last night.

They are satisfied he had nothing to do with these crimes.

# Farm Brought to Crime Lab

Gein's farm home near Plainfield. In the center picture, James Halligan, an official of the Crime Lab, is shown unloading the truck, and at the right, Jan Beck, another employe of the state investigating agency, is leaving the truck with paper bags containing other items found at the farm. (Photos by Carmie A. Thompson)

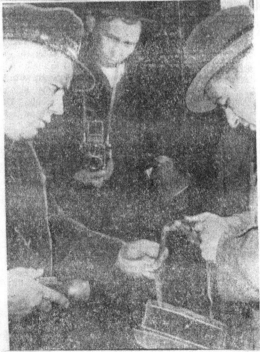

Wisconsin crime laboratory technician holding woman's handbag with a handle suspected to be of human skin, among items found in the Gein home. [United Press Telephoto]

James Halligan of crime laboratory carrying sacks of human remains into mobile laboratory at the Gein farm home.

November 19, 1957  Milwaukee Sentinel

ED GEIN (FOREGROUND) AND SHERIFF ART SCHLEY LEAVING FOR MURDER SCENE

Scores of curious persons visited the Gein farm home near Plainfield (shown above). The house appeared quite neat on the outside, but the interior was poorly kept and cluttered with items of every kind.

*November 17, 1957 Milwaukee Journal*

# Plainfield Merchant, a Widow, Found Dead

## Truck Taken From Store She Operated

### Report Cash Register Tampering; Body Is Discovered on Farm Seven Miles Away

Journal Special Correspondence
**Plainfield, Wis.**—The body of a 58 year old widow who operated a hardware store on Main st. here was found Saturday night on a farm seven miles away.

Sheriff Art Schley of Waushara county said late Saturday night that he was holding a suspect in connection with the death. He would not identify the suspect.

Mrs. Bernice Worden had been reported missing at 5 p.m. by her son, Frank, when he returned to the hardware store after a hunting trip.

Frank told Sheriff Schley that there were bloodstains on the floor of the store, a truck was missing from the garage behind the store and someone had tampered with the cash register.

The door was locked when Frank tried to enter the store shortly before 5 p.m. He used his own key to unlock the door.

### Noticed Store Closed

The Worden Hardware & Implement store is situated on one of the main corners in Plainfield, where highways 51 and 73 and Main st. intersect. Persons walking down Main st. had noticed Saturday that the store was closed, but believed that it might have something to do with the deer season.

Bernard Munchinski, Plainfield, told authorities that he had seen the Worden truck come out of the driveway next to the store about 9:30 a.m. The store usually opened at 8 a.m.

Mrs. Worden had operated the store since the death of her husband in 1931. She lived alone in her home six blocks from the store. Frank, who helped at the store, lives in another part of town with his family.

### Next to Vacant Buildings

There is an unoccupied building next to the store on one side and a vacant house on the other.

Sheriff Schley refused to give any details concerning the death of Mrs. Worden. He said that deputies had found the body on the farm of Ed Gein, who lives seven miles south west of Plainfield near the Adams county line.

The sheriff would not reveal whether any money was missing from the store.

Plainfield is less than 10 miles from the town of Pine Grove in Portage county, where a woman disappeared on Dec. 9, 1954.

Miss Mary Hogan, 54, was found missing from the tavern she operated in the town of Pine Grove. Blood was splattered around the tavern and a cash box had been emptied. No trace of Miss Hogan has ever been found.

-MONDAY, NOVEMBER 18, 1957

*Milwaukee Sentinel*

# Plainfield Widow Sliced Up, Hung By Heels on Hook

PLAINFIELD, Wis., Nov. 17 (Special) The decapitated body of a missing Plainfield widow and the skulls or other remains of four or five women have been found in a farmhouse seven miles west of here, Dist. Atty. Earl Kileen of Waushara County said Sunday.

Authorities of seven counties came upon the gruesome scene, resembling a human slaughterhouse, when a search for Mrs. Bernice Worden, 58, operator of a Plainfield hardware store, led Saturday night to the farm of Ed Gein, about 50.

## Suspect Denies Human Butchery

Gein was arrested and will be arraigned in County Court at Wautoma Monday, Kileen said, but the specific charge has not yet been determined.

Gein admitted being in the Worden store Saturday, but denied he had "hurt" her and or engaged in the butchery revealed on his farm premises.

Mrs. Worden was reported missing by her son, Frank, who returned from a hunting trip at 5 p.m. Saturday, found the store door locked, unlocked it and discovered a pool of blood on the floor. The cash register had been opened.

When authorities got to the Gein farm about 8 p.m., Gein was not there. They forced open the door of a shed and there the nude body of Mrs. Worden was discovered, hung up by the heels.

## Heart Found in Plastic Bag

The head had been severed, the stomach opened, the viscera removed and the heart put in a plastic bag, Kileen said.

It was a scene indicating one of the worst crimes ever committed in central Wisconsin, Kileen said. He added:

"It appears to be cannibalism."

The body had been washed and cleaned in much the same way animals are handled at a slaughterhouse, the district attorney said.

The Worden truck which was seen leaving the hardware store about 9:30 a.m. Saturday was found parked in a pine grove near the Gein farm.

Gein, unmarried, had lived on the farm for about 20 years.

The farm was swarming with law enforcement officers of Waushara and nearby counties when a crew of technicians arrived from the State Crime Laboratory in Madison and took charge of the investigation.

Laboratory Director Charles Wilson came in Sunday to confer with Kileen and other authorities and inspect the slaughter scene.

Authorities promptly set to work looking up details of unsolved disappearances of women and children in this area over the past few years. A child's clothing was one of the items found on the farm.

Sheriff Herbert Wanserski of Portage County was checking into the mysterious disappearance of Miss Mary Hogan, 54, Pine Grove tavern-keeper, missing since Dec. 9, 1954.

### SAME TYPE CASE

Pine Grove is seven miles from Plainfield.

When authorities investigated the Hogan case, they found blood spattered on the tavern floor and the cash box emptied.

Wilson and Sheriff Art Schley of Waushara County attempted a virtual news blackout on the macabre case. Both will release only the barest details on what was found on the farm.

Wilson admitted, however, that he had never worked on a case "quite like this one."

### NUMBER IN DOUBT

Three of Wilson's assistants spent all day Sunday at Gein's farm recovering portions of human bodies. "There is no doubt that what we found was from human bodies," said Wilson.

But Wilson said he would not know "how many bodies" are involved until the State Crime Laboratory completes its examination.

Wilson said some of the anatomical remains were "not of recent origin."

### 'IN PLAIN VIEW'

Sheriff Schley, who has released little information on his own, said "no digging" was necessary in the recovery of the remains.

Schley said "both big and little bones" and other parts of the human body were found all over the farm" and that some of them were "in plain view."

Wilson said clothing and other items such as knives will be sent to the Crime Laboratory along with the human specimens for examination.

Authorities refused to comment on their questioning of the suspect.

Wilson said, however, the farmer's manner was "a little unusual."

He said that Gein appeared "rational" during the questioning but refused to explain what the remains were doing on his farm.

Schley would not say what led authorities to the Gein farm Saturday night. An unofficial report said Gein had been seen Saturday driving Mrs. Worden's truck. The truck was found abandoned a mile east of Plainfield.

**At Top Is** the isolated farm home of Ed Gein, 50, who is being held in connection with the Saturday murder of Mrs. Bernice Worden, 58, operator of a Plainfield hardware store. So far, authorities have found 10 skulls while searching Gein's home and farm. The 50-year-old bachelor is shown in the lower photo as he walks ahead of Waushara county Sheriff Art Schley this morning shortly before Gein showed police where five skulls, neatly wrapped in plastic, were hidden. Gein has admitted "knowing something" about the macabre collection of human remains. Mrs. Worden's body was found under circumstances which indicated she had been butchered. (AP Wirephoto)

By JACK GLASNER
Post-Crescent Staff Writer

Plainfield — Discovery of the headless body of a missing Plainfield woman on a 50-year-old bachelor's farm Saturday has led police of seven counties and state crime laboratory workers into a bizarre case which may involve cannibalism.

Ed Gein, who lives on the 160-acre farm where the body of Mrs. Bernice Worden, 58, Plainfield hardware store operator, was found, was arrested Saturday night.

Police found Mrs. Worden's body hung by its heels in the summer kitchen of Gein's farm home, seven miles northwest of Plainfield, about 70 miles southwest of Appleton.

Gein would not make a statement nor explain the portions of at least four other human skeletons, thought to be women's, found on his farm. Sunday Dist. Atty. Earl Kileen said, "It appears to be cannibalism."

Gein was to appear in Waushara county court in Wautoma today, probably on a charge of robbery. A cash register taken from the blood spattered hardware store operated by Mrs. Worden was found in Gein's home. Kileen added that he thought Gein also would be charged with murder.

**Strange Rumors**

The entire Plainfield-Wautoma area was alive with rumors Sunday night, few of which were stranger than what authorities found on the Gein farm. Rumors were circulating that Gein's bedroom was decorated with furniture upholstered in human skin.

The condition of Mrs. Worden's body prompted Charles Wilson of the state crime laboratory to comment, "I've never worked on a case quite like this one."

Mrs. Worden's body had been washed and cleaned in much the same way animals are handled at a slaughterhouse, Kileen said.

A touch of horror ran through the entire community as children's clothing was found on the farm. At least four skulls were reported found and Wilson said that there was no doubt that "what we have found is from human bodies." He did not elaborate as to age of the victims.

**Search for Woman**

Mrs. Worden was the object of a search since her son, Frank, found the bloody traces in her hardware store and the cash register and a pickup truck missing. She had operated the store for 26 years, since her husband's death.

Police said crime lab workers searching Gein's home had found four other skulls and other segments of bodies—mostly in the first-floor bedroom and kitchen which Gein occupied. The rest of the house still is neatly furnished in a period of 50 years ago. Neighbors said most of the house was little used since Gein's mother died many years ago.

Sheriff Herbert Wanserski of Portage county was investigating the mysterious Dec. 9, 1954, disappearance of Miss Mary Hogan, 54, Pine Grove tavernkeeper. Law enforcement officials throughout the area were trying to relate disappearances in their area to the grisly discoveries.

*November 18th, 1957*
*Post-Crescent*

## Gein Attempts to Hide Face in First Appearance

The reaction of Gein to the popping of dozens of flashbulbs when he first appeared openly late Monday morning before the assembled press changed markedly as the day progressed

His first appearance came when he was taken from the jail to a waiting automobile about 11 a.m. As he came out of the door he attempted to hide his face behind handcuffed hands.

A short time later when he pointed out the location where he had disposed of blood behind the farm home he playfully put his hands over the lens of a moving picture camera and smiled slightly as he did it. This was about 12:45 p.m.

When he left the jail again for his arraignment on a robbery charge about 2:40, he made no attempt to evade cameras.

Also, in the courtroom itself while he was waiting for County Judge Boyd Clark to read the charge, he was docile and made no attempt to avoid photographers.

"A photograph has been prepared and is attached and we believe this photography to be in as good taste as possible under the circumstances.

"This photograph indicates the amount of physical evidence which must now be meticulously evaluated and examined.

"Release concerning the evidence in the cases enumerated must be made by proper local officers.

"No implications can be made concerning this release".

Gein was expected to be returned to Wautoma by Sheriff Arthur Schley about 4 p.m. today.

He is presently being held on a robbery charge (slightly over $40 taken from the Worden store).

District Attorney Earl Kileen told the Argus Wednesday afternoon that no change in the charges will be made until the ballistics tests on a .22 rifle being examined by the crime lab have been completed.

The rifle was found in the Worden store with a spent cartridge in the chamber.

Gein had insisted that he could not have killed Mrs Worden "because he didn't have any weapon."

William Belter, who is representing Gein, has indicated that he will waive preliminary hearing of the defendent.

Assuming that a murder indictment will be forthcoming, Gein would then be bound over to Circuit Court. Also, it is very likely that he would be submitted to sanity tests.

County Judge Boyd Clark stated Wednesday morning that if a preliminary examination was held he would disqualify himself due to the fact that the defendent had pointed out to the court the graves of persons he claims to have entered.

Gein originally maintained that the other nine skulls, found in various places throughout his bachelor quarters, were obtained from cemeteries.

However, with the confession of the slaying of Mrs. Hogan, this theory will be somewhat discredited.

A tentative identification of the head and face of Miss Hogan had been made Monday by Sheriff Herbert Wanserski of Portage County.

Wanserski has been quoted as saying, "This guy never robbed a grave in his life. There's no doubt in my mind but that he killed all of these people".

DEBUT — Ed Geins first appearance before the sizeable press representation gathered in Wautoma came about 11 a.m. Monday morning when he was taken from the jail to go to the farm southwest of Plainfield. He attempted to hide his face at first but later submitted placidly.

# Neighbors Now Remember Gein as 'a Strange One'

*November 19, 1957 Milwaukee Sentinel*

**By JOE BOTSFORD**
*Sentinel Staff Writer*

PLAINFIELD, Wis., Nov. 18—Farmer Ed Gein was "a strange one" to his Waushara County neighbors.

His home, constantly shuttered against daylight and showing signs of decay, has now become legendary here as a house of mystery.

In people's minds, the stage already was set for some drama regarding the middle-aged bachelor farmer and his old house located on a narrow dirt road six miles southwest of here.

### WORSE THAN EXPECTED

But none of his neighbors was prepared for the shocking story that has now been revealed in all its starkness—the fact that the farm was in reality a human slaughterhouse.

Again Monday, curious neighbors drove by the farmhouse where the mutilated body of a Plainfield woman and portions of other human bodies were found.

But there was little to see.

The two-story frame house looked shabby under a dull sky, and falling snow drifted through the roofs of four small barns nearby on the farm, all empty and crumbling into ruin.

### SHADES DRAWN

As usual, neighbors noticed, the windows of the house were darkened by drawn tattered shades.

But now beams of light came through the shades from spotlights being used by State Crime Laboratory personnel as they worked in secret in a front parlor.

Wherever people gathered Monday in Plainfield, a community of less than 700, or nearby Hancock, the talk was about "Ed and his house."

### THIN BUT WIRY

Gein is known here, for he had lived on the farm of his now deceased parents for about 40 years. But few people seem to know him intimately.

He was described as "pleasant" or "quiet" but also as "strange" or "odd." Gein is a little man, thin but wiry, and people pictured him as a man not capable of harming anyone.

Living alone since the death of his mother about 15 years ago, Gein was somewhat of a recluse.

He had not even visited his nearest neighbor, living only a field away, in the past two or three years. Neighbors saw him only when he drove by in his truck.

Occasionally, Gein associated with men in the local taverns. People recall him as saying little, but smiling a lot over a glass of wine.

### NO LIVESTOCK

Gein did not farm his land. He worked for other farmers or for shopkeepers in Plainfield and let his own farm deteriorate.

His house often was referred to jokingly by area residents as a "ghost house." He had no livestock.

When authorities entered the house, they found it "filthy beyond belief."

Plainfield citizens recall that Gein had been coming into town lately and pestering Mrs. Bernice Worden, as she worked in her hardware store, for a date. He had asked her to go roller skating, but the widow declined.

Gein was seen in town Saturday, and it was common knowledge that Mrs. Worden was alone in her store because her son, Frank, had gone deer hunting.

Nor was it surprising to people here that the store was closed early in the day, since it was a common practice for Mrs. Worden to close up briefly to go on an errand.

### SEEK HOGAN TIEUP

Portage County authorities sent investigators to the scene seeking a tie-in with the Dec. 9, 1954, disappearance of Miss Mary Hogan, 54, from her bloodstained Pine Grove tavern.

In the absence of definite evidence, however, authorities for the present at least were taking Gein's story at face value.

One of the most shocked of Gein's acquaintances was Lester Hill, operator of a general store at West Plainfield. He said Gein spent much time around the store, sometimes playing baseball or throwing snowballs with the children.

Linda Foster, 11, said Gein sometimes "babysat" with her 16-month-old brother at the Foster home near the store. "He bought candy for us sometimes," she said.

### SLAIN IN STORE

But residents found it shocking to learn that she apparently had been murdered in her store "in broad daylight" right in the heart of town.

Authorities went to Gein's farm Saturday night because he had been seen in town around 9 a.m. Saturday, once walking toward the store and once driving away in Mrs. Worden's truck.

Her body was found hanging in a rear workshop attached to Gein's house. He was arrested in a restaurant in Plainfield after the body was discovered.

The discovery of the murder was the first big case for Sheriff Arthur Schley.

### 2 DUCK ISSUE

In office only since Oct. 1, Schley attempted an immediate news blackout on the details of the discovery in the farmhouse.

Schley insisted it was up to the State Crime Laboratory to release even the barest details on the base, but Charles Wilson, director of the laboratory, said in turn that it was up to local authorities to release what information they wished.

Wilson returned to Madison headquarters late Monday leaving members of his staff in charge of the investigation.

**Slayer Often Asked Widow For Dates**

# Killer Tells How He 'Deer-Dressed' Widow at Farm

*By Sentinel Staff Writer*

WAUTOMA, Wis., Nov. 18—A timid, 51-year-old bachelor handyman, his hands trembling as he shielded his face, related for the first time Monday details of his butchery of a Plainfield widow and his farmstead "deathhouse" where her body and 10 other human skulls were found.

Edward Gein, longtime solitary occupant of a farm 16 miles northwest of here, ended a 30-hour silence with a statement to Waushara County District Atty. Earl Kileen in which:

- Gein admitted transporting the body of Mrs. Bernice Worden, 58, from her hardware store in the hamlet of Plainfield by truck and car to the woodshed of his farm home, where he butchered her.
- He maintained that the 10 other skulls and portions of female bodies discovered on the farm came from local cemeteries in a series of grave robberies he committed over an undetermined number of years.

## Gein to Face Lie Detector Test

Kileen released portions of Gein's confession before and after the man, described by neighbors as "a typical Casper Milquetoast," was arraigned before County Judge Boyd Clark in the Courthouse here.

He was charged with robbery and was placed under $10,000 bond. Prosecutor Kileen said a murder charge would be filed against Gein as soon as all investigative agencies have completed their investigations.

The district attorney had requested bail of only $5,000 but the court set the higher figure, explaining that if other charges should follow, the bond should be adequate.

Kileen said he was satisfied Gein was telling the truth when he claimed the 10 human skulls in his gruesome collection came only from the graves of already deceased women—and not, as previously speculated, from victims abducted and slaughtered.

However, Kileen said Gein will be taken to Madison to undergo a lie detector test in the offices of the State Crime Laboratory.

*Gein Had Sly Grin, Talked of Women*

## Explanations Branded Vague

The request was made by Crime Lab investigators on the scene, determined to use all scientific means available to get answers on one of the most shocking crimes in Wisconsin history.

The answers provided by Gein himself in his initial statement to the district attorney's office provided only the vaguest and most incomplete explanations for his behavior.

Gein said he suddenly went "into a daze" as he ordered anti-freeze for his car from Mrs. Worden Saturday morning in her store. He couldn't remember how or when he killed Mrs. Worden.

But Gein did recall bringing the body to his farm woodshed, decapitating and viscerating it with a knife he made from a file.

### 'LIKE DRESSING A DEER'

"I thought I was dressing out a deer. That's the only explanation I can think of in my mind," he said in his statement.

The same "daze" came over him, Gein told the district attorney, during his grave robbings. He would follow death notices published in the local newspaper, then would visit the graves of women who had just died.

MRS. WORDEN
*Associated Press Wirephoto*

Gein said he would unearth the coffin, decapitate the body and cut away other anatomical sections. Then he would return the headless corpse to the coffin, return it to the open grave, and cover it again with earth.

The head and other portions of anatomy Gein said he took to his home.

Of the 10 skulls discovered at the place, some appeared to be shrunken heads.

Some were found in plastic bags. Others reportedly were scattered carelessly under furniture in his littered home.

### VISIT GRAVES SCENES

District Attorney Kileen and police authorities took Gein to the farmhouse Monday morning after his first statement was obtained.

The district attorney said Gein also took him to cemeteries in the area where the grave robberies occurred.

The district attorney refused to say how many cemeteries were robbed or to identify them by name. Dates of the grave robberies also remained undetermined.

In his statement, Gein said he had committed no grave robberies "for two or three years."

Existence of the macabre farmhouse collection Sunday and Monday struck fear and apprehension across the state and stunned the tiny community of Plainfield.

Some acquaintances knew him there as a man with a sly smile who liked to talk about women.

### LONELY AND QUIET

Others pictured him as a lonely, quiet man who was friendly to children.

The Waushara County Sheriff's Department reported it was flooded by telephone calls from throughout the state.

The calls came from police authorities checking on mysterious disappearances of women in their areas, and, in some instances, from anxious relatives themselves.

A query came from La Crosse authorities, still investigating the 1953 disappearance of Evelyn Hartley, 15-year-old babysitter.

*November 19, 1957*
*Milwaukee Sentinel*

*Appleton Post-Crescent    Tues, Nov. 19, 1957*

# Gein Admits Killing Woman; Submits to Lie Detector

## Also Confesses He Robbed Graves Over Period of Years

BY DION HENDERSON

Wautoma — (AP) — A diffident, little man who admitted in puzzled tones yesterday that he had opened fresh graves over a period of years to collect human heads and finally butchered a neighbor woman — "while in a daze-like" faces a polygraph test of his story.

Edward Gein, a 51-year-old Plainfield bachelor handyman, is scheduled to go to Madison today for a lie detector test at the state crime laboratory.

Gein presently is being held under $10,000 bond for the armed robbery of Mrs. Bernice Worden last Saturday.

However, Dist. Atty. Kileen said the filing of a murder charge in the death of the 58-year-old widow, whose disemboweled body was found hanging like a deer carcass in Gein's woodshed Saturday night, awaits only a complete sifting of the gruesome remnants found on his secluded farm about 6 miles southwest of Plainfield.

Here are some of the questions the lie detector test may answer:

Did Gein mould hideous death masks from the faces of newburied dead?

Did he fabricate upholstery for furniture in his cluttered farm house from human skin?

Did he intend to eat the one victim he admits killing, the one of whom he said, almost apologetically, "I am not too sure that I killed her"?

"What is what I can't remember," Gein said in a ques-

Edward Gein

## X-Ray of Skull To be Examined At Crime Lab

BY RICHARD GLAMAN
Post-Crescent Staff Writer

Plainfield — An X-ray of the skull of a woman tavern owner who disappeared Dec. 8, 1954, was turned over Monday to the state crime laboratory to be compared with the skulls found in the farm home of Edward Gein.

The X-ray is that of Miss Mary Hogan who operated a tavern in the town of Pine Grove about six miles north of Gein's farm. Blood was found on the floor of the tavern along with evidence of a fight at the time of the 54-year-old woman's disappearance.

### Showed Gold Tooth

Crime lab officials and Portage county police picked up the X-ray Monday afternoon from Mr. and Mrs. Henry Sherman, who have taken over operation of the tavern.

Mrs. Sherman said the X-ray was taken in Chicago in 1929 when Miss Hogan feared she had a skull fracture. A doctor's comment on the X-ray showed there was no fracture, Mrs. Sherman said. But, she added that a gold tooth showed very plainly on the X-ray.

Waushara County Sheriff Art Schley Monday night said he didn't know if the X-ray had been compared with the 10 skulls found in Gein's house. "That's in the hands of the crime lab," he said.

### Claimed Killing

Mrs. Donald Foster, who lives three miles west of Plainfield and about three miles from Gein's farm, said Gein had often claimed he had killed Miss Hogan and hauled her away in his truck.

But, everyone wrote off Gein's remarks because he followed crime news closely and when they were talking about a crime he often claimed to have done it, Mrs. Foster said.

The Shermans found the X-ray among Miss Hogan's belongings after they took over the tavern. They attempted to turn it over to Sheriff Schley Monday night, but he refused to take it saying it came from Portage county where the tavern is located.

In another development, Waushara County Deputy Sheriff Arthur Judge, said Monday afternoon that embalming fluid, syringes and books on embalming had been found at Gein's home.

This might throw a block in tory director, said that when all the human segments had been collected from Gein's farm, technicians would study them in an effort to identify the victims of the grave robberies.

Gein said he had followed death notices published in the local newspaper and then opened the graves of women who had just died.

### Robbed 10 Graves

The handyman said he had visited cemeteries about 40 times, robbing at least 10 graves from 1944 to 1952. He indicated that on other occasions he snapped out of his "daze" and went home without violating a grave.

Gein said the pillaging of graves always had been done "when I was in a daze like when I killed Mrs. Worden."

In his statement, Gein recalled visiting the Worden Hardware store Saturday morning and paying 99 cents for some anti-freeze. He also remembered transporting Mrs. Worden's body to his farm home.

Asked whether he remembered killing her, he said, "No, that is what I can't remember; my memory is a little vague."

Gein said he did remember hanging the body from its heels in the shed and butchering it

"because I thought I was dressing out a deer."

In the statement, he said, "That is as close as I can remember. I was in a regular daze-like and I can't swear to it."

Mrs. Worden's disappearance was discovered by her son, Frank.

Funeral services for Mrs. Worden will be held at the Plainfield Methodist church at 2 p.m. Wednesday.

—THE CAPITAL TIMES, Tuesday, Nov. 19, 1957

# State, Local Officials Search Farmhome of Slayer
# Knives, Many Curious Items Found In Gein's Home

A truckload of boxes and barrels, many containing mutilated human remains, is unloaded at the Wisconsin State Crime Laboratory, Madison, from the home of Edward Gein, butcher of women. One box shockingly reads: "Seasons Greetings An Assortment of Delicious Chocol-

An unidentified deputy is shown here carrying out of the Gein home one of the wooden chairs which appeared to have the seat made of woman skin.

# SHERIFF SAYS HEAD MAY BE MRS. HOGAN'S

## She Disappeared Late in 1954

Gein in police car en route to Madison.

[Chicago Tribune Press Service]

Madison, Wis., Nov. 19—Tentative identification of the head and face of a second woman victim at the murder farm of Ed Gein, 51, confessed butcherer of a Plainfield, Wis., business woman, today prompted authorities to the belief he killed all of his victims and didn't take their bodies from graves, as he has contended.

Investigators also expressed belief his victims are more numerous than the 10 skulls found in his home indicates and they revealed they are searching for a second murder farm he may have operated.

### Has No Doubts of Killings

"This guy never robbed a grave in his life," insisted Sheriff Herbert Wanserski of Portage county. "There's no doubt in my mind but that he killed all of these people."

The sheriff said "we believe we have found the head and face of Mary Hogan" among the parts of bodies found in Gein's farm home.

The statement of the sheriff, who came here with authorities who brought Gein from Wautoma to Madison for a lie detector test, contradicted the farmer's contention that he hadn't killed anyone altho he admitted butchering the body of Mrs. Bernice Worden, 58.

### Pool of Blood Only Clew

Mary Hogan, 54, who operated a tavern in Bancroft, Portage county, about 10 miles from Gein's home, disappeared in December, 1954. The only clew authorities found was a pool of blood at the tavern.

Charles Wilson, director of the state crime laboratory, said he had learned from questioning Gein in preparing for the lie test, that he knew Mrs. Hogan both by reputation and by sight.

Sheriff Wanserski told newsmen that Mrs. Hogan's features were recognized in one of the grisly relics found by police who searched the cluttered farmhouse where Gein, a bachelor, has lived alone since the death of his mother in 1945.

### Fragments of Bodies

It was there sheriff's deputies found Mrs. Worden's body, decapitated and eviscerated and strung up by the heels like an animal carcass, and 10 human skulls. They also found furniture upholstered in human skin, bones, and other fragments of bodies.

Sheriff Wanserski's disclosures broke a news blackout that previously had confined mainly to rumors the details of the horrifying objects found in the murder house.

"The heads found had been skinned," he related. "The detached portion made up faces of a regular size, well

### Tell Mysterious Trips

The interest of two Chicago detectives, who went to Wautoma to question Gein, in the possibility he may have been involved in recent unsolved Chicago slayings was heightened today when it was learned that the farmer frequently made mysterious trips away from home.

Lester Hill, 45, who operates a general store and gasoline station between Wautoma and Plainfield, said he is well acquainted with Gein. He said Gein was known among his neighbors as a man who disappeared from his home for two or three weeks at a time, often breaking agreements to work as a handy man. When he reappeared, no explanation for his whereabouts in the interim was offered.

'He Didn't Talk Much'

# Plainfield People Thought Killer 'A Little Strange—but Harmless'

**BY RICHARD GLAMAN**
*Post-Crescent Staff Writer*

Plainfield — "He's harmless" — that was the phrase most often used by people in and around Plainfield to describe Edward Gein before he killed and butchered Mrs. Bernice Worden, 58-year-old widow-store owner.

The entire community of 680 persons was still in a state of shock Monday afternoon, two days after the gruesome discovery on the 51-year-old bachelor's farm home.

### Acted Normal

Everyone who knew Gein, and nearly everyone did, said he was a mild-mannered man although "a little odd" or "strange."

"He never talked much, just stood around and smiled," said Banker Charles Legrand. Gein kept a small savings account in the bank, but seldom came in to deposit or withdraw money, Legrand said.

"There wasn't anybody believed it when they first heard it," was the comment of Lester Hill, one of Gein's closest friends, and in whose home Gein ate the evening after the murder. "He acted just the same as always," Hill said.

"I've known Eddie for 35 years and you could've knocked me over with a feather when I first heard about it," said Clyde Ellis who owns a filling station on Plainfield's main street. "I sold him a couple of gallons of kerosene about 10 o'clock Saturday morning and he must have gone from here right to Mrs. Worden's store."

### Was In Store

Roy Scanlon, who operates a hardware and general store across the street from the Worden store said Gein came in the store about 4 o'clock Saturday afternoon with another man and bought an auto battery. Scanlon said Gein seemed the same as always and didn't remark about the Worden store being closed.

At this time the body of Mrs. Worden was hanging by the heels from a rafter in the summer kitchen at the farmhouse.

Bernie Muchinski, Jr., a partner in a filling station across the street from Worden's Hardware store, and other men who knew Gein said he liked to talk about women, but seldom talked to them.

Tavern operators said Gein seldom drank anything in their places. Other people who knew him better said he drank an occasional beer, but wasn't much of a drinker.

### Sat With Baby

Few people had ever been inside Gein's home in recent years, only a few men who worked with him on the roads and his closest neighbors, and then only the men. Gein worked for the town of Plainfield occasionally and for nearby farmers when they needed extra help.

One woman was in the farm home last April. She was Mrs. Donald Foster, who lives near Hill's country store at West Plainfield, three miles west of the village.

Gein and the Fosters were friends and last summer Mrs. Foster had Gein stay with her 16-month-old son. "He was strange, but we got used to him and he always played with the kids," Mrs. Foster said.

The Fosters went through Gein's house last April because they had talked about trading their home for the farm.

"He didn't come out for quite awhile when we were there, and then he said we wouldn't want to go through the house because it was so dirty," Mrs. Foster said in recalling the visit. "After we told him we wouldn't mind the dirt he let us in."

Mrs. Foster said she noticed nothing unusual in the house although it was piled high with trash of all descriptions. "There were one or two rooms we didn't see because he said they were too dirty," Mrs. Foster said.

### 'Shrunken Heads'

Both Hill and Mrs. Foster said Gein had often teased their children by inviting them over to see "shrunken heads."

When approaching a closed door during the tour of the house Mrs. Foster asked Gein if that was where he kept his shrunken heads.

"He gave me a funny look and then smiled and said 'No, they're in another room.'"

Gein appeared to be quite well read on many subjects, according to both Hill and Mrs. Foster. He apparently followed crime news closely and when they talked about something he often said he had done it.

### Claimed Other Killing

When Miss Mary Hogan, a town of Pine Grove tavern owner who lived about eight miles northwest of Plainfield disappeared on Dec. 8, 1954, Gein said he had killed her and hauled her away in his truck.

Mrs. Foster said everyone wrote this off as one of Gein's eccentricities, and often kidded him about it.

The downstairs of the house was an almost unbelievable mess Monday afternoon when reporters and photographers were permitted in the house. Books and magazines on crime, love stories, men's features, mechanics and other subjects were strewn about by the hundreds.

Gein talked with Sheriff Art Schley (left) as the slayer was led from the farm Monday after a visit to the place with law officers. Later, Gein was arraigned before Judge Boyd Clark (right). —United Press Telephoto

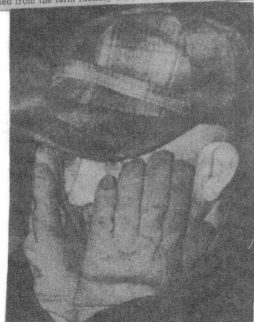

—Journal Staff by Fred L. Tonne

Gein covered his face with his gloved hands as authorities prepared to take him to his farm Monday.

## Describes Events in Store

By Sentinel Staff Writer

WAUTOMA, Wis., Nov. 18 — "My memory is vague..."

These and other phrases of a similar nature recur in the confession of Edward Gein, 51, handyman who admitted Monday the butchery of a Plainfield, Wis., widow, and ownership of a macabre collection of female skulls.

**RELEASED DETAILS**

The statement was released Monday afternoon by Dist. Atty. Earl Kileen.

In his statement, Gein admitted going to Mrs. Bernice Worden's hardware store at Plainfield Saturday morning.

"I went into the store with a glass jug to order some antifreeze," Gein was quoted by Kileen. "Mrs. Worden said, 'Do you want a gallon of antifreeze?' 'No,' I said. 'A half gallon.'

"I held the glass jug for her while she poured the antifreeze into it. It was 99 cents. I gave her a dollar and got one cent in change.

"I don't know just what happened then. She glanced out the window and said, 'they are checking deer out there.'" (This was a reference to a deer checking station within sight of the Worden store.)

**DROVE TRUCK**

(Gein was asked at this point, "did you stab her or shoot her?" "My memory is vague," he replied. "I do remember dragging her across the floor. I remember loading her body into the truck." This referred to the store delivery truck, parked behind the building.)

"Then I drove the truck out on the east road. I drove the truck into pine trees (apparently the pine grove about one mile east of Plainfield where the truck was recovered later)."

"Then I got out of the truck and walked to town. And I got my car and drove it out there. And loaded her body into the back end of the car."

(At this point Gein said he also put the cash register from the store into the car as well.)

"Then I drove out to my farm and took the body out of my car and hung it up by its heels in my woodshed."

(Gein said he decapitated the body and put the head into a box.)

(Gein said he used a knife he "made from a file" as he eviscerated the body.)

**'EXPLAINS' ACT**

"I thought I was dressing out a deer," he said in his statement. "It's the only explanation I can think of in my mind."

(Gein was asked if he had killed anyone else.)

"Not to my knowledge," he said.

"The only thing is, I'm not too sure that I killed her (Mrs. Worden) because didn't have any weapons with me."

Kileen said a bullet wound was found in Mrs. Worden's head. A revolver and several rifles were discovered in his house, the district attorney added.

## New Sheriff Gets 'Rough Initiation'

By Sentinel Staff Writer

WAUTOMA, Wis., Nov. 18 — "Believe me, it was a rough initiation."

Art Schley, appointed sheriff of Waushara County only six weeks ago, made this comment Monday night after being handed Wisconsin's most macabre murder case in years.

Schley has snatched only five hours sleep in the past three nights in his investigation of the murder and grave robbings confessed here by Edward Gein, 51 year old bachelor handyman who lives on a farm 16 miles north of this county seat community.

But Schley is a big man, 6 feet, 240 pounds, and was unbending as a bulldog in the face of nearly 40 newsmen who descended on his office here to write the Gein story.

Right from the start, Schley told newsmen he would give out little information on the case until the State Crime Laboratory helped solve the mystery of 10 skulls discovered in the Gein home.

Schley never backed down.

"Cooperation is important," he said. "And on such a case as this, it would have been foolish to commit yourself without the backing of expert knowledge provided by the state lab."

The 32-year-old sheriff had five years experience in law enforcement as a deputy, when he was appointed Oct. 1 by Gov. Thomson to fill the vacancy created by the resignation of Sheriff Edward Jester.

Schley worked in the highway department, pushing around bulldozers and other highway equipment, before becoming a deputy.

He works in a "poor county," as far as financing extensive law enforcement is concerned.

He has an undersheriff, Arthur Schwandt, and two full-time deputies, Daniel Chase and Arnold Fritz.

Schwandt, Chase and Fritz — plus 11 special deputies on call — patrol the county's 628 square miles.

Born here, married, and the father of three girls, 8 to 14, Schley is grateful for at least one thing in the Gein case.

"Fortunately we had no deer hunting fatalities while all this was going on," he said.

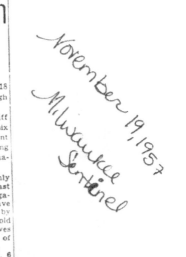

*November 19, 1957 Milwaukee Sentinel*

Gein talked with Sheriff Art Schley (left) as the slayer was led from the farm Monday after a visit to the place with law officers. Later, Gein was arraigned before Judge Boyd Clark (right).
—United Press Telephoto

November 19, 1957. Milwaukee Sentinel

ISOLATED FARMHOUSE WHERE GEIN CARRIED ON HIS GRISLY WORK

INTERIOR OF SHED IN WHICH MRS. WORDEN'S BODY WAS FOUND

November 20, 1957
Appleton Post Crescent

## State Attorney Warns on Gein News Releases

**Fear Trial Prejudice; Dist. Atty. Says He Plans No Grave Check**

Waushara Dist. Atty. Earl Kileen has been warned about releasing information on the Edward Gein murder case lest Gein's rights to a fair trial should be violated.

Atty. Gen. Stewart Honeck said he personally did not issue the warning to Kileen, but acknowledged that it came from his office.

In Wautoma, Kileen said today that he did not intend opening any graves to determine if Gein, in fact, took skulls and parts of human bodies from cadavers.

"I want no part in opening graves to prove anything," Kileen said. "Just think how the poor relatives would feel."

However, he said graves could be opened on the order the state crime laboratory or some other authority.

**No News Blackout**

On the advice from the attorney general's office, a spokesman said that the warning to Kileen was not intended to impose a news blackout, but was designed to head off the possibility that the sensational stories of the slaying and butchering of Mrs. Bernice Worden and the grisly hoard of humans remains found in Gein's home would prejudice Gein's trial, if one is held.

Kileen did not ask for the advice.

He later said that he had tried to cooperate with newspapermen, but all that happened was that he got in trouble. He then declined to say any more on the subject.

## Woman Says She Almost Married Gein

Plainfield —(P)— Ed Gein, bachelor recluse who has admitted butchering a Plainfield woman, was "good and kind and sweet" to the woman who said she almost married him, the Minneapolis Tribune said in a copyrighted interview.

**Miss Watkins** Adeline Watkins, 50, who lives with her mother in a small apartment here, said that during a 20-year romance with Gein he "was so nice about doing things I wanted to do, that sometimes I felt I was taking advantage of him."

A Tribune reporter quoted her as saying she had her last date with Gein Feb. 6, 1955.

"That night he proposed to me. Not in so many words, but I knew what he meant."

Miss Watkins, described by the Tribune as a plain woman with graying bangs and horn-rimmed glasses, said "I turned him down, but not because there was anything wrong with him. It was something wrong with me. I guess I was afraid I wouldn't be able to live up to what he expected of me."

The Tribune quoted Miss Watkins' widowed mother as saying Gein was a "sweet, polite man," and that she told him to have her daughter in from dates by 10 p.m. and "he never failed me once."

Miss Watkins, the story related, said she and Gein used to discuss books. "We never read the same ones, but we liked to talk about them anyway. Eddie liked books about lions and tigers and Africa and India. I never read that kind of books.

"I guess we discussed every murder we ever heard about. Eddie told how the murderer did wrong, what mistakes he had made. I thought it was interesting."

When they went out, the story said, they usually went to a movie at nearby Wautoma. Sometimes they visited taverns between Plainfield and Wisconsin Rapids.

"I liked to drink beer sometimes, but I would almost have to drag Eddie into a tavern," Miss Watkins was quoted as saying. "He would much rather have gone to a drugstore for a milk shake."

## Sheriff Says He's Sure Ghastly Death Mask Is That of Mrs. Mary Hogan

BY JACK GLASNER
Post-Crescent Staff Writer

(From Press Dispatches)
A face and head found in the macabre hoard of human remains amassed in the lonely farmhouse of 51-year-old Edward Gein, has been identified as that of a missing Pine Grove woman.

Portage County Sheriff Herbert Wanserski emphatically said the remains were  Wanserski those of Mrs. Mary Hogan, 54-year-old divorcee, who disappeared in December of 1954 from her rural tavern at Bancroft, six miles from Gein's farm.

A source close to the Wisconsin State Crime Laboratory disclosed today that questioning of Gein thus far, in a lie detector test that began Tuesday, indicates that he killed two women.

Joseph Wilimowski, the lab's lie detector expert, said that Gein so far has spent a total of 30 minutes under polygraph recording—19 minutes Tuesday and 11 today.

Wanserski has been on the case since Saturday when the butchered body of Mrs. Bernice Worden, 58, a widowed Plainfield hardware store operator, was found hanging by its heels in the summer kitchen of Gein's home. Gein has admitted butchering Mrs. Worden but insists he does not remember killing her in her store Saturday morning.

Gein was equally emphatic in saying that he "didn't know anything" about Mrs. Hogan's disappearance. But he said he had been in her tavern two days after she vanished, leaving behind marks of blood and signs of violence.

### 'In Daze-Like'

Gein, a handyman and sometime babysitter, has maintained that the skulls and other human relics found in his house had been looted from graves "while I was in a daze-like."

Gein's attorney, William Belter, of Wautoma, said he had not verified reports that parts of 15 female bodies had been found in Gein's house. He said an officer at the Gein farm, whom he did not know, had told him yesterday there were some "extra" human noses found. Belter added the officer told him "they didn't seem to go with the faces."

The Portage sheriff said the heads found in the debris littered farmhouse had been skinned and the detached portions "made up faces of a regular size, well preserved." Wan-

Mrs. Mary Hogan

serski said he examined 10 such grisly objects, apart from the skulls found in the farmhouse, commenting that all but two were faces. The others were scalps, the sheriff said.

Gein, a bachelor who has lived alone in the farmhouse since the death of his mother in 1945, appeared to show no remorse after four hours of questioning by state criminologist Charles Wilson Tuesday night. Wilson, head of the state crime lab, said Gein faces more grilling today.

Wilson characterized Gein's attitude as one of detachment, adding that he was a responsive, capable subject and suitable for polygraph (lie detector) examination. "I'll have a definite opinion on the subject Wednesday," he said.

### Death Weapon

Meanwhile, authorities believe they have found the death weapon in the killing of Mrs. Worden. A .22 caliber rifle, new with a spent cartridge in the firing chamber, was found in a gun rack in Mrs. Worden's store. What has been identified as a .22 caliber bullet hole was found in Mrs. Worden's head by pathological examination.

Gein has told authorities he dragged Mrs. Worden's body through a pool of blood to her pickup truck, later butchering the body as though it were an animal. He has said he dressed the body "in a kind of daze" and thought it was a deer.

The element of cannabalism has not been verified with Gein refusing to indicate what he intended to do with Mrs. Worden's body.

### Second Murder?

The identification of one of the skulls and faces found as that of Mrs. Hogan throws doubt on Gein's story that he got the ghastly collection from robbing graves between 1944 to 1952. He maintained that he robbed the graves in the same sort of daze which he recalls came over him during the Mrs. Worden murder.

Mrs. Hogan's disappearance was marked by blood spattered in her tavern and a spent .32 caliber cartridge on the floor.

Wilson, meanwhile, said the gristly face masks did not preserve the facial features. He added that "in my opinion, you can't tell who they were."

Wanserski said "I absolutely do not believe Gein's story that he got all the heads in graveyard robberies."

Missing persons records are being checked throughout the Plainfield area in an effort to identify the human remains found in Gein's home.

One case mentioned is that of Evelyn Hartley, 15-year-old babysitter who disappeared from a LaCrosse home in 1953.

### Relatives in LaCrosse

A Post-Crescent staff reporter, interviewing persons who knew Gein, Monday found that Gein had relatives in LaCrosse and had been known to visit the city. No further connection with the girl's disappearance has been made.

Among the filth, litter, trash and human remains in Gein's home were found clippings of crimes, including the Hogan and Hartley cases. Police also found clippings about the 1947 disappearance of Georgia Jean Weckler, 8, from Fort Atkinson and the disappearance from Adams county of two men, one known as Buck Travis.

Wilson said that results of examinations by the crime laboratory will be disclosed only if authorized by officials of Waushara county, in which Gein's home is located.

He said the Mobile unit of the crime laboratory had gathered "all sorts of things" from Gein's home.

There are crime detective books, a medical anatomical volume, chairs covered with human skin. There are skulls found under chairs in boxes in the home. There are also 10 whistles and toys similar to those found in cereal boxes.

There are even cans of used chewing gum.

Wilson said it is already known that some of the human heads contain embalming fluid because of their odor.

But Wilson said this did not necessarily support Gein's contention that he got the heads from graves.

"It's embalming fluid, but he may have put it there. Maybe he's an amateur taxidermist. We don't know," Wilson said.

Formaldehyde and an old embalming needle were among the items found in Gein's home.

### 7 Tons of Evidence

Wilson said there were so many items of possible value as evidence in Gein's home that two Crime Lab technicians barely had room in their 14,000-pound truck to drive it back to Madison.

Wilson has recommended that any inquest into the death of Mrs. Worden be delayed unless charges are pressed immediately.

Officials fear that an open inquest would arouse public opinion at Wautoma, where the county jail is located.

"They'll lynch me too, and all my deputies first," Sheriff Arthur Schley has said. "This man is innocent until proven guilty. Mrs. Worden's son Frank is a deputy, so I don't have anything to worry about on that score."

### Family Farm

Gein's mother, Augusta W. Gein, bought the 160-acre farm for $3,600 in 1914. His father died of cancer in the early 1940s. His brother died in 1944. His mother died in 1945 of a stroke.

Gein did not farm the place, but worked for the town of Plainfield, doing odd jobs such as clearing debris from town road ditches.

Gein's attorney said that he will enter a plea of innocent by reason of insanity when Gein is arraigned in Waushara county court Monday on a charge of armed robbery. He is being held under $10,000 bond on the charge in connection with the theft of a cash register in Mrs. Worden's store.

# Gein Admits Killing Woman Bar Owner

## Confesses as Mrs. Worden Is Buried

BY JACK GLASNER
Post-Crescent Staff Writer

(From Press Dispatches)
Edward Gein, Plainfield, admitted butcher-slayer of Mrs. Bernice Worden, this morning pleaded innocent by reason of insanity at his arraignment in Wautoma on a first degree murder charge.

He was ordered held without bond for trial in circuit court.

Waushara County Judge Boyd Clark, after accepting the plea, found "probable cause" that the crime had been committed.

The case now goes before Circuit Judge Herbert A. Bunde, Wisconsin Rapids, who will decide whether Gein is sane and capable of standing trial or is insane and should be committed to the Central State hospital at Waupun state prison without standing trial for murder.

### Gein Confession

Judge Bunde also could permit Gein to go on trial but has the authority to stop the proceedings at any time he finds Gein incompetent to stand trial.

Today's county court proceedings lasted only five minutes. Gein, clean-shaven, glassy-eyed and trembling slightly, stood before the judge in company with his attorney, William Belter, and a clergyman, the Rev. Kenneth Engelman, pastor of the Methodist church, who Wednesday conducted funeral services for Mrs. Worden.

Gein spoke only two words. He acknowledged his identity and said "Yes" when Judge Clark asked him if he was represented by an attorney.

Gein admitted his second murder Wednesday as hundreds of friends and relatives of Mrs. Worden attended funeral services for her at Plainfield.

Edward Gein, 51, Who Wednesday admitted killing two women near his rural Plainfield home, leaves the state crime lab in Madison with Waushara County Sheriff Arthur Schley, left. Gein arrived Monday for lie detector tests and interrogation at the lab. (AP Wirephoto)

Appleton Post-Crescent
Thursday November 21, 1957

*MILWAUKEE SENTINEL — NOVEMBER 21, 1957*

Ed Gein wears a slight smile as he leaves the state crime lab in Madison with Waushara County Sheriff Arthur Schley (left) for return to Waushara jail.

## Keating Quiz Results Inconclusive

*By Sentinel Staff Writer*

MADISON, Nov. 20—Almost two days of examination at the State Crime Laboratory has eliminated Edward Gein "as the person responsible for and/or involved in" three major unsolved disappearances in Wisconsin.

But Charles Wilson, director of the Crime Laboratory, said the lie detector test to which Gein submitted showed no conclusive result in another disappearance, that of Mrs. Irene Keating, 30, Fort Atkinson, last Aug. 20.

The disappearances in which Gein was cleared are:

● Evelyn Hartley, 15, from a baby sitting job at a college professor's home in La Crosse on Oct. 24, 1953.

● Abduction of Georgia Jean Wechler, 8, from the driveway of her farm home near Fort Atkinson on May 1, 1947.

● Victor Travis, 51, an Adams County resident who vanished while deer hunting on Nov. 1, 1952.

The map locates Plainfield and Wautoma, Wis., and the area in which the Edward Gein farm is situated. Ten human skulls, other human bones and the body of Mrs. Bernice Worden, 58, Plainfield widow who was slain last Saturday, were found in and around the Gein farm house. (Associated Press-Capital Times Wirephoto)

## Ed Gein: Bluebeard Or Ghoul?

PLAINFIELD, Wis., Nov. 20 — Did mild mannered, quiet spoken Edward Gein, under the influence of an inner drive he can define only as a "daze," actually rob graves for most of his gruesome human trophies?

Or did he employ even more horrible means, and assemble his grotesque collection of at least 10 and possibly 15 human heads by murdering living victims, as he has confessed doing to Mrs. Bernice Worden and Miss Mary Hogan?

**THESE ARE QUESTIONS**

These are the questions that are still unanswered — questions that are still agitating this tiny hamlet not far from the Gein "horror farm," where the ghoulish discoveries of one of Wisconsin's most horrifying crimes were discovered Saturday.

The questions were becoming more pointed Wednesday, when it was learned that Ed Gein, the genial handyman, after repeated denials, had admitted in Madison he is the murderer of Miss Mary Hogan, the Town of Pine Grove tavern keeper.

If Gein had killed not once but twice in answer to the dictates of his mysterious "daze," maybe all of the human remains found in his ramshackle farmhouse came from living victims.

**DOUBT GRAVE THEFTS**

Residents here and elsewhere in the area believe it improbable that Gein could have dug into fresh graves, as he has declared, for most of his victims.

Their reasoning makes sense.

In the first place, they point out that Gein is a small man, scaling not more than 140 pounds. And while he is accustomed to manual labor as a sometime street cleaner, they doubt if he could withstand, alone, the physical demands of unearthing a grave, removing the casket, mutilating the body, and then returning it and the casket to the excavation, and re-covering it with earth — all in the course of a single night.

Gein has claimed he has done just this — not once, but on at least 10 different occasions between 1944 and 1952.

Another reason for skepticism lies in the soil itself which Gein admits he has desecrated. It is admittedly poor soil, sandy in texture, resistant to most crops. When you dig into this earth, the excavation soon crumbles as the sandy soil seeks to return to its original form.

Perhaps the most compelling argument has been the fact that in the last decade, roughly covering the period of the alleged grave robbings, it has become a common practice to encase caskets in heavy concrete vaults before they are covered with earth for the last time.

*November 21, 1957 Milwaukee Sentinel*

## OPENING ANY AS CHECK UP TO RELATIVES

11-22-57

### Gein Enters an Insanity Plea

BY PAUL HOLMES
[Chicago Tribune Press Service]

Wautoma, Wis., Nov. 21 — Opening of at least one and possibly a dozen graves became an imminent prospect today with disclosure by Sheriff Arthur Schley of Waushara county that he has what he calls a complete list of graves said to have been robbed by Ed Gein, 51, butcher-ghoul and slayer.

Schley made the disclosure to Ralph Wing, Plainfield township board chairman and member of the Waushara county board, when Wing called at the sheriff's office to demand an explanation of reports that the grave of Mrs. Eleanore M. Adams, Wing's sister-in-law, was one of those violated.

—Journal Staff by Fred L. Tonne
Slayer Ed Gein stood bareheaded as he was arraigned Monday before County Judge Boyd Clark at Wautoma.

# THE CHICAGO AMERICAN
MONDAY—NOVEMBER 25—1957

# Graves to Be Opened

## Gein Story of Thefts Faces Test

WAUTOMA, Wis., Nov. 24 (INS)—Waushara County officials prepared for a series of exhumations which could settle the question of whether Wisconsin's "mad butcher," Edward Gein, murdered two persons—or many more.

The first grave probably could not be opened until Tuesday.

District Attorney Earl Kileen said mounting pressure by the public definitely precludes any further delay in testing Gein's assertion that nine skulls and various other human parts found in his home were trophies of moonlight grave-robbing forays.

A 30-day mental examination of the 51-year-old hermit-farmer at the state hospital at Waupun for the criminally insane has interrupted legal action on the murder of Mrs. Bernice Worden, whose mutilated body was found hanging a week ago in Gein's home near Plainfield.

**CITIZENS STUNNED**

Gein also confessed the murder of Mrs. Mary Hogan, 54, a tavern operator in neighboring Portage County. Last night, shortly before he was taken to the state hospital, Gein took Portage County officials along the route he drove with Mrs. Hogan's body Dec. 9, 1954.

The townspeople of Plainfield, stunned by day after day of grisly disclosures, have demanded that Kileen open the graves Gein said he plundered. A county board official, Floyd Wing, led those who insisted on knowing the whole story of their neighbor's depradations.

Kileen, who estimated that "four, perhaps five" graves be opened, overruled urging by Charles Wilson, head of the state's crime laboratory at Madison, that the exhumations be delayed "a week or two" while the laboratory completes examination of the skulls.

**FIRST GRAVE CHOSEN**

The district attorney said the first grave to be opened will be that of Mrs. Eleanor Adams, 51, Wing's sister-in-law, whose body Gein said he disturbed. She died in 1951.

District Attorney John J. Haka of Portage County said s will obtain a warrant charging Gein with the Hogan slaying, but that warrant may never be used.

If doctors at the state hospital pronounce Gein insane, he probably would be committed to the hospital until he died or recovered. And if he is declared competent to stand trial, Kileen explained, Gein faces a maximum life sentence for the murder of Mrs. Worden.

Wisconsin has no death penalty.

Waushara Circuit Judge Herbert A. Bunde already has heard a plea of not guilty by reason of insanity in the Worden case.

# Sheriff Cites Co-operation As Key Factor in Arrest

*Nov. 27, 1957*

The important role played by law officers from neighboring counties and local Plainfield residents in the apprehension of Ed Gein less than two hours after evidence of the crime had been made known, was recognized Wednesday by Sheriff Arthur Schley in a letter to the co-operating agencies.

The sheriff's office at Wautoma received the call from Plainfield at 5:10 p.m. Saturday. Gein had been arrested by 7 p.m. and was housed in a jail cell at Wautoma by 7:40 p.m.

The letter from the sheriff read as follows:

"Gentlemen:

"We wish to sincerely thank all persons who assisted in any manner in the recent investigation at Plainfield.

"All neighboring sheriff's departments which were contacted responded promptly and gave us their utmost co-operation.

"We also wish to thank the crime laboratory for their quick response and expert handling of their phase of the investigation.

"It is also true, that without the help and assistance of the volunteers in and around Plainfield, our investigation would not have been successful.

"To each and every one who assisted in any way we wish to repeat our thanks.

Waushara Co. Sheriff's Dept.
Arthur Schley, Sheriff"

Sheriff Schley told The Argus Wednesday morning that if even a few hours had elapsed allowing Gein time to completely dispose of the body, it would have been much more difficult to have solved the crime.

What took place in those first few hours, according to the sheriff, was essentially as follows:

Sheriff Schley and Deputy Arnold Fritz went directly to the Worden Store after receiving the call.

At the store there was obvious evidence of foul play with blood found on the floor, the fact that Mrs. Worden was missing, the truck belonging to the store was nowhere in the area, the cash register in the store was missing.

After a hurried conference, sheriff's offices in adjoining counties were called and the state crime laboratory notified.

The first search was for the truck, which was found just east of the village on a "lover's lane" road. Village residents went with officers from other areas to help guide them to possible hiding places.

A pattern of tires from the Worden truck was obtained from the place where the tires had been purchased.

Also, at the outset, there were at least "three or four" suspects, who for one reason or another there was cause to check. Gein was one of these.

The suspect was found and taken into custody at Hill's Grocery. While he was being questioned by Traffic Officer Dan Chase, Sheriff Schley and Captain Lloyd Schoephoester of the Green Lake County Traffic Department went to the Gein farm.

While Capt. Schoephoester searched another part of the house, Sheriff Schley opened the door to the summer kitchen and found the mutilated body.

He radioed Officer Chase to bring Gein in.

## Grave Findings Touch Off Mass Exodus of Press

The findings on opening two graves in the Plainfield cemetery Monday morning has cleared the air on the truth of at least some of confessed murderer Ed Gein's story.

In the two graves opened, no body was found in the grave of Mrs. Eleanore Adams and only a few bones on the casket of the other, that of Mrs. Mabel Everson.

Both Sheriff Arthur Schley and District Attorney Earl Kileen have stated that no more graves will be opened unless relatives of persons on the Gein list request that it be done.

Whether or not other graves will be opened will also depend on the findings of the state crime laboratory and what their investigators deem necessary.

The state attorney general's office has assumed some of the responsibility in the case and have been directed by the governor to examine facts as to whether Gein might have committed other crimes.

Gein was taken to the state hospital at Waupun for 30 days of mental observation Saturday by Sheriff Schley and Deputy Arnold Fritz.

The findings at Plainfield Monday touched off a mass exodus of reporters and photographers from the area and as of Wednesday morning Sheriff Schley, who has been pursued by the press since the first news of the murder broke, stated that there were only a few Chicago reporters still in the city.

The sheriff told the Argus Wednesday morning that reporters had been kept from the Plainfield cemetery as a protection to the relatives of deceased persons whose graves Gein has said that he entered.

He said that one photographer attempted to take pictures from atop a ladder at the edge of the cemetery and others were taken from an airplane hovering over the scene.

[United Press Telephoto]
Scene at Ed Gein farm as workman boarded up house where grisly relics of women were found.

# Inside Ghoul's Farmhouse

Cluttered kitchen in farm home of bachelor slayer Edward Gein. (AP Wirephoto.)

## Skull-Bowl on Table in Kitchen

PLAINFIELD, Wis., Nov. 19 (AP)—You step through the kitchen door and here is an ordinary kitchen chair, except that its seat is upholstered with human skin. There is what appears to be a small bowl on the table, but it is not a bowl, it is the top half of a human skull.

This is the home of Edward Gein, 50, handyman and babysitter. It is inside the sagging old farmhouse where he has lived alone since his mother died of a stroke in 1945.

Gein is charged with the robbery of a Plainfield widow. He has admitted robbing her, and has admitted killing her —and somehow, but just how he says he doesn't remember —and bringing her to his home last Saturday to be dressed out like a beef.

### 10 SKULLS FOUND

Officers who went to the house and found the eviscerated corpse hanging from its heels in a summer kitchen, found that only the first of a series of grisly testimonials to Gein's necrogenic obsession.

(Necrogenic is defined as "living with the dead.")

They found also 10 human skulls. Gein says he dug them up out of new graves in the area and authorities are inclined to believe him.

They found the chair with its horrid upholstery.

They found a box piled with scraps and tatters of human skin, and a ghastly pair of puttees apparently made from the skin of two human legs.

## Officers Tend to Accept His Story as True

### But Investigation of Plainfield Horrors Is Continued; Lie Test Slated at Madison

By RICHARD C. KIENITZ
Of The Journal Staff

Plainfield, Wis. — Authorities Tuesday were trying to check Edward Gein's claim that he murdered only Mrs. Bernice Worden and that he got the rest of his grisly collection of human heads and skulls in a series of ghoulish grave robberies.

Waushara county authorities appeared to be convinced by Gein's story.

"Our case is pretty well cleaned up," said Dist. Atty. Earl Kileen. "We have no missing persons in our county. The only thing here is the murder rap."

Neither Kileen nor Sheriff Art Schley would say whether they had checked the cemeteries where Gein said he robbed graves—or that they intended to. They jokingly claimed that they "didn't remember" if they had checked any of the supposedly violated graves Monday.

### No Visitors Allowed

When asked Tuesday morning if he planned to check the cemeteries, Schley looked out a window at snow that was falling. "I wouldn't know about that," he said, implying that it was too nasty outside.

The sheriff did say that the snow and icy roads might prevent him from taking Gein to Madison, where the 51 year old farm recluse was scheduled to undergo a lie detector test at the state crime laboratory.

A news blackout imposed by Schley as soon as the butchered body of Mrs. Worden was found Saturday in a summer kitchen of Gein's ramshackle farm home remains in force. The sheriff refused to let reporters or photographers visit Gein in his jail cell, saying that they would upset Gein and that they hadn't finished talking to the suspect.

### "Very Annoying Fellow"

Kileen added that Gein was "a very annoying fellow to talk to—sometimes he'll want to go into great detail and other times he'll shut up and won't say anything." Kileen explained that Schley feared that the presence of reporters and photographers might frighten Gein into a sustained silence.

Gein was returned to jail after his arraignment Monday in Wautoma on an armed robbery charge. The charge was filed by Kileen to hold Gein until the crime laboratory had completed its investigation.

Gein told County Judge Boyd Clark that he wanted an attorney and could afford to hire one. He selected Atty. William N. Belter of Wautoma, a former assemblyman. Belter said Tuesday that he didn't know whether he would defend Gein. He said he hadn't talked to him yet.

### Bond Set at $10,000

Gein's bond was set at $10,000. Kileen had asked for $5,000 but Schley suggested it be doubled. The armed robbery charge arose from that fact that a cash register containing $41 or $42 was taken from Mrs. Worden's store at the time of the slaying. It was found in Gein's home.

The preliminary hearing on the charge was set for next Monday. However, Kileen said he expected Gein's lawyer (whoever he may be) to ask for a delay.

At Madison, Charles Wilson, director of the state crime laboratory, said that a check of cemeteries wasn't necessary yet.

"There's no sense going out with a pick and shovel to check the graveyards near Plainfield until we have exhausted the possibilities of evidence we already have," Wilson said.

Wilson said that if Gein's grisly collection of human heads, skulls and bones came from graves "there will be

*Turn to page 3, col. 1*

## Single Killing Theory Told

### Officers in Waushara County Think Others Were From Graves

*From page 1, column 8*

traces of embalming fluid and we'll find them."

Wilson also said that detailed physical descriptions of persons who had disappeared in recent years would be checked against what was found in Gein's farm home. He said the department had gathered such descriptions in many cases of disappearing persons.

Gein told authorities that he committed the grave robberies while in a "daze." He was quoted as saying that he committed at least 10 grave robberies from 1944 to 1952 and that each grave was that of a woman.

### He Read Obituaries

He was also quoted as saying he read obituaries in the newspapers and then went out to dig up the new graves. It was reported that some of the grave robberies were at cemeteries near his home.

There have been conflicting reports about what authorities found in Gein's home. Lt. Vern Weber, chief of detectives at La Crosse, said he saw part of the collection in the crime laboratory truck.

He said there were 10 women's heads, some with eyes and some without. He said some were complete with skulls, others were merely skin.

Weber said that all of the heads appeared to be those of women of middle age or older.

Weber said he was told that no full skulls were recovered—"just pieces"—and that other patches of skin had been recovered.

He said he saw with his own eyes a chair with a seat which appeared to be made of human skin, and a knife with a handle that appeared to have a skin covering. He said the chair was a typical kitchen chair which probably once had a rattan seat.

### Inclined to Believe Him

Weber said that the heads were in a very good state of preservation and that they had been found behind chairs and other furniture in Gein's home.

Weber said that he had talked to Gein twice and that he was inclined to believe his story about the grave robberies. He said that Gein said he had wanted to be a doctor in his youth. He said Gein said he had cured the heads in a brine solution.

Weber said that he had asked Gein "strong questions" about rumors of cannibalism.

"That's out," Weber said. "He said he never ate a bit of that stuff and I don't believe he did."

### "He Needs Help"

Weber said that Gein was "a very sincere, very meek fellow—you'd never believe he'd be the kind of guy to do such a thing—you feel like he needs help awful bad."

The La Crosse detective said Gein said that he could feel his grave robbing spells coming on.

"He said he would pray and that sometimes the prayers would snap him out of it. He said he came out of a spell one time while he was digging up a grave and that he stopped."

Weber said that Gein insisted that he hadn't robbed a grave since 1952. "He said maybe his prayers had been answered."

Gein also claims that he was in a spell when he murdered Mrs. Worden, although he admits he must have done it. "He says he only remembers carrying her out of the store — not

butchered like a hunter would butcher a deer. Her heart was found inside the farm home. One official pointed out that deer hunters customarily saved the heart and that this would lend some credence to Gein's claim that he thought he was dressing a deer at the time.

### Shoes Don't Fit

Weber came to Plainfield to check if Gein had any connection with the violent disappearance of baby sitter Evelyn Hartley in October, 1953. He said he was inclined to doubt a connection.

Weber said that tennis shoes found after the disappearance and linked to the murder were too large for Gein. "The shoes we found are size 11½; Gein wears about an 8," the detective chief said.

Weber said that Gein was a native of La Crosse but had left there with his parents when he was 7. "He claims he hasn't been back since," Weber said. "He has some relatives here and we're going to check with them."

Chicago police interviewed Gein for almost three hours until 3 a.m. Tuesday, seeking a connection with unsolved Chicago crimes, notably the Judith Anderson slaying. Gein told them that he hadn't ever traveled south of Milwaukee.

Sheriff Roger Reinel and Dist. Atty. Harold A. Eberhard of Jefferson county came here Tuesday to check any connection with the disappearance of Georgia Jean Weckler in 1947.

Authorities are still trying to establish the details of Mrs. Worden's slaying. She was shot in the head with a .22 caliber bullet. Gein claims that he doesn't own a gun of that caliber although two guns of another caliber were found in his home.

Many persons have been wondering how a person as slight as Gein could dig up so many graves and remove bodies without help. Gein claims that he never took a complete body.

Weber said the chair seat made of skin looked like skin from the chest or back of a human. Where Gein got this skin, he never took a complete body and murdered only Mrs. Worden, has not been answered.

Gein has been questioned about the disappearance of Miss Mary Hogan, 54, from her tavern at the nearby town of Pine Grove (Portage county).

Gein said he was at the tavern two days after her disappearance but admitted no other connection with that disappearance.

Funeral services for Mrs. Worden will be held at 2 p.m.

# Bachelor, 50, Held After Missing Plainfield Woman's Body Discovered in Home

Plainfield — (AP) — The Waushara County district attorney said today that five more human heads have been found on an isolated farm near Plainfield, raising to 10 the number of cadavers discovered so far in the house where a mild-mannered handy man lived alone.

Prosecutor Earl Kileen said that Edward Gein had broken a stubborn 30-hour silence and admitted that he "knew something" about the macabre collection.

Kileen said that Gein told him he "might of" killed the victims, and admitted the ghastly butchering of a 58-year-old Plainfield business woman Saturday.

Gein was asked whether, in connection with the disemboweling of Mrs. Bernice Worden, he had intended to eat his victim.

"On that point he still has a lapse of memory," the district attorney said.

**Heads in Plastic Bags**

The five latest heads to be found were wrapped neatly in plastic bags.

Shortly after 11 a.m. the 51-year-old Gein—a frail looking 140-pound bachelor — wearing rubber boots, and with his red cloth gloves handcuffed before him, was taken from the Waushara county jail at Wautoma by Kileen, Sheriff Art Schley and County Judge Boyd Clark.

"He has something he wants to show us," Kileen said.

The farm scene where the grisly discoveries were made laid under a four-inch blanket of snow today but State Crime Laboratory officials continued their chilling work of searching the buildings.

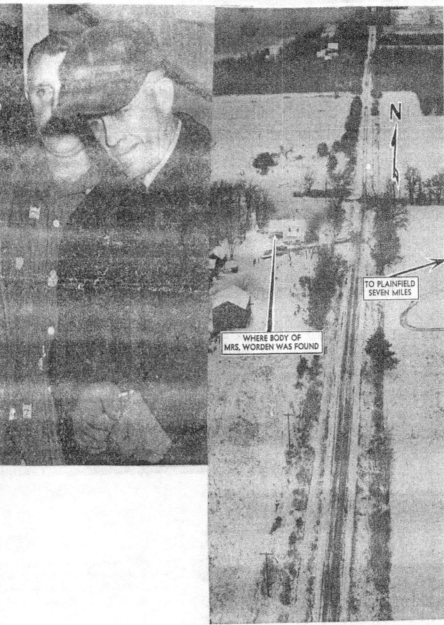

[TRIBUNE Photo]
Air view of the Ed Gein farm where discovery of Mrs. Worden's body started inquiry.

[TRIBUNE Photo by Dan Tortorell]

Tribune aerial view of the small town of Plainfield, Wis., site of the slaying of Mrs. Bernice Worden in the hardware store which she operated. Ed Gein, bachelor recluse farmer, has admitted her slaying and that of another woman. Unidentified are remnants of 13 other bodies.

SHERIFF ART SCHLEY (LEFT) AND EDWARD GEIN

A saw found along with portions of human bodies on the rural Plainfield farm of confessed slayer Ed Gein is taken into the State Crime Laboratory at Madison. Lab workers brought in a truck load of evidence from the Gein farm, with the unloading watched by University of Wisconsin students.
Sentinel photo.

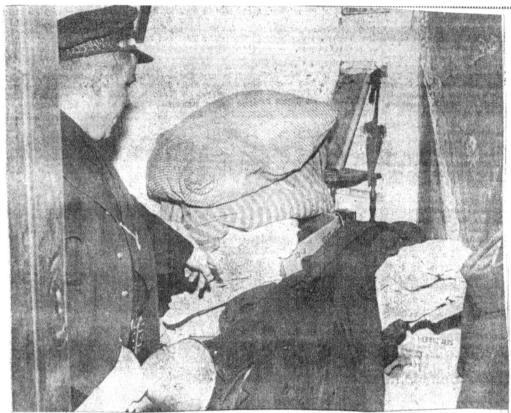

Dave Sharkey, Wood County deputy, points to a pile of clothes under which authorities found a box of human skulls in a junk-laden room of Ed Gein's farmhouse near Plainfield.

### DA CONFERS WITH REPORTERS

Waushara County Dist. Atty. Earl F. Kileen, center, talks to reporters outside the sheriff's office at Wautoma just before Edward Gein, confessed slayer of a Plainfield widow, was returned to his ramshackle farm home for a tour. It was during this conference with reporters that Kileen said Gein had broken a stubborn silence and admitted "knowing something" about the slaying. (Daily Northwestern photo)

# Incredibly Dirty House Was Home of Slayer

## Grave Robber Saved Everything — Books, Gum, Magazines — Amid Filth

By ROBERT W. WELLS
Of The Journal Staff

Plainfield, Wis.—Until Saturday, when he was arrested following the murder and decapitation of Mrs. Bernice Worden, this is the way the small, inoffensive village handyman named Ed Gein lived.

When he came home at night —perhaps from an odd job, perhaps from sitting with a child as a favor to a mother—he stood on the sagging rear porch and opened the back door into the room where the widow's butchered body was found Saturday, hanging from one of two blocks and tackles.

There was no electricity, no telephone—no sign, in fact, that this was 1957 instead of the 1917 of Gein's boyhood on the bleak farm. So when the little man came home, blinking his watery blue eyes against the gathering darkness, he must have lit one of the old lanterns or dusty kerosene lamps.

### Piles of Debris

Stepping inside the rude summer kitchen, he stepped over and around the piles upon piles of debris that filled four of the 10 rooms in the decaying house. This was home to Ed Gein, so he would not have noticed the cobwebs festooned from the ceiling or the mice peering from the rafters.

Judging from a tour of the house the reporter made Tuesday morning, Gein would have gone from the summer kitchen into the regular kitchen. At his left, as he moved through the door, was a chair with a bottom made of human skin. On a table was the top half of a human skull, turned over so that it formed a grisly bowl.

Near a window, partially covered by a curtain so old it was hanging in shreds, was an old-fashioned cook stove. Gein did not use it, though, except to store some of his accumulations —everything from used chewing gum saved in a neat but dusty collection to fine sets of hand tools.

### Mostly Pork and Beans

He apparently did his rudimentary cooking on top of the pot bellied stove in the living room. Next to it was an iron bedstead with an incredibly dirty mattress and coverings. Near the bed was the only object in the entire house that investigators found not covered by dust and dirt that had accumulated for months or perhaps years.

This was a table, covered with fresh newspapers, where Gein ate. Judging from the empty cans scattered on the floor, pork and beans and canned fruit formed the mainstays of his diet.

Next to the table was an old couch. On it was a violin with two strings, one broken; a small accordion, and a collection of books that included "Dorothy Dale, a Girl of Today" and "A Little Girl in Old Detroit."

Presumably, these children's books of a bygone day were not read but only saved. Gein saved literally everything he laid his hands on, judging from his house. His own reading tastes, presumably, were better reflected by the men's cheap magazines, some with lurid pictures, that were scattered about. One, showing an American soldier about to stab a Japanese, also armed with a long knife, was on the bed.

### Pieces of Skin Found

Some of the magazines were in boxes. Below them, investigators found pieces of human skin. Deputy Dave Sharkey of the Wood county sheriff's department said that these mementoes included a pair of macabre puttees made from the skin of the lower half of two human legs.

On the wall of the kitchen were pictures, including several pinups. Calendars, some of them from bygone years, helped hide the dirty wallpaper and the bare spots of plaster from which the wallpaper had been stripped.

It was in this shedlike wing of the Gein farm that the decapitated body of Mrs. Worden was found. The trailer (right), belonging to the Wood county sheriff's department, contains a portable generator used to supply electricity during the investigation of the house. The Gein home has no lights or telephone. —Journal Staff

Gein talked with Sheriff Art Schley (left) as the slayer was led from the farm Monday after a visit to the place with law officers. Later, Gein was arraigned before Judge Boyd Clark (right). —United Press Telephoto

Gein covered his face with his gloved hands as authorities prepared to take him to his farm Monday. —Journal Staff by Fred L. Toone

ISOLATED FARMHOUSE WHERE GEIN CARRIED ON HIS GRISLY WORK
Associated Press Wirephoto.

# Gein's Statement Tells of Butchering Widow

## Slayer at Plainfield Can't Remember the Actual Killing; Describes 'Daze'

WAUTOMA, WIS.—Æ—Waushara County Dist. Atty. Earl Kileen nhas released the following stenographic record of a statement made Monday afternoon by Edward Gein, 51, when questioned by county authorities.

Kileen: Now you start from the time you went into the Worden implement store. Tell us exactly what happened, the best you can recall.

### Wanted Antifreeze

Gein: When I went into Mrs. Worden's, I took a glass jug for permanent antifreeze. When I entered the hardware store she came toward me and said, "Do you want a gallon a antifreeze?" and I said, "No, a half gallon."

She got the antifreeze and pumped it out, and I held the jug for her to pour it in and then she pumped out another quart and I was still holding the jug while she poured that. Then I paid her with a dollar bill. She gave me back 1c because it was 99c.

This is what I can't say from now on because I don't know just what happened from now on, you see.

She glanced out of the window toward the filling station across the street and said, "They are checking deer there." Then she looked toward the west, out of the west and north windows, and said, "There are more people up town than I thought there would be." She might have said something about opening of the season, she might have said that.

Kileen: Do you remember striking her or shooting her?

### Can't Recall Slaying

Gein: No. That is what got me; whether I took my antifreeze out. That is what I can't remember. It is hard for me to say from now on. My memory was a little vague, but I do remember dragging her across the floor.

I remember loading her body in the truck; then I drove the truck out on the east road at the intersection, where 51 and 73 separate east of Plainfield. I drove the truck up in the pine trees.

Then I walked to town and got my car and drove it out there and loaded her body in the back end of the car, and also the cash register. I loaded the cash register in the truck when I put her body in there.

Then I drove out to my farm and took the body out of the car and hung it up by its heels in my woodshed.

Kileen: You used the knife you made from the file to cut her up?

Gein: That is what is as close as I can remember, I was in a regular dazelike and I can't swear to it. . . .

Kileen: Then you proceeded to dress out the body? You told me that you thought you were dressing out a deer.

Gein: That is the only explanation that I can think was in my mind.

Kileen: Do you remember if you had the body all dressed before those people came out, or after?

Gein: You mean the girl and her brother? Yes, it had to be.

Kileen: How about Mr. Ueck?

Gein: He came before; before the girl and her brother came.

Kileen: Before the body was dressed and hung up? On these other 10 skulls found in your house or shrunken heads —those other 10 shrunken heads. You got them from a cemetery—or cemeteries?

Gein: Yes. (Nods his head.)

### No Other Killings

Kileen: Did you ever kill anyone else besides Mrs. Worden?

Gein: Not to my knowledge. The only thing I am not too sure that I killed her; that is the only thing, because I didn't have any weapons with me or on my property.

Slaying victim Mrs. Bernice Worden was pictured in her hardware store at Plainfield in 1956. The photograph appeared in the Plainfield Sun, a weekly newspaper, along with a story about her.

# GEIN ADMITS SLAYING OF MARY HOGAN

## Burned Most of Her Body, He Confesses

### Act to End Conjecture

"Mr. Gein has now admitted that he is responsible for the death of Mary Hogan in Portage county on Dec. 8, 1954, and Bernice Worden in Waushara county, Nov. 16, 1957.

"This release, jointly concurred in by the interested local officials, is being made to eliminate Mr. Gein from unnecessary suspicion and conjecture.

"An avalanche of physical evidence has been recovered, which may take weeks and probably months to completely evaluate and process. When this is done the result will be made known to the proper local officials.

"No amplifications can be made concerning this release. The success of the investigative efforts in the five cases referred to are due principally to the coöperation of all interested law enforcement agencies."

### Says He Burned Body

Additional information about Gein's confession in the Hogan case was learned from the source close to the case.

He said Gein admitted ripping off Mrs. Hogan's face and making a mask of it. He said the farmer asserted he burned parts of the woman's body in the stove in his home and insisted he had no other parts of her body in his home.

Authorities, however, indicated a belief one of the skulls found in the home was that of Mrs. Hogan. They said marks on it matched those believed borne by Mrs. Hogan as a result of a head injury she incurred and of which she had X-rays taken.

### Back Grave Digging Story

The source also said authorities believe Gein is telling the truth in his insistence that he took from graves all of the other bodies, except those of Mrs. Worden and Mrs. Hogan, whose parts were found in his home.

Gein's lie detector examination was conducted over a two day period during which he was subjected to many hours of questioning, but reportedly was examined with the aid of the polygraph only 19 minutes yesterday and 11 minutes today. Joseph C. Wilimovsky, expert employed by the state crime laboratory, operated the machine and did most of the interrogating.

When Gein emerged from the laboratory today, to be returned to the Waushara county jail at Wautoma, he appeared bright and was smiling. He was clean shaven for the first time since his arrest last Saturday. He spent the night in the city jail here.

Members of the entourage guarding the confessed killer said he appeared to relish the food supplied him while he was in custody here and that he told his guards he "feels better" since admitting his slaying of Mrs. Hogan.

### Recall Disappearance
[Chicago Tribune Press Service]

Bancroft, Wis., Nov. 20 — The roadside saloon near here in which Mrs. Mary Hogan held forth as propietor, bartender, and bouncer for five years prior to January, 1955, is now owned and operated by Mr. and Mrs. Hank Sherman. It has a sign proclaiming that it is "Hank's Place."

The Shermans came to the saloon as owners in the early part of 1955 following the disappearance of Mrs. Hogan, whom Ed Gein of nearby Plainfield today confessed slaying.

### Lived in Chicago

They recall many details of this disappearance.

Mary Hogan, they said, was a 200 pound woman about 5 feet 8 inches tall who had told acquaintances that she was twice married and twice divorced when she arrived in this area after spending previous years in Chicago and other middle western cities.

Mrs. Hogan had a reputation, the Shermans said, of being able to handle herself in dealings with frequently intoxicated steady customers. When customers got obstreperous, they said, Mrs. Hogan would order them out. If the did not go willingly, she woul walk from behind the bar an throw them out.

Mrs. Hogan is last known to have been seen at 4:30 p. m on Dec. 8, 1954. At that hour the last customers of the day staggered out. Mrs. Hogan was seen by them to lock the door after they left. Presumably she intended to go to her adjoining living quarters to make her supper.

### Find Pool of Blood

The saloon did not open for business the next day. Puzzled patrons reported to the Portage county sheriff, Harold [Topper] Thompson, that something was wrong. A day later Thompson forced the front door and found a pool of blood on the barroom floor. No one had been found who thereafter saw Mrs. Hogan alive until Gein confessed.

Sherman said that when he and his wife moved into the saloon they found many belongings of Mrs. Hogan, including an X-ray film of Mrs. Hogan's head. He displayed this film to interviewers, pointing to a name, "Mrs. Mary Hogan," and a date, "1927." The film had the appearance of an X-ray which may have been ordered by a physician, rather than by a dentist, and may have been taken to enable a physician to diagnose a nasal obstruction or sinus trouble.

### Finds Stained Cap

Sherman said when he found the X-ray film he told Portage county authorities about it and offered to surrender it to them. The sheriff told him he had no use for the film.

Sherman said he also found a man's cap, stained with what might be blood, but that so far as he knows no tests were ever made by authorities to ascertain the cause of the stain.

### Daughter Gets News

Carlinville, Ill., Nov. 20 (AP) — A Wisconsin's sheriff's recognition of a skull has apparently brought to a shocking end the search of a Carlinville woman for her mother.

Mrs. Christine Selvo, 37, who last saw her mother, Mrs. Mary Hogan, about 27 years ago in Carlinville, began to search again for her two years ago when she learned Mrs. Hogan was reported missing in Wisconsin.

### Slayer Confesses

Mrs. Hogan, 54, was a Portage county, Wis., divorcee who disappeared in December, 1954, from the rural tavern she operated at Bancroft, about six miles from the farm of Ed Gein, 51, who today confessed the slaying after one of a number of human skulls found on his farm was identified by Wisconsin authorities as that of Mary Hogan.

### Insurance Beneficiary

Victor Selvo, husband of Christine, told a reporter today an administrator of Mrs. Hogan's estate brought the first word in years to his wife of her mother's whereabouts in 1955. Mrs. Selvo was named in an insurance policy held by Mrs. Hogan.

Selvo said his wife had been adopted by foster parents in her childhood. Since that time, he said, Mrs. Selvo knew only that her mother had lived at various times in Springfield, Joliet, and Chicago.

**UNDERGOES LIE DETECTOR TEST**
Edward Gein, 51-year-old bachelor farmer, sits in a police car with bowed head enroute to Madison from Wautoma Tuesday for a lie detector test. Gein is being held on a robbery charge and for questioning in the death of Mrs. Bernice Worden of Plainfield. He is also being questioned regarding parts of human bodies found on his farm, Waushara County Dist. Atty. Earl Kileen stated. (AP Wirephoto)

Edward Gein (right) walks with Sheriff Art Schley to the preliminary hearing Thursday in Wautoma in the death of Mrs. Bernice Worden last Saturday.
Associated Press Wirephoto.

### ...dy Found Hanging by Heels

He said that the decapitated body of Mrs. Bernice ...orden, 58, widowed proprietor of a hardware store ...ainfield, was found hanging by the heels from a hook in ...ein's woodshed with all vital organs removed.

"The body was cleaned and dressed like a freshly ...tchered animal," he said. "Gein has admitted that he

Map shows location of the Gein farm in relation to Plain...eld and Wautoma.

...id the butchering and tells us he thought he was dressing ...deer."

Kileen disclosed that the woman's heart was found in ... dish on a table in a room adjoining the woodshed which ...ein apparently used as his dining table.

## Killer's Young Friend Says He Saw Heads

Journal Staff Correspondence

Plainfield, Wis.—Bob Hill, 16, a junior at Tri-County high school, said Tuesday that he had been shown two of the heads fuond in the Ed Gein horror house some time ago.

He said Gein told him that they had been sent to him from the Philippines by a cousin, saying that they were like shrunken heads.

He said he had not noticed any of the other ghastly items in the Gein house.

Hill had been friendly with Gein, going to the movies with the slayer and attending baseball games with him. When Gein was arrested Saturday night, he had been eating dinner at the Hill home. Bob's parents, Mr. and Mrs. Lester Hill, run a grocery store and gasoline station at West Plainfield, a community about three miles west of Plainfield.

said Tuesday morning that the county had no cases of missing persons.

However, Murty, who was sheriff for six years and whose wife was sheriff for two years, said that a man named Victor Travis disappeared in 1953. He said that at the time he got calls about fresh graves being found in wooded sections.

Murty said he checked these reports and found two freshly dug graves. He said one was empty; the other contained a dead dog.

Murty, now a deputy and village marshal at Wild Rose, was one of the lawmen who brought Edward Gein here for a lie test at the state crime laboratory.

Sheriff Herbert Wanserski of Portage county, who Tuesday afternoon expanded the investigation by identifying one of the faces or heads found in the house as that of a missing woman tavern keeper, said he had been told that Gein had a habit of disappearing at times. He reported an Elmer Ueech of Plainfield, who claimed to know Gein had said that Gein would occasionally be absent from his usual haunts for a couple of weeks at a time—usually in the winter.

## Sheriff Cites Co-operation As Key Factor in Arrest

*Waushara Argus*

The important role played by law officers from neighboring counties and local Plainfield residents in the apprehension of Ed Gein less than two hours after evidence of the crime had been made known, was recognized Wednesday by Sheriff Arthur Schley in a letter to the co-operating agencies.

The sheriff's office at Wautoma received the call from Plainfield at 5:10 p.m. Saturday. Gein had been arrested by 7 p.m. and was housed in a jail cell at Wautoma by 7:40 p.m.

The letter from the sheriff read as follows:

"Gentlemen:

"We wish to sincerely thank all persons who assisted in any manner in the recent investigation at Plainfield.

"All neighboring sheriff's departments which were contacted responded promptly and gave us their utmost co-operation.

"We also wish to thank the crime laboratory for their quick response and expert handling of their phase of the investigation.

"It is also true, that without the help and assistance of the volunteers in and around Plainfield, our investigation would not have been successful.

"To each and every one who assisted in any way we wish to repeat our thanks.

Waushara Co. Sheriff's Dept.
Arthur Schley, Sheriff"

Sheriff Schley told The Argus Wednesday morning that if even a few hours had elapsed allowing Gein time to completely dispose of the body, it would have been much more difficult to have solved the crime.

What took place in those first few hours, according to the sheriff, was essentially as follows:

Sheriff Schley and Deputy Arnold Fritz went directly to the Worden Store after receiving the call.

At the store there was obvious evidence of foul play with blood found on the floor, the fact that Mrs. Worden was missing, the truck belonging to the store was nowhere in the area, the cash register in the store was missing.

After a hurried conference, sheriff's offices in adjoining counties were called and the state crime laboratory notified.

The first search was for the truck, which was found just east of the village on a "lover's lane" road. Village residents went with officers from other areas to help guide them to possible hiding places.

A pattern of tires from the Worden truck was obtained from the place where the tires had been purchased.

Also, at the outset, there were at least "three or four" suspects, who for one reason or another there was cause to check. Gein was one of these.

The suspect was found and taken into custody at Hill's Grocery. While he was being questioned by Traffic Officer Dan Chase, Sheriff Schley and Captain Lloyd Schoephoester of the Green Lake County Traffic Department went to the Gein farm.

While Capt. Schoephoester searched another part of the house, Sheriff Schley opened the door to the summer kitchen and found the mutilated body.

He radioed Officer Chase to bring Gein in.

PAPER BAGS AND BOXES CONTAIN EVIDENCE FOUND IN THE RURAL PLAINFIELD HOME OF ED GEIN

## Shy Gein Feared Women, Pal Says

A Milwaukee man who claims "I knew Ed Gein better than any othe living man" Wednesday described the Plainfield farmer as "very bashful" and the "first to offer to help anyone who asked him."

Ira Turner, 39, of 3720 S. Pennsylvania Av., a yardman at the Ladish Co., said:

"Ed was the best friend I had. As a boy the Gein farm was my second home. I stopped there practically every day after school. And I ate as many meals there as I did at my own home."

Turner said his family moved to a farm about half a mile south of the Gein place when he was 5 years old. When he was 16 Turner moved to Milwaukee and has been here since. Turner and Gein have remained friends through the years and the Milwaukeean has seen Gein "many times" since moving here.

Turner said there was one part of the Gein case which puzzled him:

Following his arrest for his macabre activities, Gein said his "memory is vague" and that he must have been in a daze.

Turner said that in all the years he has known him, Gein "never suffered from dazes."

### HUNTED TOGETHER

"Ed taught me to hunt, fish and play the accordion and the flute. We went hunting together lots of times. We hunted rabbits and birds, but never deer. Ed was a very nice fellow. He would do anything for you," Turner said.

Turner said the last time he saw Gein was about three weeks ago.

"I went up there (Plainfield) to hunt and took my son along," he said. "After the hunting I wanted my son to meet Ed so we went over to the Gein place. Before we could knock on the door Ed came out and we talked for a while outside.

"He didn't invite me in like he used to but at the time I didn't think anything of it. Ed seemed about the same as he always did."

"When I first found out about the murder I was shocked and at first I figured they (police) had the wrong man. Later the sheriff told me the whole story. I just couldn't understand what came into that man's mind."

Gein was always a "little slower" than other youngsters, Turner declared, and he never spoke of violence.

When asked if Gein ever went out with girls, Turner answered:

Never. Ed was shy. The most bashful man I have ever seen. If a girl talked to him, Ed would look down at the ground. Very bashful.

### READ CRIME STORIES

"The gun, which he used to let me shoot some times, was to take care of crows and other birds on the farm. I guess he took the gun to town with him just as a force of habit.

"When Ed's mother was alive the Gein place was always kept nice and clean. I remember how we—my father and I—often went to the Gein house to play cards. Ed used to get great pleasure out of reading detective magazines, but I never thought anything of that, lots of people do.

"When I knew Ed up north he never touched smokes or drink. He was just a very nice fella."

*Wautoma Argus* — Wednesday, November 20, 1957

# Worden, Hogan Slayings

The first real break in the Gein case came at approximately 2 p.m. today when the suspect confessed to State Crime investigators that he had slain Mrs. Bernice Worden of Plainfield and Miss Mary Hogan, former operator of a tavern near Bancroft.

To this time he had made no definite statement as to the actual slaying of Mrs. Worden and had denied implication in the Hogan murder.

He had told District Attorney Earl Kileen and law officers that he could recall dragging Mrs. Worden's body from her Plainfield store, but his mind was "hazy" on any violence.

The statement released by Charles Wilson, director of the State Crime Laboratory, read as follows:

"The lie detector tests of Ed Gein have been completed and after consultation with the several district attorneys we are able at this time to state that the results of the test referred to eliminate the subject, Ed Gein, 51, as the person responsible and / or involved in the disappearance of Evelyn Hartley in LaCrosse County on Oct. 24, 1953; the disappearance of Georgia Jean Weckler in Jefferson County on May 1, 1947, and Victor Travis in Adams County on Nov. 1, 1952.

"Mr. Gein has now admitted that he is responsible for the death of Mary Hogan in Portage County on Dec. 8, 1954 and Bernice Worden in Waushara County on Nov. 16, 1957.

"This release is jointly concurred in by the interested local officers to eliminate Mr. Gein from unnecessary suspicion and conjecture.

"An avalanche of physical evidence has been recovered which will take weeks and possibly months to completely evaluate and process.

"When this is done the results will be made known to the proper local officials.

"A photograph has been prepared and is attached and we believe this photography to be in as good taste as possible under the circumstances.

"This photograph indicates the amount of physical evidence which must now be meticulously evaluated and examined.

"Release concerning the evidence in the cases enumerated must be made by proper local officers.

"No implications can be made concerning this release".

Gein was expected to be returned to Wautoma by Sheriff Arthur Schley about 4 p.m. today.

He is presently being held on a robbery charge (slightly over $40 taken from the Worden store).

District Attorney Earl Kileen told the Argus Wednesday afternoon that no change in the charges will be made until the ballistics tests on a .22 rifle being examined by the crime lab have been completed.

The rifle was found in the Worden store with a spent cartridge in the chamber.

Gein had insisted that he could not have killed Mrs Worden "because he didn't have any weapon."

William Belter, who is representing Gein, has indicated that he will waive preliminary hearing of the defendent.

Assuming that a murder indictment will be forthcoming, Gein would then be bound over to Circuit Court. Also, it is very likely that he would be submitted to sanity tests.

County Judge Boyd Clark stated Wednesday morning that if a preliminary examination was held he would disqualify himself due to the fact that the defendent had pointed out to the court the graves of persons he claims to have entered.

Gein originally maintained that the other nine skulls, found in various places throughout his bachelor quarters, were obtained from cemeteries.

However, with the confession of the slaying of Mrs. Hogan, this theory will be somewhat discredited.

A tentative identification of the head and face of Miss Hogan had been made Monday by Sheriff Herbert Wanserski of Portage County.

Wanserski has been quoted as saying, "This guy never robbed a grave in his life. There's no doubt in my mind but that he killed all of these people".

## Missing Person Probe Revives Travis Mystery

Waushara County law enforcement agencies and the district attorney's office are primarily interested in one thing presently regarding the Ed Gein case. That is proving conclusively, with all possible evidence, that he is responsible for the death of Mrs. Bernice Worden.

The identifying of the remains of 9 other skulls found on the Gein farm will be left to the State Crime Laboratory and to officials of other counties who have missing persons on record.

The investigation will be carried further, however, only if it is definitely proven that the bodies were not taken from various cemeteries as Gein states is the case.

In addition to the Mary Hougan case, which the local authorities were involved in to a more or less minor degree since the tavern was located in Pine Grove Township in Portage County, there is one other area "missing person" case that received considerable publicity at the time.

The latter involved the disappearance of Victor "Bunk" Travis who disappeared from a Plainfield tavern on Nov. 1, 1952.

The story, which appeared in The Argus issue of December 3, 1952 read as follows:

"The search for Victor "Bunk" Travis, Adams County man who mysteriously disappeared Nov. 1 with a stranger after leaving Mac's Bar in Plainfield, reached into Waushara County this week with Sheriff Leon Murty checking movements of the men before they were last seen.

"Travis formerly lived in Waushara County west of Hancock. For some time, however, he lived about four miles south and east of Big Flats tavern and store on state highway 13.

"His disappearance has raised many questions:

"What has happened to Travis?

"Who was the stranger in whose company Travis was last seen about 7 p.m., Nov. 1?

"Why would he leave his pretty young bride of two months without telling her, or his mother, that he didn't expect to be back within a few hours?

"These questions are stirring the imaginations of the natives in sparsely settled Adams County, a county that has thousands of acres of wilderness. A wilderness that is seldom traversed except in limited fashion during deer hunting season. It is wild country that could hide violence for years and perhaps never give up its secret."

The final appearance of Travis and the stranger was at the Plainfield bar (they had been visiting other bars in the area over a period of about a week)

In their last visit to Plainfield they were reported to have stayed at the bar about three hours. They left saying they were going to return to the Lars Thomsen farm in the Town of Plainfield to hunt. Neither of the two men has been seen since.

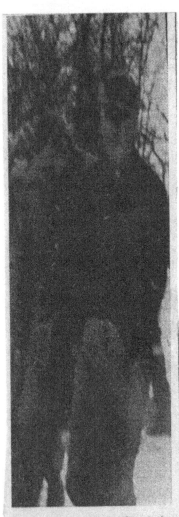

Ed Gein is shown leading Arthur Schley to the place behind his farm home where he disposed of the blood. In the investigating party were District Attorney Earl Kileen Judge Boyd Clark and Charles Wilson, head of the State Crime Laboratory.

GEIN'S HOME — This rather plain looking farm home of Ed Gein has been referred to on television and by the press as everything from a "murder factory" to "ramshackle hovel". Mrs. Worden's body was found in the shed only partially visible at left. No photographers were allowed on the scene until mid-morning Monday. A few minutes after this picture was taken Gein was brought to the scene and pointed out to officials where he had disposed of blood.

# Plainfield Killer Lived in Run Down House Amid Piles of Debris and Filth

Debris filled four of the 10 rooms of the decaying house Ed Gein called home. The building was incredibly dirty. Deputy Sheriff William Radomski of Wood county searched through litter in the kitchen. —United Press.

# Murder Factory on Farm!

# Find Remains of 5 Slain Women

## Plainfield Widow Sliced Up, Hung By Heels on Hook

*1957*

PLAINFIELD, Wis., Nov. 17 (Special) The decapitated body of a missing Plainfield widow and the skulls or other remains of four or five women have been found in a farmhouse seven miles west of here, Dist. Atty. Earl Kileen of Waushara County said Sunday.

Authorities of seven counties came upon the gruesome scene, resembling a human slaughterhouse, when a search for Mrs. Bernice Worden, 58, operator of a Plainfield hardware store, led Saturday night to the farm of Ed Gein, about 50.

### Suspect Denies Human Butchery

Gein was arrested and will be charged in County Court at Wautoma Monday with first degree murder, Kileen said.

Gein admitted being in the Worden store Saturday, but denied he had "hurt" her and or engaged in the butchery revealed on his farm premises.

Mrs. Worden was reported missing by her son, Frank, who returned from a hunting trip at 5 p.m. Saturday, found the store door locked, unlocked it and discovered a pool of blood on the floor. The cash register had been opened.

When authorities got to the Gein farm about 8 p.m., Gein was not there. They forced open the door of a shed and there the nude body of Mrs. Worden was discovered, hung up by the heels.

### Heart Found in Plastic Bag

The head had been severed, the stomach opened, the viscera removed and the heart put in a plastic bag, Kileen said.

It was a horrible scene, indicating one of the worst crimes ever committed in central Wisconsin, Kileen said. He added:

"It appears to be cannibalism."

The body had been washed and cleaned in much the same way animals are handled at a slaughterhouse, the district attorney said.

The Worden truck which was seen leaving the hardware store about 9:30 a.m. Saturday

Waushara County Deputy Sheriff Art Judge uses his flashlight to point out the rafter where the body of Mrs. Bernice Worden was hung after she was killed.
Associated Press Wirephoto.

A VIEW OF THE KITCHEN IN THE FARM HOME OF EDWARD GEIN

Associated Press Wirephoto.

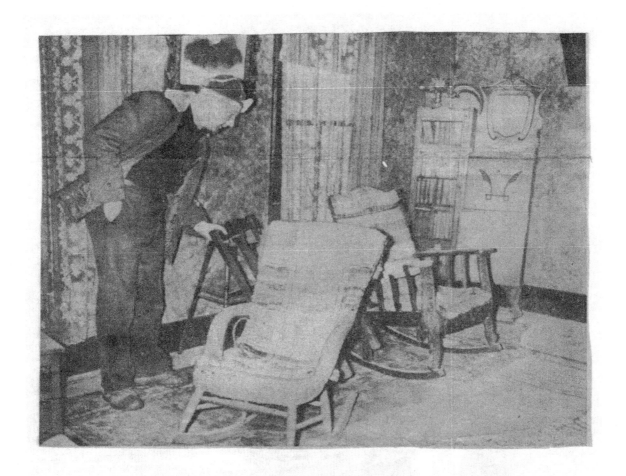

—Journal Staff
Sheriff Art Schley (upper) and Dist. Atty. Earl Kileen of Waushara county played key roles in the investigation of the Worden slaying and the questioning of Ed Gein.

By JOE BOTSFORD
*Sentinel Staff Writer*

PLAINFIELD, Wis., Nov. 18 — Farmer Ed Gein was "a strange one" to his Waushara County neighbors.

His home, constantly shuttered against daylight and showing signs of decay, has now become legendary here as a house of mystery.

In people's minds, the stage already was set for some drama regarding the middle-aged bachelor farmer and his old house located on a narrow dirt road six miles southwest of here.

## WORSE THAN EXPECTED

But none of his neighbors was prepared for the shocking story that has now been revealed in all its starkness—the fact that the farm was in reality a human slaughterhouse.

Again Monday, curious neighbors drove by the farmhouse where the mutilated body of a Plainfield woman and portions of other human bodies were found.

But there was little to see.

The two-story frame house looked shabby under a dull sky, and falling snow drifted through the roofs of four small barns nearby on the farm, all empty and crumbling into ruin.

## SHADES DRAWN

As usual, neighbors noticed, the windows of the house were darkened by drawn tattered shades.

But now beams of light came through the shades from spotlights being used by State Crime Laboratory personnel as they worked in secret in a front parlor.

Wherever people gathered Monday in Plainfield, a community of less than 700, or nearby Hancock, the talk was about "Ed and his house."

## THIN BUT WIRY

Gein is known here, for he had lived on the farm of his now deceased parents for about 40 years. But few people seem to know him intimately.

He was described as "pleasant" or "quiet" but also as "strange" or "odd." Gein is a little man, thin but wiry, and people pictured him as a man not capable of harming anyone.

Living alone since the death of his mother about 15 years ago, Gein was somewhat of a recluse.

He had not even visited his nearest neighbor, living only a field away, in the past two or three years. Neighbors saw him only when he drove by in his truck.

Occasionally, Gein associated with men in the local taverns. People recall him as saying little, but smiling a lot over a glass of wine.

## NO LIVESTOCK

Gein did not farm his land. He worked for other farmers or for shopkeepers in Plainfield and let his own farm deteriorate.

His house often was referred to jokingly by area residents as a "ghost house." He had no livestock.

When authorities entered the house, they found it "filthy beyond belief."

Plainfield citizens recall that Gein had been coming into town lately and pestering Mrs. Bernice Worden, as she worked in her hardware store, for a date. He had asked her to go roller skating, but the widow declined.

Gein was seen in town Saturday, and it was common knowledge that Mrs. Worden was alone in her store because

(Please Turn to Page 2, Col. 4)

## NEIGHBORS
# Slayer Often Asked Widow For Dates

(Continued From Page 1)
her son, Frank, had gone deer hunting.

Nor was it surprising to people here that the store was closed early in the day, since it was a common practice for Mrs. Worden to close up briefly to go on an errand.

## SLAIN IN STORE

But residents found it shocking to learn that she apparently had been murdered in her store "in broad daylight" right in the heart of town.

Authorities went to Gein's farm Saturday night because he had been seen in town around 9 a.m. Saturday, once walking toward the store and once driving away in Mrs. Worden's truck.

Her body was found hanging in a rear workshop attached to Gein's house. He was arrested in a restaurant in Plainfield after the body was discovered.

The discovery of the murder was the first big case for Sheriff Arthur Schley.

## 2 DUCK ISSUE

In office only since Oct. 1, Schley attempted an immediate news blackout on the details of the discovery in the farmhouse.

Schley insisted it was up to the State Crime Laboratory to release even the barest details on the base, but Charles Wilson, director of the laboratory, said in turn that it was up to local authorities to release what information they wished.

Wilson returned to Madison headquarters late Monday letting members of his staff in charge of the investigation.

# Killer Tells How He 'Deer-Dressed' Widow at Farm

*By Sentinel Staff Writer*

WAUTOMA, Wis., Nov. 18—A timid, 51-year-old bachelor handyman, his hands trembling as he shielded his face, related for the first time Monday details of his butchery of a Plainfield widow and his farmstead "deathhouse" where her body and 10 other human skulls were found.

Edward Gein, longtime solitary occupant of a farm 16 miles northwest of here, ended a 30-hour silence with a statement to Waushara County District Atty. Earl Kileen in which:

- Gein admitted transporting the body of Mrs. Bernice Worden, 58, from her hardware store in the hamlet of Plainfield by truck and car to the woodshed of his farm home, where he butchered her.
- He maintained that the 10 other skulls and portions of female bodies discovered on the farm came from local cemeteries in a series of grave robberies he committed over an undetermined number of years.

## Gein to Face Lie Detector Test

Kileen released portions of Gein's confession before and after the man, described by neighbors as "a typical Casper Milquetoast," was arraigned before County Judge Boyd Clark in the Courthouse here.

He was charged with robbery and was placed under $10,000 bond. Prosecutor Kileen said a murder charge would be filed against Gein as soon as all investigative agencies have completed their investigations.

The district attorney had requested bail of only $5,000 but the court set the higher figure, explaining that if other charges should follow, the bond should be adequate.

Kileen said he was satisfied Gein was telling the truth when he claimed the 10 human skulls in his gruesome collection came only from the graves of already deceased women—and not, as previously speculated, from victims abducted and slaughtered.

However, Kileen said Gein will be taken to Madison to undergo a lie detector test in the offices of the State Crime Laboratory.

## Explanations Branded Vague

The request was made by Crime Lab investigators on the scene, determined to use all scientific means available to get answers on one of the most shocking crimes in Wisconsin history.

The answers provided by Gein himself in his initial statement to the district attorney's office provided only the vaguest and most incomplete explanations for his behavior.

Gein said he suddenly went "into a daze" as he ordered anti-freeze for his car from Mrs. Worden Saturday morning in her store. He couldn't remember how or when he killed Mrs. Worden.

But Gein did recall bringing the body to his farm woodshed, decapitating and viscerating it with a knife he made from a file.

### 'LIKE DRESSING A DEER'

"I thought I was dressing out a deer. That's the only explanation I can think of in my mind," he said in his statement.

The same "daze" came over him, Gein told the district attorney, during his grave robbings. He would follow death notices published in the local newspaper, then would visit the graves of women who had just died.

Gein said he would unearth the coffin, decapitate the body and cut away other anatomical sections. Then he would return the headless corpse to the coffin, return it to the open grave, and cover it again with earth.

The head and other portions of anatomy Gein said he took to his home.

Of the 10 skulls discovered at the place, some appeared to be shrunken heads.

Some were found in plastic bags. Others reportedly were scattered carelessly under furniture in his littered home.

### VISIT GRAVES SCENES

District Attorney Kileen and police authorities took Gein to the farmhouse Monday morning after his first statement was obtained.

The district attorney said Gein also took him to cemeteries in the area where the grave robberies occurred.

The district attorney refused to say how many cemeteries were robbed or to identify them by name. Dates of the grave robberies also remained undetermined.

In his statement, Gein said he had committed no grave robberies "for two or three years."

Existence of the macabre (Please Turn to Page 2, Col. 5)

*(Continued From Page 1)* farmhouse collection Sunday and Monday struck fear and apprehension across the state and stunned the tiny community of Plainfield.

Some acquaintances knew him there as a man with a sly smile who liked to talk about women.

### LONELY AND QUIET

Others pictured him as a lonely, quiet man who was friendly to children.

The Waushara County Sheriff's Department reported it was flooded by telephone calls from throughout the state.

The calls came from police authorities checking on mysterious disappearances of women in their areas, and, in some instances, from anxious relatives themselves.

A query came from La Crosse authorities, still investigating the 1953 disappearance of Evelyn Hartley, 15-year-old babysitter.

### SEEK HOGAN TIEUP

Portage County authorities sent investigators to the scene seeking a tie-in with the Dec. 9, 1954, disappearance of Miss Mary Hogan, 54, from her bloodstained Pine Grove tavern.

In the absence of definite evidence, however, authorities for the present at least were taking Gein's story at face value.

One of the most shocked of Gein's acquaintances was Lester Hill, operator of a general store at West Plainfield. He said Gein spent much time around the store, sometimes playing baseball or throwing snowballs with the children.

Linda Foster, 11, said Gein sometimes "babysat" with her 16-month-old brother at the Foster home near the store. "He bought candy for us sometimes," she said.

**MURDER**
# Gein Had Sly Grin, Talked of Women

## The Uncluttered Room in Ghoulish Home

Deputy Sheriff William Radomski in doorway of the one uncluttered room in farm home of Ed Gein near Plainfield, Wis. This room had been closed and unused since the death of Gein's mother. (United Press Telephoto)

Gein talked with Sheriff Art Schley (left) as the slayer was led from the farm Monday after a visit to the place with law officers. Later, Gein was arraigned before Judge Boyd Clark (right). —United Press Telephoto

# Plainfield 'Butcher' Story!

TUESDAY, NOVEMBER 19, 1957

## Admits Murder, Grave Robbings

### Neighbors Now Remember Gein as 'a Strange One'

# Gein Lived in Incredibly Filthy, Junk-Littered House

**By VERNE HOHL**
*Sentinel Staff Writer*

PLAINFIELD, Wis., Nov. 19 — The two story frame building where Edward Gein "existed" houses the most bizarre, cluttered and filthy collection of junk and debris imaginable.

"Exist" is the only word that can describe the incredible conditions found inside the building.

The regular entrance opens into a shed-like wing of the building where the body of Mrs. Bernice Worden, 58, was found hung by the heels from rafters.

## JUNK COLLECTION

The room, framed only by beams and siding, contained, among other litter:

A pair of 8-foot home-made skis, an old pot-bellied stove, a small oil space heater, lanterns, a scythe, stacks of burlap bags, heaps of empty cans, cardboard boxes filled with old papers and magazines, a funeral wreath and hundreds of odds and ends.

The entrance to a basement leads from the room. Nothing but old vegetable crates were found there.

The next room you enter probably was destined to be a kitchen.

In it are some cupboards and an old fashioned cooking stove, stacks of empty cans, utensils, tools and other pieces of trash including a jar lid full of chewing gum.

## KNEE-DEEP IN LITTER

The floor is knee-deep with broken chairs, bottles, newspapers, pails, tool chests and rags.

Also found in the "kitchen" were some formaldehyde and an old-fashioned embalming needle, a deer hide, and two sets of deer antlers above door-ways.

From the empty cans and cartons spotting the "kitchen" it would seem that Gein had lived on oatmeal, canned soup and peanut butter. There were no milk bottles or coffee cans evident or anything in which food was stored.

Deputies pointed out places in the building where skulls, pieces of facial skin and scalps and other human remains were found.

Wood County Deputy Dave Sharkey verified that odd pieces of human skin had been found in the building, some lying in the open and some in boxes beneath magazines.

## SKIN FROM TORSO

The pieces included sections from a woman's upper torso and strips from backs, legs and necks.

Toy planes, marbles and other cereal box prizes were scattered about the kitchen.

In Gein's bedroom, one corner is occupied by an ancient bedspread and a mattress usually seen only in junk yards.

Nine calendars were nailed above the bed. Men's magazines littered the room.

Five filthy rags — monogramed handkerchiefs — hung from a clothes line.

Three straight back chairs, a stuffed one and a sofa all hidden under a variety of debris and the only connected stove in the building are the other sizable objects in the room.

## CURTAINS IN SHREDS

The wall paper is cracked and peeled to a line half-way down to the floor. Lace curtains hang in dirty shreds and the shades are riddled with holes.

The only thing resembling a cleared area is the top of a table, covered with newspaper pages.

A violin, a zither, an old fashioned accordion, a harmonica and an extensive collection of whistles are also spread about.

Two ancient radios stand in a corner. Pictures of a little boy, a dog and a religious scene hang on the walls.

## PARLOR SHUT OFF

A paper partition was broken to gain entrance to the living room and what used to be Gein's mother's bedroom.

The living room holds a collection of porch chairs, another old radio and a book case containing many Horatio Alger and Bible-study books.

Apparently unused for years, it was the only first floor room approaching neatness. Its floor was cluttered with only dirt and dust.

Some bed clothes and women's hats were scattered around the adjoining bedroom. Another small room was heaped with pillows, mattresses and boxes of other junk, some of which had contained the pieces of human hair and skin.

## 4 ROOMS UPSTAIRS

Four rooms make up the second story. One, used for storage, held two egg incubators and cream separator equipment—and a pair of boxing gloves.

The stuffings of two mattresses blanketed the floor in another room, fallen plaster and pile of butter nuts in a corner completed its contents.

Two other bedrooms, one minus a bed, each contained dressers and a few chairs. The floors were bare.

State Crime Laboratory experts checking the house termed it "the worst mess we have ever seen."

A shed behind the building held another interesting item —a 1942 blue Chevrolet pickup truck.

Deputy Sharkey said it answered the description of a vehicle sought as the one seen in the Pine Grove area when a 54-year-old tavernkeeper, Miss Mary Hogan, disappeared in December, 1954.

TUESDAY, NOVEMBER 19, 1957

# Gein 'Didn't Know What Happened, Was in Daze'

## Describes Events in Store

*Sentinel Staff Writer*

WAUTOMA, Wis., Nov. 18 — "My memory is vague . . ."

These and other phrases of a similar nature recur in the confession of Edward Gein, 51, ......or handyman who admitted Monday the butchery of a Plainfield, Wis., widow, and ownership of a macabre collection of female skulls.

**RELEASED DETAILS**

The statement was released Monday afternoon by Dist. Atty. Earl Kileen.

In his statement, Gein admitted going to Mrs. Bernice Worden's hardware store at Plainfield Saturday morning.

"I went into the store with a glass jug to order some antifreeze," Gein was quoted by Kileen. "Mrs. Worden said, 'Do you want a gallon of antifreeze?' 'No,' I said. 'A half gallon.'

**HELD GLASS JUG**

"I held the glass jug for her while she poured the antifreeze into it. It was 99 cents. I gave her a dollar and got one cent in change.

"I don't know just what happened then. She glanced out the window and said, 'they are checking deer out there.'"

(This was a reference to a deer checking station within sight of the Worden store.)

**DROVE TRUCK**

(Gein was asked at this point, "did you stab her or shoot her?" "My memory is vague," he replied. "I do remember dragging her across the floor. I remember loading her body into the truck." This referred to the store delivery truck, parked behind the building.)

"Then I drove the truck out on the east road. I drove the truck into pine trees (apparently the pine grove about one mile east of Plainfield where the truck was recovered later)."

"Then I got out of the truck and walked to town. And I got my car and drove it out there. And loaded her body into the back end of the car."

(At this point Gein said he also put the cash register from the store into the car as well.)

"Then I drove out to my farm and took the body out of my car and hung it up by its heels in my woodshed."

(Gein said he decapitated the body and put the head into a box.)

NOVEMBER 20, 1957

# D. A. Refuses Probe Of Gein Grave Raids

## Fears He'll Upset Kin, Kileen Says

*Sentinel Staff Writer*

WAUTOMA, Wis., Nov. 19 — Further delving into the grave digging activities of Plainfield handyman and confessed murderer Edward Gein will not be instituted by the district attorney's office, Earl F. Kileen, Waushara County district attorney, said Tuesday.

Kileen said he is not interested in opening any graves and has no intention of upsetting the whole community of Plainfield—"which would result if wholesale grave openings occurred."

**ON OFFICIAL ORDER**

Kileen added, however, that a grave or graves would be opened at the order of some other authority, such as the State Crime Laboratory.

Gein has admitted robbing graves in at least two cemeteries. He has pointed out one grave in the Plainfield Cemetery which he opened he said, to remove the head of a 60-year-old woman who died in 1949.

Under Wisconsin law body snatching carries a term of one to three years.

"I want no part in opening graves to prove anything. Just think how the poor relatives would feel," said Kileen.

**8-YEAR 'CAREER'**

The district attorney said Gein began opening graves about 1949. Gein supposedly ended the ghoulish practice about three years ago.

Gein told authorities he was only interested in the bodies of women and that all 10 skulls and heads found in his farm home were female. He kept the skulls in cardboard boxes around his home.

The farmer said he opened the graves at night, removed the heads and other parts of the corpses and then re-filled the graves.

Gein said he may have done the grave robberies by the light of a "full moon."

**NEW GRAVES, TOO**

But he always spoke of "being in a daze" when opening a grave and said he was not fully aware of what he was doing in these periods.

The farmer also said he opened "new graves," usually two or three days after reading of burial notices in the newspaper.

Kileen continued to insist he is only interested in "pinning the murder rap on Gein and leaving the cemeteries undisturbed."

Tuesday, November 19, 1957 — THE MILWAUKEE JOURNAL

Gein talked with Sheriff Art Schley (left) as the slayer was led from the farm Monday after a visit to the place with law officers. Later, Gein was arraigned before Judge Boyd Clark (right).
—United Press Telephoto

Gein covered his face with his gloved hands as authorities prepared to take him to his farm Monday.
—Journal Staff by Fred L. Toone

November 19, 1957     Appleton Post-Crescent

This Is the Kitchen of the Farm Home of Edward Gein, 51, Plainfield bachelor, who is being held for murdering and butchering Mrs. Bernice Worden, 58-year-old widow-storekeeper in Plainfield. The body of Mrs. Worden was found hanging in an adjacent summer kitchen Saturday night. (Post-Crescent Photo)

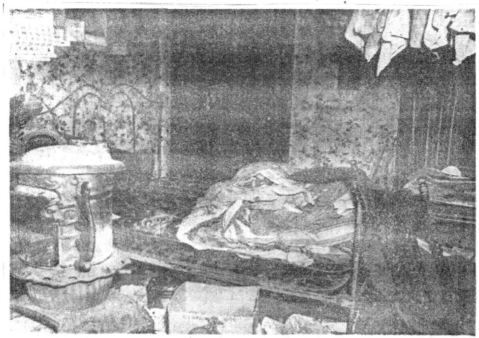

Part of the Incredible Litter found in the home of Edward Gein, six miles southwest of Plainfield, is shown in this picture of what he used as a bedroom. Hundreds of books and magazines were strewn about the home where the headless body of a Plainfield widow and parts of 10 other bodies were found. (Post-Crescent Photo)

## Officers Tend to Accept His Story as True

### But Investigation of Plainfield Horrors Is Continued; Lie Test Slated at Madison

By RICHARD C. KIENITZ
Of The Journal Staff

Plainfield, Wis. — Authorities Tuesday were trying to check Edward Gein's claim that he murdered only Mrs. Bernice Worden and that he got the rest of his grisly collection of human heads and skulls in a series of ghoulish grave robberies.

Waushara county authorities appeared to be convinced by Gein's story.

"Our case is pretty well cleaned up," said Dist. Atty. Earl Kileen. "We have no missing persons in our county. The only thing here is the murder rap."

Neither Kileen nor Sheriff Art Schley would say whether they had checked the cemeteries where Gein said he robbed graves—or that they intended to. They jokingly claimed that they "didn't remember" if they had checked any of the supposedly violated graves Monday.

### No Visitors Allowed

When asked Tuesday morning if he planned to check the cemeteries, Schley looked out a window at snow that was falling. "I wouldn't know about that," he said, implying that it was too nasty outside.

The sheriff did say that the snow and icy roads might prevent him from taking Gein to Madison, where the 51 year old farm recluse was scheduled to undergo a lie detector test at the state crime laboratory.

A news blackout imposed by Schley as soon as the butchered body of Mrs. Worden was found Saturday in a summer kitchen of Gein's ramshackle farm home remains in force. The sheriff refused to let reporters or photographers visit Gein in his jail cell, saying that they would upset Gein and that they hadn't finished talking to the suspect.

### "Very Annoying Fellow"

Kileen added that Gein was "a very annoying fellow to talk to—sometimes he'll want to go into great detail and other times he'll shut up and won't say anything." Kileen explained that Schley feared that the presence of reporters and photographers might frighten Gein into a sustained silence.

Gein was returned to jail after his arraignment Monday in Wautoma on an armed robbery charge. The charge was filed by Kileen to hold Gein until the crime laboratory had completed its investigation.

Gein told County Judge Boyd Clark that he wanted an attorney and could afford to hire one. He selected Atty. William N. Belter of Wautoma, a former assemblyman. Belter said Tuesday that he didn't know whether he would defend Gein. He said he hadn't talked to him yet.

### Bond Set at $10,000

Gein's bond was set at $10,000. Kileen had asked for $5,000 but Schley suggested it be doubled. The armed robbery charge arose from that fact that a cash register containing $41 or $42 was taken from Mrs. Worden's store at the time of the slaying. It was found in Gein's home.

The preliminary hearing on the charge was set for next Monday. However, Kileen said he expected Gein's lawyer (whoever he may be) to ask for a delay.

At Madison, Charles Wilson, director of the state crime laboratory, said that a check of cemeteries wasn't necessary yet.

"There's no sense going out with a pick and shovel to check the graveyards near Plainfield until we have exhausted the possibilities of evidence we already have," Wilson said.

Wilson said that if Gein's grisly collection of human heads, skulls and bones came from graves "there will be

Turn to page 3, col. 1

## Single Killing Theory Told

### Officers in Waushara County Think Others Were From Graves

From page 1, column 8

traces of embalming fluid and we'll find them."

Wilson also said that detailed physical descriptions of persons who had disappeared in recent years would be checked against what was found in Gein's farm home. He said the department had gathered such descriptions in many cases of disappearing persons.

Gein told authorities that he committed the grave robberies while in a "daze." He was quoted as saying that he committed at least 10 grave robberies from 1944 to 1952 and that each grave was that of a woman.

### He Read Obituaries

He was also quoted as saying he read obituaries in the newspapers and then went out to dig up the new graves. It was reported that some of the grave robberies were at cemeteries near his home.

There have been conflicting reports about what authorities found in Gein's home. Lt. Vern Weber, chief of detectives at La Crosse, said he saw part of the collection in the crime laboratory truck.

He said there were 10 women's heads, some with eyes and some without. He said some were complete with skulls, others were merely skin.

Weber said that all of the heads appeared to be those of women of middle age or older.

Weber said he was told that no full skulls were recovered—"just pieces"—and that other patches of skin had been recovered.

He said he saw with his own eyes a chair with a seat which appeared to be made of human skin, and a knife with a handle that appeared to have a skin covering. He said the chair was a typical kitchen chair which probably once had a rattan seat.

### Inclined to Believe Him

Weber said that the heads were in a very good state of preservation and that they had been found behind chairs and other furniture in Gein's home.

Weber said that he had talked to Gein twice and that he was inclined to believe his story about the grave robberies. He said that Gein said he had wanted to be a doctor in his youth. He said Gein said he had cured the heads in a brine solution.

Weber said that he had asked Gein "strong questions" about rumors of cannibalism.

"That's out," Weber said. "He said he never ate a bit of that stuff and I don't believe he did."

### "He Needs Help"

Weber said that Gein was "a very sincere, very meek fellow—you'd never believe he'd be the kind of guy to do such a thing—you feel like he needs help awful bad."

The La Crosse detective said Gein said that he could feel his grave robbing spells coming on.

"He said he would pray and that sometimes the prayers would snap him out of it. He said he came out of a spell one time while he was digging up a grave and that he stopped."

Weber said that Gein insisted that he hadn't robbed a grave since 1952. "He said maybe his prayers had been answered."

Gein also claims that he was in a spell when he murdered Mrs. Worden, although he admits he must have done it. "He says he only remembers carrying her out of the store — not the killing or the butchering," Weber said.

Mrs. Worden's body was found hanging by the heels and butchered like a hunter would butcher a deer. Her heart was found inside the farm home. One official pointed out that deer hunters customarily saved the heart and that this would lend some credence to Gein's claim that he thought he was dressing a deer at the time.

### Shoes Don't Fit

Weber came to Plainfield to check if Gein had any connection with the violent disappearance of baby sitter Evelyn Hartley in October, 1953. He said he was inclined to doubt a connection.

Weber said that tennis shoes found after the disappearance and linked to the murder were too large for Gein. "The shoes we found are size 11½; Gein wears about an 8," the detective chief said.

Weber said that Gein was a native of La Crosse but had left there with his parents when he was 7. "He claims he hasn't been back since," Weber said. "He has some relatives here and we're going to check with them."

Chicago police interviewed Gein for almost three hours until 3 a.m. Tuesday, seeking a connection with unsolved Chicago crimes, notably the Judith Anderson slaying. Gein told them that he hadn't ever traveled south of Milwaukee.

Sheriff Roger Reinel and Dist. Atty. Harold A. Eberhard of Jefferson county came here Tuesday to check any connection with the disappearance of Georgia Jean Weckler in 1947.

Authorities are still trying to establish the details of Mrs. Worden's slaying. She was shot in the head with a .22 caliber bullet. Gein claims that he doesn't own a gun of that caliber although two guns of another caliber were found in his home.

Many persons have been wondering how a person as slight as Gein could dig up so many graves and remove bodies without help. Gein claims that he never took a complete body.

Weber said the chair seat made of skin looked like skin from the chest or back of a human. Where Gein got this skin, he never took a complete body and murdered only Mrs. Worden, has not been answered.

Gein has been questioned about the disappearance of Miss Mary Hogan, 54, from her tavern at the near-by town of Pine Grove (Portage county).

Gein said he was at the tavern two days after her disappearance but admitted no other connection with that disappearance.

Funeral services for Mrs. Worden will be held at 2 p.m. Wednesday at the Plainfield Methodist church.

## Gruesome Story Brings Record Press Coverage

Wautoma Argus 11-20-57

The nation-wide impact of the gruesome Gein story has brought to this area more reporters, photographers and television news personnel than has decended on a small community in perhaps the history of the state.

Art Tittle of the Associated Press Chicago bureau estimates that at the height of activity there were at least 55 newsmen working on the story.

To facilitate the moving of pictures from Wautoma the AP has set up a portable photo transmitter at Wagler's Studio in the city.

Comparison wise, Mr. Tittle stated that he had recently covered the Katy-Jane Rest Home disaster in southern Missouri where 71 persons died and there were about 30 newsmen covering.

Some of the newspapers have as many as five newsmen covering various angels of the story.

Publications represented include the Milwaukee Journal, Milwaukee Sentinel, Capitol Times, Chicago Tribune, Chicago Sun-Times, Minneapolis Star, St. Paul Pioneer Press, Life and Time publications, at least four television stations and numerous other smaller dailies and few weeklies.

**UNLOAD EVIDENCE AT LAB**
Jan Beck, State Crime Lab official, carries cash register found at home of Ed Gein, 51, Plainfield, into lab. The cash register was taken from a hardware store operated by Mrs. Bernice Worden, 58, whose body was found Saturday night hanging in Gein's farm house. Gein is being held on charge of theft of the register. Crime lab mobile unit, loaded with cargo of parts of human bodies and other evidence being studied by technicians, arrived late last night. (AP Wirephoto)

## Gein Attempts to Hide Face in First Appearance

The reaction of Gein to the popping of dozens of flashbulbs when he first appeared openly late Monday morning before the assembled press changed markedly as the day progressed.

His first appearance came when he was taken from the jail to a waiting automobile about 11 a.m. As he came out of the door he attempted to hide his face behind handcuffed hands.

A short time later when he pointed out the location where he had disposed of blood behind the farm home he playfully put his hands over the lens of a moving picture camera and smiled slightly as he did it. This was about 12:45 p.m.

When he left the jail again for his arraignment on a robbery charge about 2:40, he made no attempt to evade cameras.

Also, in the courtroom itself while he was waiting for County Judge Boyd Clark to read the charge, he was docile and made no attempt to avoid photographers.

## Two Caskets Looted; Gein Believed Now

### Workmen Discover Bones on Top of One Wooden Coffin; DA Is Satisfied Now

By RICHARD C. KIENITZ
Of The Journal Staff

Plainfield, Wis. — Plainfield and Waushara county officials Monday opened two graves in the Plainfield cemetery to check on Ed Gein's story that he robbed bodies from various graves, in addition to committing two murders.

They found one body missing and bones from the second body scattered in the earth above the coffin. Both caskets were empty.

Officials said they did not plan to open other graves unless local people got an inkling that their relatives' graves might have been pillaged. County officials said they would tell any who asked if their relatives' names were on the list which Gein gave them.

However, the names will not be divulged otherwise, Scheriff Art Schley of Waushara county said.

### Near Parents' Graves

The first grave opened was that of Mrs. Eleanor Adams, who died in August, 1951. The other was that of Mrs. Mabel Everson, who died in April, 1951.

Mrs. Everson was 69 years old when she died. Mrs. Adams was 53.

The Adams grave was on the lot west of the cemetery lots in which Gein's mother, father and brother, Henry, are buried. Mrs. Everson's grave was 100 feet southeast of the Adams grave and about 50 feet northeast of the grave of Mrs. Bernice Worden, slain by Gein here a week ago Saturday.

Wautoma Argus — Wednesday, November 20, 1957

...AWAITS HEARING — Gein was arraigned before County Judge Boyd Clark at 2:45 p.m. Monday and charged with robbery of the Worden store. At left with him is Sheriff Arthur Schley, who took him to Madison Tuesday for the lie detector tests that resulted in his confessing the murder of Mrs. Worden and Miss Hogan.

GEIN'S HOME — This rather plain looking farm home of Ed Gein has been referred to on television and by the press as everything from a "murder factory" to "ramshackle hovel". Mrs. Worden's body was found in the shed only partially visible at left. No photographers were allowed on the scene until mid-morning Monday. A few minutes after this picture was taken Gein was brought to the scene and pointed out to officials where he had disposed of blood.

DEBUT — Ed Geins first appearance before the sizeable press representation gathered in Wautoma came about 11 a.m. Monday morning when he was taken from the jail to go to the farm southwest of Plainfield. He attempted to hide his face at first but later submitted placidly.

## Find Gein Wasn't Joking About Killings

11-20-57

PLAINFIELD, Wis. (UP)—Edward Gein's neighbors remember now. They believed he was joking when he told them of doing away with persons who were reported missing. Gein, a 51-year-old bachelor described as bashful and mild, has admitted two murders. Both of his victims were women, Mrs. Bernice Worden of Plainfield, and Miss Mary Hogan of Bancroft.

Bob Hill, a 16-year-old high school student from Plainfield, said he had been shown what appeared to be "two shrunken heads" at Gein's farm some time ago.

**Sent By Cousin**

"He said they were sent to him by a cousin from the Philippines," Hill recalled. "I didn't think anything about it at the time."

Authorities came upon a collection of skulls Gein kept on the farm. He told police he robbed graves.

"He was a little peculiar," Mrs. Morris Diggles said. "Like that time Mary Hogan disappeared. People would kid Ed about it and he'd say, sure, he did it. Whenever there was any crime anywhere Ed would confess to it. Everybody thought it was a big joke."

Mrs. Donald Foster said, "He's admitted to us he did away with Mary Hogan. We'd kid him about it, like everybody else, and he'd say, 'Yes, I went and got her in my little pickup truck and took her home.' And then he'd grin. Of course, nobody believed him. Not then."

### Gein Eats Hearty At Wautoma Jail

WAUTOMA, Wis. (UP)—Confessed killer Ed Gein isn't bothered with any loss of appetite, Sheriff Art Schley said today.

Schley said Gein "dug into" a meal of lettuce salad, lamb, potatoes, corn, apple pie and coffee Wednesday afternoon after returning from Madison, where he had confessed the slaying of two women.

This morning, Schley said, Gein had a bowl of corn flakes, pork links, toast, and two cups of coffee.

11-20-57

**CLAIMS GRUESOME FIND**

Sheriff Herbert Wanserski of Portage County as he told reporters one of 10 or more skulls found at the home of the recluse handyman, Ed Gein of Plainfield in Waushara County, was that of a Portage County woman missing for two years. Wanserski was in Madison where Gein was questioned at the State Crime laboratory.

## Sheriffs Disagree on Value Of Further Gein Farm Digging

12-4-57

PLAINFIELD, Wis. (UP)—The sheriffs of Waushara and Portage counties disagreed today on the value of continued digging around confessed killer and butcher of women Ed Gein's "house of horrors" near here. They also disputed the reliability of a "hot tip" in Wisconsin's most bizarre crime case.

Sheriff Art Schley of Waushara County, where the rundown farm of 51-year-old bachelor Gein is located, said "as far as I am concerned" digging for possible human remains has finished."

Sheriff Herbert Wanserski of Portage County, where one of Gein's two known women victims lived, said he will continue hacking through the frozen soil in hopes of finding remains taken from disturbed graves.

Wanserski also said again that Gein may have killed others besides Mrs. Bernice Worden, 58, a Plainfield store keeper, and Miss Mary Hogan, 54, a tavernkeeper near Bancroft.

When Mrs. Worden's butchered and dressed out body was found in Gein's summer kitchen more than two weeks ago it turned up the frail-appearing farmer's grisly activities over the past years. Miss Hogan was killed in 1954.

The Portage County sheriff, who had announced the "hot tip" in the case to newsmen earlier in the week said Tuesday night it concerned a possible missing person who lived in the area near Gein's farm four miles west of here. He said further investigation was needed to substantiate it.

Schley said earlier that Wanserski's "hot tip" concerned a possible burial site for other human remains on the farm and that it was "a big flop." Schley said Wanserski's announcement meant only a lot of hard work and no results.

"I don't see how there could be any other conclusion but that the man is insane," said William Belter, counsel for the 51 year old bachelor who has told authorities that he killed two women and robbed graves to obtain parts of other bodies.

### No Hartley Case Link

Charles Wilson, head of the state crime laboratory, said at Madison Wednesday that the lie detector test had eliminated Gein as a suspect in the disappearance of three other persons—Evelyn Hartley, 15, La Crosse baby sitter, Oct. 24, 1953; Georgia Jean Weckler, 8, Fort Atkinson, May 1, 1947, and Victor Travis, Adams county resident, Nov. 1, 1952.

"The district attorney appears to be willing to go along with me on a mental test," Belter said. "I don't doubt what the results of the examination will be. I don't see how there could be any other conclusion but that the man is insane."

Gein, who previously had admitted killing Mrs. Bernice Worden, 58 year old Plainfield (Waushara county) storekeeper, confessed the second slaying in Madison Wednesday during questioning preliminary to a lie detector test at the state crime laboratory.

### Hogan Slaying Confessed

He admitted killing Mary Hogan, 54 year old Portage county tavern keeper, on Dec. 8, 1954. Miss Hogan had been missing for three years.

Earlier in the week, Gein admitted killing Mrs. Bernice Worden, 58, a storekeeper at Plainfield (Waushara county).

Mrs. Worden's decapitated and eviscerated body was found Saturday in Gein's farmhouse near Plainfield. The house was littered with parts of other bodies, and Gein claimed that he had taken them from graves.

Gein Wednesday said he intended to do the same thing with Mrs. Worden's body as he did with Miss Hogan's—kept the head and several other parts of the body, and burned the rest.

**ADELINE WATKINS**
He was "good and kind and sweet"
Associated Press Wirephoto.

# Almost Wed Gein; He's 'Good, Kind'

PLAINFIELD, Wis., Nov. 20 (AP) Ed Gein, bachelor recluse who has admitted butchering a Plainfield woman, was "good and kind and sweet" to the woman who said she almost married him, the Minneapolis Tribune said in a copyrighted interview.

Adeline Watkins, 50, who lives with her mother in a small apartment here, said that during a 20-year romance with Gein he "was so nice about doing things I wanted to do, that sometimes I felt I was taking advantage of him."

A Tribune reporter quoted her as saying she had her last date with Gein Feb. 6, 1955.

"That night he proposed to me. Not in so many words, but I knew what he meant."

"Miss Watkins, described by the Tribune as a plain woman with graying bangs and horn-rimmed glasses, said "I turned him down, but not because there was anything wrong with him. It was something wrong with me. I guess I was afraid I wouldn't be able to live up to what he expected of me."

The Tribune quoted Miss Watkins' widowed mother as saying Gein was a "sweet, polite man," and that she told him to have her daughter in from dates by 10 p.m. and "he never failed me once."

Miss Watkins, the story related, said she and Gein used to discuss books. "We never read the same ones, but we liked to talk about them anyway. Eddie liked books about lions and tigers and Africa and India. I never read that kind of books.

"I guess we discussed every murder we ever heard about. Eddie told how the murderer did wrong, what mistakes he had made. I thought it was interesting."

When they went out, the story said, they usually went to a movie at nearby Wautoma. Sometimes they visited taverns between Plainfield and Wisconsin Rapids.

"I liked to drink beer sometimes, but I would almost have to drag Eddie into a tavern," Miss Watkins was quoted as saying. "He would much rather have gone to a drugstore for a milk shake."

PAPER BAGS AND BOXES CONTAIN EVIDENCE FOUND IN THE RURAL PLAINFIELD HOME OF ED GEIN

Sentinel photo

## Friends Crowd Church at Worden Rites

*By Sentinel Staff Writer*

PLAINFIELD, Wis., Nov. 20 — Merchants and businessmen of this little village closed their stores and offices Wednesday afternoon to join other friends and relatives of Mrs. Bernice Worden at funeral services for the slain widow.

Close to 250 people — Plainfield has a population of 680 — filled the church and connected Sunday School of the Methodist Church, to which Mrs. Worden belonged.

### PLEA FOR FAITH

They heard the church pastor, the Rev. Gerald Tanquist, give a funeral sermon in which he used the first words of the Twenty Third Psalm — "The Lord is my Shepherd" — as his theme in a plea for continued faith in God and remembrance "in the face of the horrible incidents of the past few days, that the Lord has not abandoned us."

Before the service the congregation filed past the open gold-colored casket, set in a semi-circle of flowers. The casket was closed when the service began.

Funeral ritual by the Plainfield chapter of the Order of the Eastern Star followed the brief church service.

### NOT FAR FROM CHURCH

Six pallbearers carried the casket to the waiting hearse. They were Albert Walter, Jesse Wood, Franklin Rothermel, Cyle Ellis, Arden Spees and James Severns.

In the little Plainfield cemetery, a mile and a half from the church, the Rev. Mr. Tanquist spoke a few final words as the casket was lowered into the grave.

Mrs. Worden's survivors are a son, Frank, Plainfield; a daughter, Mrs. Miriam Walker, Lincoln, Neb.; three brothers, Lloyd Conover, Leola, Wis.; Lester Conover, Almond, Wis., and Burrel Conover, Aurora, Ill.; a sister, Mrs. Clifton Johnson, Leola, and four grandchildren.

# Identify 2nd Gein Victim

NOVEMBER 20, 1957

## Death Mask Solves '54 Murder

*Sentinel Staff Writer*
MADISON, Nov. 19 — A woman tavernkeeper who disappeared in 1954 was a victim of Edward Gein, the 51-year-old bachelor handyman, Portage County Sheriff Herbert J. Wanserski declared here Tuesday.

Wanserski made his emphatic statement to newsmen after hours of questioning Gein and a close inspection of one of the death masks found Saturday in the man's ramshackle "house of death."

"There is no question in my mind that this facial skin and hair was Miss Mary Hogan," Wanserski said.

### AN UNBELIEVER

"I absolutely do not believe Gein's story that he got all the heads in graveyard robberies."

Miss Hogan disappeared Dec. 8, 1954, from her blood spattered tavern in the Town of Pine Grove, Portage County, which is 10 miles from Gein's home.

The cash drawer was rifled, and a spent .32 caliber cartridge was found on the tavern floor.

There were striking similarities in Miss Hogan's disappearance and the murder of Mrs. Bernice Worden, 58, Plainfield hardware store operator whom Gein has admitted slaying.

## MURDER FACTORY
## 'Butcher' Smiles at Lie Test

The Worden store, like Miss Hogan's, was splattered with blood and the cash register was taken.

### MAY BE MORE HEADS

Discovery Saturday of Mrs. Worden's eviscerated body in Gein's home led to the further discovery of a grisly collection of human heads, skulls and death masks.

Gein contended Monday he got the heads in a series of grave robberies from 1944 to 1952.

Authorities said at least 10 heads have been found, but Charles Wilson, director of the State Crime Laboratory, said Tuesday "there may be more." Wilson said his office will not be able to determine the exact number until an inventory and analysis is completed of the human remains found in the Gein home.

### KNEW MISS HOGAN

Wanserski said he knew Miss Hogan on sight before her mysterious disappearance. His identification was based, he indicated, on similarities he noted in one of three death masks he examined and Miss Hogan's face as he remembered it.

The sheriff said the death mask included hair, skin and "facial features," but no eyes.

Previously, Wanserski submitted Gein to intensive questioning on the Hogan case after his ghoulish collection was discovered, and said he was not satisfied with the answers he got from Gein.

Gein "showed familiarity with certain aspects of the case," but steadfastly denied any connection with Miss Hogan's disappearance, Wanserski said.

Another factor was the discovery of a 1942 blue pickup truck in one of the sheds on Gein's farm.

Portage County authorities said it tallied with the description of a small truck seen in the neighborhood of Miss Hogan's tavern after her disappearance.

Wanserski was interviewed by newsmen here after he arrived with the group of lawmen who accompanied Gein to the State Crime Laboratory, where the confessed killer underwent a lie detector examination late Tuesday.

Gein, unshaven and haggard from lack of sleep, checked into the crime laboratory at 1:46 p.m. A half smile played on his lips, but he winced when waiting photographers snapped his picture.

Charles Wilson, director of the laboratory, said it is already known that some of the human heads contain embalming fluid because of their odor.

But Wilson said this did not necessarily support Gein's contention that he got the heads from graves.

"It's embalming fluid, but he may have put it there. Maybe he's an amateur taxidermist. We don't know," Wilson said.

Formaldehyde and an old embalming needle were among the items found in Gein's home.

Wood County Deputy Dave Sharkey examines one of the many newspapers and crime magazines found in the farmhouse of Ed Gein. Most of the newspapers were dated during the years 1942-44.

## Killer Tried to Date Victim

Special to The Chicago American

PLAINFIELD, Wis., Nov. 19—Edward Gein, owner of the "ghost farm" where the body of Mrs. Bernice Worden and 10 human skulls were found, tried repeatedly to make dates with the slain woman, neighbors disclosed today.

Mrs. Worden's hacked body was found in a shed at Gein's lonely, filthy farm home.

She never accepted any of his repeated invitations, the neighbors said.

Citizens of this town recall that Gein had been coming in to town lately and "pestering" Mrs. Worden in the hardware store she operated.

He asked her to go roller skating and to go out on numerous other occasions friends of Mrs. Worden said but she refused.

Gein was seen in Plainfield Saturday at a time when Mrs. Worden is believed to have been alone in her store.

Townfolk were not suspicious when her store was closed early in the day, because Mrs. Worden frequently closed up briefly to go on errands.

Then came the shocking word that the respected widow had been murdered in her own store in broad daylight.

## Lured to Graves by Moon—Farmer

*Chicago Tribune*

Special to The Chicago American.

MADISON, Wis., Nov. 20—Edward Gein, hermit farmer who confessed butchering a woman neighbor, said last night he believes he robbed graves "by the light of a full moon."

The 51-year-old bachelor, who remained on his 190-acre farm near Plainfield after the deaths of his mother and brother, told Earl F. Kileen, district attorney, he had opened graves in at least two cemeteries. Ten skulls were found scattered around Gein's delapidated frame house, and he said all the skulls belonged to women.

Kileen said Gein has pointed out one grave in the Plainfield Cemetery from which he removed the head of a 60-year-old woman who died in 1949.

Kileen said Gein told him he began opening graves in the Plainfield area "about 1949 and quit it about three years ago."

Gein told the prosecutor he was "interested only in the bodies of women," Kileen said. He added:

"He said he opened the graves at night, removed the heads and other parts of the bodies, then refilled the graves.

"He said he always was in a daze while robbing the graves, but thought he had dug by the light of a full moon."

Kileen said Gein admitted he "always went to fresh graves after reading about burials of women in the papers." Kileen added:

"I am interested only in prosecuting this man for the murder of Mrs. Worden of Plainfield. The grave-robbing penalty is a term of one to three years. To press that charge would necessitate the opening of graves, and I want no part of that. Think how the poor relatives would feel."

Kileen said a woman neighbor who has known Gein all her life told him she "would not be surprised if one of the 10 skulls was his mother's, or that another was that of his brother."

The neighbor told the prosecutor that the mother, Augusta, a widow who died in 1945, ruled her sons with an iron hand. The elder brother, Henry, died in 1944, apparently after a heart attack that followed exertion at a brush fire, which Edward helped him extinguish. Henry was planning to marry at the time, Kileen said.

Kileen said other neighbors have told how Mrs. Gein frequently lectured her sons about the "dangers of meeting up with women who curl their hair or wear corsets."

Plainfield residents have described the Geins as very clannish people "who never attended church but often were heard mouthing references to God and the Bible."

James E. Halligan of the State Crime Laboratory at Madison examines litter found in the kitchen of Ed Gein's farmhouse. He is holding a small balsam airplane. Many small tin whistles were found among the litter.

Nov. 20, 1957 Chicago Tribune

## Machine Clears Him in 3 Other Missing Cases

BY GEORGE BLISS
[Chicago Tribune Press Service]

Madison, Wis., Nov. 20—Farmer Ed Gein, 51, today confessed during a lie detector examination the killing of a second woman at his murder farm near Plainfield, Wis.

The sly and shy bachelor previously had admitted the butchery of Mrs. Bernice Worden, 58, last Saturday but had insisted that parts of bodies of 15 or more persons found in his horror filled home were assembled from graves he robbed. However, he admitted during his lie test that he also had slain Mrs. Mary Hogan, 54, who disappeared nearly three years ago from the rural barroom she operated about six miles from Gein's farm.

**Details Called Ghastly**

Sheriff Herbert Wanserski of Portage county had told newsmen earlier that he recognized Mrs. Hogan's face mask—the flesh and skin pulled away from her skull—among the human heads, portions of heads, and other grisly relics found in Gein's living quarters.

## London Paper Asks News of Murder

A call received by Max Koon, Dane County radio dispatcher, from the London Daily Sketch today, revealed the interest of the people living in the locale of Sherlock Holmes' great exploits, in the macabre murder story near Plainfield, Wis.

At 5:30 a.m. today Koon received a telephone call from a Mr. Lewis for the London Sketch, inquiring about the diet of Ed Gein, the confessed murderer of Mrs. Worden.

Mr. Lewis asked for the "Governor of Dane County jail."

Koon said after the call he was a bit suspicious about the call thinking someone was "pulling his leg." He said the telephone operator interceded to tell him the call was genuine.

Lewis was most interested in the "cannibalism" aspect of the gruesome story, Koon said.

The Sketch reporter asked Koon if the jailer here "will have to supply Gein with an all-meat diet."

Koon said he told Lewis that he was certain that Gein would receive a normal food diet if he were brought here. He told Lewis that Gein was eating a normal dinner when he was apprehended by police.

Koon told Lewis that there was no proof that Gein was cannibalistic.

He said he talked with Lewis for about five minutes and that the call was clear, as if made in Madison.

Part 1  Wednesday, November 20, 1957

## Face Masks Detail Told

### Gein Attorney Tours Farm Where Heads Were Found

Journal Staff Correspondence

Wautoma, Wis. — Former Assemblyman William Belter of Wautoma, the attorney for Ed Gein, Tuesday got a vivid description of the "death masks" found in the Gein horror house west of Plainfield.

Belter accompanied an officer and several other persons through the Gein house Tuesday after informing authorities that he had accepted the slayer's case.

He said that the officer had described the "death masks" found in the house this way:

The tops of the skulls apparently had been sawed or cut off. The cranial bones and other internal tissues of the heads were removed from the skins. The skins then were stuffed with newspaper and other material to form lifelike death masks, easily recognizable by persons who knew the victims in life.

#### "More Noses Than Faces"

He said he was told that "there were more noses than faces," but added that he did not recall any specific number being mentioned. Until now, the numbers usually cited were 10 and 11, depending on whether Mrs. Worden's head was counted. But one reporter said he heard the officer indicate that a total 15 victims was arrived at because of the presence of 10 faces, four extra noses and Mrs. Worden's severed head.

Belter said that the officer who escorted him through the trim 10 room house was a Wood county deputy sheriff.

Belter said that the officer reported that a pair of human lips was found among the ghastly collection. Two long bones also were found, Belter quoted the officer as saying. The attorney said the officer presumed they were human shin bones.

#### Skull Tops Missing

Belter said the officer told him that with the death masks were found five skull tops, but that the other skull tops could not be located.

Gein's attorney said the deputy informed him that there were four straight backed chairs on which strips of a leathery material resembling human skin were stretched to replace broken cane. Belter said that previously he had heard of only one such chair.

In an upstairs room, Belter said, the officer pointed out a doubled up mattress leaning against a wall. It was atop this mattress, at about eye level, that one of the heads was found, the officer told him.

#### Officials Co-operative

Belter said that he encountered no opposition from authorities when he told them he wanted to tour the Gein home. He said he merely stated that he was the defense attorney and officials arranged for the tour.

He said he understood that officials had resisted others' attempts to see the house because they were "trying to keep out curiosity seekers and people who had no business there."

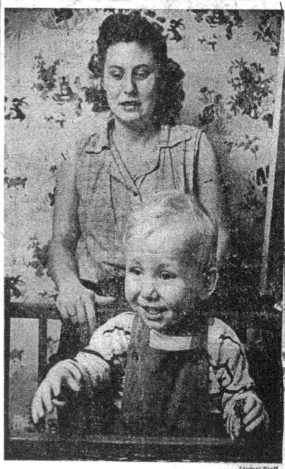
—Journal Staff

Slayer Edward Gein at times baby sat for Howard Foster, 21 months, son of Mrs. Donald Foster of West Plainfield.

# Won't Dig Up Graves, Waushara DA Insists

## 'It Would Just Upset Relatives,' He Says in Refusing Check of Ghoulish Tale

Journal Staff Correspondence

**Wautoma, Wis.** — Dist. Atty. Earl F. Kileen said Wednesday that Waushara county would not make any effort to check Edward Gein's story that he got most of his horrible collection of human remains by robbing graves.

"We're not going to dig up any graves," Kileen said. "I want no part in opening graves to prove anything. Just think how the poor relatives would feel."

Kileen repeated his earlier statement that Waushara county had no missing persons cases and that, because of this, a check of the cemeteries supposedly robbed by Gein "isn't necessary."

### "It's Up to Them"

"If other counties want to get court orders to open graves it's up to them," Kileen said, adding that "if the people concerned (the survivors) don't like it, I'll do everything possible to help them stop it."

Kileen has appeared willing to accept Gein's story that he slew only Mrs. Bernice Worden of Plainfield and that the rest of his grisly collection came from a series of ghoulish expeditions.

Revelations Tuesday that one of the heads found in the Gein house was that of a missing woman tavern keeper from Portage county and a charge that Waushara county did have a missing person case, had failed to sway Kileen in his stand.

### "I Want to Help"

Briefly, Kileen thinks that there is a clear cut case against Gein in the murder and butchery of Mrs. Worden.

"If we get a conviction for murder what use is there to stir up anything more?" he asked. "Of course, if other counties want to solve their cases I want to help, but they'll have to get permission (from survivors) to open any graves."

The charge that Waushara county did have a case of a missing person was made Tuesday afternoon in Madison by former Sheriff Leon Murty, one of the lawmen who brought Gein to the state crime laboratory for a lie test. Murty now is a deputy and village marshal at Wild Rose.

Murty, who was sheriff for six years and whose wife was sheriff for two years, told newsmen that a man named Victor (Bunk) Travis disappeared in Waushara county in 1953.

### Gein Reported Burglary

Kileen insisted Wednesday that Travis' disappearance was an Adams county case even though the man reportedly was last seen in a Plainfield tavern. He said Travis resided in Adams county. Local rumor was to the effect that Travis might have been abducted by a Chicago gang.

Murty said at the time of Travis' disappearance he got several calls about fresh graves being found in wooded sections. Murty said he checked the reports and found two freshly dug graves. He said one was empty; the other contained a dead dog.

The ex-sheriff also recalled that Gein two years ago reported a burglary at his house. He said Gein complained that someone had stolen an antique kerosene lamp and that he wanted authorities to check tire tracks and footprints he found in the yard.

### "I Wouldn't Know"

Murty said he went to the house to check the report but that Gein wasn't home. He said he didn't enter the house in Gein's absence. Later, he said, he found Gein working on a road job and talked to him about the case. The burglary never was solved and Murty said he never again had an opportunity to enter the house.

As to the identification of one of the heads as that of another slaying victim and reports that the number of bodies Gein used in making his horrible collection might reach 15, Kileen said, "I wouldn't know about that."

Kileen was reminded that it was reported earlier that Gein committed only 10 grave robberies and that he only took the head and another small piece of the human anatomy when he robbed a grave. It was pointed out that too many articles made of skin were found in Gein's home to substantiate the story that he took only the head and the other small portion of skin—if he did rob graves.

Kileen said this discrepancy had not occurred to him. He said he didn't look too closely at Gein's ghastly collection.

"I don't know where he got them from," he said. "He said he got them from cemeteries."

But asked if he intended to check any graves to see if they actually were robbed, Kileen stuck by his earlier statement that Waushara county—at least —wouldn't.

# To His Girl Friend, Gein Seemed 'Good and Sweet'

**Plainfield, Wis.** —(AP)— Ed Gein, bachelor recluse who has admitted butchering a Plainfield woman, was "good and kind and sweet" to Adeline Watkins, who said she almost married him.

Miss Watkins, 50, who lives with her mother in a small apartment here, said that during a 20 year romance with Gein he "was so nice about doing things I wanted to do that sometimes I felt I was taking advantage of him."

A Minneapolis Tribune reporter quoted her as saying she had her last date with Gein Feb. 6, 1955.

### "He Proposed to Me"

"That night he proposed to me. Not in so many words, but I knew what he meant."

Miss Watkins, a plain woman with graying bangs and horn rimmed glasses, said, "I turned him down, but not because there was anything wrong with him. I guess I was afraid I wouldn't be able to live up to what he expected of me."

The Tribune quoted Miss Watkins' widowed mother as saying Gein was a "sweet, polite man," and that she told him to have her daughter in from dates by 10 p.m. and "he never failed me once."

Miss Watkins said she and Gein used to discuss books. "We never read the same ones, but we liked to talk about them anyway. Eddie liked books about lions and tigers and Africa and India. I never read that kind of books.

### Talked About Murder

"I guess we discussed every murder we ever heard about. Eddie told how the murderer did wrong, what mistakes he had made. I thought it was interesting."

When they went out, Miss Watkins said, they usually went to a movie at near-by Wautoma.

"I liked to drink beer sometimes, but I would almost have to drag Eddie into a tavern," Miss Watkins was quoted as saying. "He would much rather have gone to a drugstore for a milk shake."

# Woman Vanished From Bar in 1954

MADISON, Nov. 20—A second murder — that of Miss Mary Hogan, who disappeared Dec. 8, 1954, from her blood-splattered Portage County tavern — has been admitted by Edward Gein, it was announced here Wednesday.

Charles Wilson, director of the State Crime Laboratory, revealed Gein's latest confession at 2 p.m. in a brief, written statement issued by investigating authorities at the conclusion of two days of interrogation here of the 51-year-old bachelor handyman who already has admitted the slaughter-slaying of Mrs. Bernice Worden.

"Mr. Gein has now admitted that he is responsible for the deaths of Mary Hogan in Portage County on Dec. 8, 1954, and Bernice Worden in Waushara County Nov. 16, 1957," the statement said.

"This release, jointly concurred in by the interested local officials, is being made to eliminate Mr. Gein from unnecessary suspicion and conjecture."

Wilson issued no further details of Gein's confession to the slaying of Miss Hogan, 54, a twice divorced tavernkeeper who once lived in Cicero, Ill. "Gein is a human being and deserves a fair trial," Wilson said.

## Information Can Do Harm

"It does a great deal of harm to release information unless we have the concurrence of local authorities."

Joseph Wilimovsky, assistant Crime Lab superintendent who directed the interrogation of Gein, indicated the confession to the Hogan murder was not obtained while the man was on the "lie box."

This would be an important consideration if Portage County authorities decide to press their own murder charges against Gein. Evidence obtained through a lie detector is not admissible in court.

"The information we obtained was the result of interviews and skilled interrogation with Gein," Vilimovsky said. "The lie detector results had nothing to do with it."

Wilimovsky said Gein spent only 19 minutes Tuesday and 11 minutes Wednesday on the lie detector.

Gein left Madison at 2 p.m. and by nightfall was again in the Waushara County Jail at Wautoma, where District Atty. Earl Kileen said he would file a murder charge against the confessed slayer as soon as he receives a ballistics report from the crime laboratory.

### FIRST MURDER CASE

Gein's attorney, William N. Belter, 30-year-old former assemblyman who is handling his first murder case, has said his client will plead not guilty and not guilty by reason of insanity at the arraignment.

Wilson's statement said the "success of the investigative efforts" in the Hogan and Worden cases, and in determining Gein had no knowledge of the Hartley, Weckler and Travis disappearances, was "due principally to the cooperation of all interested law enforcement agencies."

## Connection to Rifle Sought

Wilson was unable to say Wednesday when the ballistics test would be completed. It will seek to establish a connection between the .22 caliber bullet found in Mrs. Worden's head, and a rifle, containing a spent cartridge of the same caliber, discovered later in her hardware store.

Technicians at the Crime Lab, meanwhile, began the arduous task of analyzing what Wilson termed "an avalanche" of physical evidence found in Gein's home, including at least 10 human heads, some death masks, and other articles believed to have been fashioned from human skin.

Wilson said it would take "weeks, and possibly months, to completely evaluate and process" the evidence. Except for the Degnan murder case in Chicago and another Illinois case, he said he had never seen a larger assemblage of evidence.

### CARRIED IN TRUCK

Gein has admitted carrying Mrs. Worden's body from the store in the store's pickup truck. In the Hogan case, a pickup truck was seen in the area shortly before Miss Hogan disappeared — similar to the 1942 blue pickup truck found by authorities behind Gein's home.

District Atty. Kileen, as he announced his decision to file a murder charge against Gein, said he will "move immediately for a sanity hearing when he is arraigned."

Gein's arraignment is scheduled to resume Monday before County Judge Boyd Clark. At the opening of his arraignment three days ago, he was held under $10,000 bond on a robbery charge stemming from the $41 he took from the Worden store. This was a maneuver designed to keep Gein in custody until the murder investigation is completed.

## CITES ASSISTANTS

The statement cited in particular Kileen; Waushara County Sheriff Arthur Schley, Special Deputy Leon Murty, and Deputies Arnold Fritz, Dan Chase, Franklin Wetmore, Bert Carlson and Arden Spees.

Also Portage County District Atty. John Haka, Sheriff Wanserski, Undersheriff Myron Groshek and Deputies Sam Cleveland, Harold Fix and Miles Burchum; Wood County Sheriff Thomas Forsythe, Undersheriff Don Caylor and Deputy David Sharkey; Adams County Sheriff Frank B. Serles; Green Lake County Deputy Lloyd Schoephoester, Marquette County Deputy Don Nielson, and the crime laboratory staff.

### HANDLING DIFFICULT

"The mass of material makes handling difficult in our cramped quarters," Wilson said.

The analysis will strive to confirm or refute Gein's story that except for the Worden and Hogan slayings, he got the rest of his human trophies in a series of grave robberies from 1944 to 1952.

Sheriff Herbert Wanserski of Portage County, who on Tuesday made the first identification of Mrs. Hogan as a victim of Gein from a death mask he viewed in the Gein home, has expressed doubt that the handyman was physically able to commit the grave robberies.

Wanserski said the land in the Waushara area is so sandy that it requires shoring up for any excavations.

Gein's admission of the Hogan slaying clears up a mystery which had striking similarities to the killing of Mrs. Worden in her Plainfield hardware store Saturday.

In both instances, money was taken along with the bodies of the victims. In the Hogan case, a spent .32 caliber cartridge (Gein says he owns a .32 Mauser pistol) was found on the tavern floor. In the Worden case, the rifle was found in a rack with other weapons.

*November 21, 1957*
*Milwaukee Sentinel*

THURSDAY, NOVEMBER 21, 1957

# Shy Gein Feared Women, Milwaukee 'Best Pal' Says

A Milwaukee man who claims "I knew Ed Gein better than any other living man" Wednesday descrbed the Plainfield farmer as "every bashful" and the "first to offer to help anyone who asked him."

Ira Turner, 39, of 3720 S. Pennsylvania Av., a yardman at the Ladish Co., said:

"Ed was the best friend I had. As a boy the Gein farm was my second home. I stopped there practically every day after school. And I ate as many meals there as I did at my own home."

**FAMILY HAD FARM**

Turner said his family moved to a farm about half a mile south of the Gein place when he was 5 years old. When he was 16 Turner moved to Milwaukee and has been here since. Turner and Gein have remained friends through the years and the Milwaukeean has seen Gein "many times" since moving here.

Turner said there was one part of the Gein case which puzzled him:

Following his arrest for his macabre activities, Gein said his "memory is vague" and that he must have been in a daze.

Turner said that in all the years he has known him, Gein "never suffered from dazes."

**HUNTED TOGETHER**

"Ed taught me to hunt, fish and play the accordion and the flute. We went hunting together lots of times. We hunted rabbits and birds, but never deer. Ed was a very nice fellow. He would do anything for you," Turner said.

Turner said the last time he saw Gein was about three weeks ago.

"I went up there (Plainfield) to hunt and took my son along," he said. "After the hunting I wanted my son to meet Ed so we went over to the Gein place. Before we could knock on the door Ed came out and we talked for a while outside.

**DIDN'T BELIEVE IT**

"He didn't invite me in like he used to but at the time I didn't think anything of it. Ed seemed about the same as he always did."

"When I first found out about the murder I was shocked and at first I figured they (police) had the wrong man. Later the sheriff told me the whole story. I just couldn't understand what came into that man's mind."

Gein was always a "little slower" than other youngsters, Turner declared, and he never spoke of violence.

When asked if Gein ever went out with girls, Turner answered:

NNever. Ed was shy. The most bashful man I have ever seen. If a girl talked to him, Ed would look down at the ground. Very bashful.

**READ CRIME STORIES**

"The gun, which he used to let me shoot some times, was to take care of crows and other birds on the farm. I guess he took the gun to town with him just as a force of habit.

"When Ed's mother was alive the Gein place was always kept nice and clean. I remember how we—my father and I—often went to the Gein house to play cards. Ed used to get great pleasure out of reading detective magazines, but I never thought anything of that, lots of people do.

"When I knew Ed up north he never touched smokes or drink. He was just a very nice fella."

—Thurs., Nov. 21, 1957

# Gein 'Smart' as Boy, but Odd, Simple

**BY LEE CHESLEY**
State Editor, The Chicago American.

PLAINFIELD, Wis., Nov. 20—Just who is this little man named Edward Gein?

Gein—slaughterer of at least one woman and robber of his own account of at least nine graves—first came to here in the dense woods near here before World War I.

His father, George, brought his wife and his two sons—Edward and Henry—from their home town of LaCrosse, Wis.

### SCARED CHILDREN

When recollections of Lester Hill and his wife, Irene, are collected along with the memories of Milton Johnson and his wife Ethel — and others like them — there emerges this picture of Gein: He was always calm, but he always leered at women. Gein didn't swear or use vulgar language. He drank an occasional glass of beer. He didn't drink hard liquor.

When Gein was just a youngster he delighted in scaring other youngsters by telling them ghost stories.

Mrs. Gein—the mother—was a strongly religious woman but she didn't send her boys to Sunday School or to church. No one recalls when Edward had last been in church—and yet he claimed he was a devout Lutheran.

Gein wasn't old enough to go into service during World War I, but he was childishly critical of America's entry into the war against the Kaiser.

During World War II Gein more than on one occasion lauded Adolf Hitler. He was especially laudatory of the German dictator's purge of Jews.

Gein had piles of detective magazines in his home. He is an ardent reader of mystery stories—especially the exceptionally violent kind.

Before death struck down his father, his brother, Henry, and finally in 1945, his mother, Edward was an eager fisherman and huntsman.

The father died of cancer in 1940 in a Madison hospital. Four years later Henry died, supposedly of a heart attack, while fighting a brush fire that flared out of control.

A year later the mother suffered a stroke leaving her partly paralyzed. She died in 1945.

A handful of relatives from LaCrosse and Minneapolis came here to Mrs. Gein's funeral. But the relatives refused to stay in the Gein home "because it hadn't been kept clean."

The house, explained Mrs. Johnson, was described by relatives as "filthy."

Throughout the years, Milton Johnson recalls, Gein remained close to his farm home. But he didn't till the soil after his mother died. He let the equipment rust. There is no livestock on the farm today. The only crops were raised by tenant farmers.

Gein found odd jobs occasionally. Sometimes he helped Elmo Ueeck who has a sawmill. Sometimes he helped clear the county roads of snow in winter and he spread gravel on roads occasionally in summer. Infrequently he helped other farmers harvest or plant their crops.

Ueeck said that during past winters Gein had disappeared from his home for "days on end."

The Mills, who operate the West Plainfield store, said he might visit them several times a day and then not return for two weeks. Gein never offered any explanation.

Lester Hill said that Gein liked to play football with Hill's son, Bob, 16. Shortly before Gein was seized at Hill's store last Saturday Gein and Bob went hunting.

Bob agreed with his parents that Gein was "simple" and, therefore, frequently was the butt of jokes.

Nobody seems to remember why they came to Plainfield. They had no relatives here. Neither did they have friends.

The Johnson family knew them well—especially Milton Johnson. Milton and Edward were schoolmates during their childhood days.

### SMART AT SCHOOL

Milton recalled that Gein was "always smart" at school. But, he added:

"He was always odd, too. Kind of simple."

Milton lives just 30 rods from the house of horrors where Gein lived with the skulls he says he dug from graves.

A handful of horrified friends and neighbors — all living along Route 73 west of town or on County Road K leading to Gein's 190-acre farm—tried to fit together bits of Gein's life.

**Admitted murderer** Ed Gein, 51, looked bewildered as he arrived at the state crime laboratory in Madison Tuesday for a lie detector test. The butchered body of Mrs. Bernice Worden was found by authorities at the Plainfield handy man's run down home, interior views of which are shown here.

THURSDAY, NOVEMBER 21, 1957

# Lie Tests Clear Gein In 3 State Mysteries

## Keating Case Results Inconclusive

*By Sentinel Staff Writer*

MADISON, Nov. 20—Almost two days of examination at the State Crime Laboratory has eliminated Edward Gein "as the person responsible for and/or involved in" three major unsolved disappearances in Wisconsin.

The vanishings are:

• Evelyn Hartley, 15, from a baby sitting job at a college professor's home in La Crosse on Oct. 24, 1953.

• Abduction of Georgia Jean Wechler, 8, from the driveway of her farm home near Fort Atkinson on May 1, 1947.

• Victor Travis, 51, an Adams County resident who disappeared while deer hunting on Nov. 1, 1952.

Charles Wilson, director of the Crime Laboratory, said the lie detector test to which Gein submitted showed no conclusive result in another disappearance, that of Mrs. Irene Keating, 30, Fort Atkinson, last Aug. 20.

Ed Gein wears a slight smile as he leaves the state crime lab in Madison with Waushara County Sheriff Arthur Schley (left) for return to Waushara jail.
*Associated Press Wirephoto.*

# Gein Admits 2nd Slaying

*ER 21, 1957*

## Woman Vanished From Bar in 1954

*By Sentinel Staff Writer*

MADISON, Nov. 20—A second murder — that of Miss Mary Hogan who disappeared Dec. 8, 1954, from her blood-splattered Portage County tavern — has been admitted by Edward Gein, it was announced here Wednesday.

Charles Wilson, director of the State Crime Laboratory, revealed Gein's latest confession at 2 p.m. in a brief written statement issued by investigating authorities at the conclusion of two days of interrogation here of the 51-year-old bachelor handyman who already has admitted the slaughter-slaying of Mrs. Bernice Worden.

"Mr. Gein has now admitted that he is responsible for the deaths of Mary Hogan in Portage County on Dec. 8, 1954, and Bernice Worden in Waushara County Nov. 16, 1957," the statement said.

"This release, jointly concurred in by the interested local officials, is being made to eliminate Mr. Gein from unnecessary suspicion and conjecture."

Wilson issued no further details of Gein's confession to the slaying of Miss Hogan, 54, a twice divorced tavernkeeper who once lived in Cicero, Ill. "Gein is a human being and deserves a fair trial," Wilson said.

### Information Can Do Harm

"It does a great deal of harm to release information unless we have the concurrence of local authorities."

Joseph Wilimovsky, assistant Crime Lab superintendent who directed the interrogation of Gein, indicated the confession to the Hogan murder was not obtained while the man was on the "lie box."

This would be an important consideration if Portage County authorities decide to press their own murder charges against Gein. Evidence obtained through a lie detector is not admissible in court.

"The information we obtained was the result of interviews and skilled interrogation with Gein," Wilimovsky said. "The lie detector results had nothing to do with it."

Wilimovsky said Gein spent only 19 minutes Tuesday and 11 minutes Wednesday on the lie detector.

Gein left Madison at 2 p.m. for the Waushara County Jail at Wautoma, where District Atty. Earl Kileen said he would file a murder charge against the confessed slayer as soon as he receives a ballistics report from the crime laboratory.

Relatives of Mrs. Bernice Worden left the Plainfield Methodist church in a group after funeral services for the slain woman Wednesday. From left are her daughter, Mrs. Donald Walker, and her husband of Lincoln, Neb.; her brother-in-law, Mac Worden of Little Rock, Ark.; her son, Frank, a deputy sheriff, and his son, Frank, jr., 14.
—Journal Staff (UP Telephoto)

## Victim's Casket Carr

The casket containing the body of Mrs. Bernice Worden, Plainfield widow whom Edward Gein confessed he killed last Saturday, is carried from the Plainfield Methodist Church Wednesday following funeral services. (Associated Press-Capital Times Wirephoto)

## Macabre Discoveries Follow Wisconsin Slaying

[Associated Press Wirephoto]
The farm house of Ed Gein near Plainfield, Wis., where body of Mrs. Bernice Worden, slain in her hardware store, and the remains of other humans were found.

The truck of Mrs. Worden in which Gein admitted transporting her body from her store to a point outside of Plainfield where he transferred it to his own automobile.

Evelyn Hartley, school girl long missing from LaCrosse, Wis., whose disappearance was recalled yesterday as remains of unidentified humans were found on Gein farm.

Mrs. Worden, the identified slaying victim.

The hardware store of Mrs. Worden, where she was slain.

**FUNERAL PASSES HARDWARE STORE**
The funeral procession bearing the body of Mrs. Bernice Worden comes down the main street of Plainfield on the way to the cemetery and passes the hardware store in which law enforcement officials say she was slain last Saturday. At about the same hour, State Crime Laboratory officials announced that Ed Gein had admitted the killing of Mrs. Worden and also the 1954 slaying of Mrs. Mary Hogan. (AP Wirephoto)

## Sex Mania Drove Gein To Murder

MADISON, Nov. 21—Farmer Ed Gein murdered two women because he developed feminine tendencies arising out of an unnatural attachment for his mother, it was confirmed Thursday by Charles Wilson, director of the State Crime Laboratory.

Wilson said the bachelor farmer admitted in questioning at the crime laboratory that he killed and butchered Mrs. Bernice Worden, Plainfield hardware dealer, and Mrs. Mary Hogan, Portage County tavern operator, because he thought they resembled his mother, who died in 1945.

### OEDIPUS COMPLEX

Gein's sexual abnormality is known medically as an Oedipus complex, an unnatural attachment for the mother on the part of the son.

The Plainfield murderer revealed he became disconsolate after the death of his mother whom he nursed after two paralytic strokes.

After his mother's death, Gein said he felt an urge to visit cemeteries and later to dig into new graves. Outside of one instance in which he dug up an entire body, Gein said he usually only took heads and parts of bodies of women.

### CUT, BURNED BODY

Gein said he disposed of Mrs. Hogan's body by cutting it up into small pieces and burning them in a stove. He said he saved the head and parts of her body.

Authorities discovered at least 10 skulls or death masks in the sadist's lonely house, located six miles outside of Plainfield on a narrow dirt road.

Gein said he stripped the facial skin and hair from the skulls, stuffed the face masks with newspapers and kept them preserved by rubbing oil on them.

The farmer said he noticed that Mrs. Hogan resembled his mother when he first saw her in her tavern when he stopped there to have coffee with a man who had employed him for an odd job.

## Weeping Gein Prays in Cell With Minister

*By Sentinel Staff Writer*

WAUTOMA, Wis., Nov. 21—Edward Gein, the Plainfield, Wis., "butcher," wept and prayed in his jail cell in Wautoma Thursday afternoon with a young minister who had never seen him before but sought him out as "a citizen of God."

The Rev. Kenneth Engelman, 33, pastor of the Wautoma Methodist Church for the past four years, told newsmen who clustered around him in the jail lobby that Gein had shown "definite remorse" in the half hour interview.

### BREAKS INTO TEARS

He said Gein broke into tears when the clergyman walked into the cell remarking, "This is a difficult day for you." Gein wept again convulsively during the interview, the Rev. Mr. Engelman said, and expressed concern about those who have been troubled by his actions. The clergyman said he assumed Gein meant the relatives and home communities of his victims.

Gein told him he had already prayed for forgiveness, the clergyman said, adding that he and the accused murderer knelt together beside the bunk in the cell "and prayed for his comfort and forgiveness."

The Rev. Mr. Engelman said he had decided to make the call because "I am a Christian minister and here is a man who needs help."

### THANKED FOR COMING

He said Gein had thanked him for coming, and showed by his manner that the visit was welcome."

"He asked me to pray for him," said the clergyman.

After the clergymen had left, Gein told Sheriff Arthur Schley, "I hope he comes again."

The Rev. Mr. Engelman told reporters he intended to repeat the visit, possibly Thursday night.

November 21, 1957 Milwaukee Sentinel

The funeral procession containing the body of Mrs. Bernice Worden comes down the main street of Plainfield on the way to the cemetery and passes her hardware was found slain Saturday.
—Associated [Press]

## Friends Crowd Church at Worden Rites

By Sentinel Staff Writer

PLAINFIELD, Wis., Nov. 20 —Merchants and businessmen of this little village closed their stores and offices Wednesday afternoon to join other friends and relatives of Mrs. Bernice Worden at funeral services for the slain widow.

Close to 250 people—Plainfield has a population of 680—filled the church and connected Sunday School of the Methodist Church, to which Mrs. Worden belonged.

**PLEA FOR FAITH**

They heard the church pastor, the Rev. Gerald Tanquist, give a funeral sermon in which he used the first words of the Twenty Third Psalm — "The Lord is my Shepherd" — as his theme in a plea for continued faith in God and remembrance "in the face of the horrible incidents of the past few days, that the Lord has not abandoned us."

Before the service the congregation filed past the open gold-colored casket, set in a semi-circle of flowers. The casket was closed when the service began.

Funeral ritual by the Plainfield chapter of the Order of the Eastern Star followed the brief church service.

**NOT FAR FROM CHURCH**

Six pallbearers carried the casket to the waiting hearse. They were Albert Walter, Jesse Wood, Franklin Rothermel, Cyle Ellis, Arden Spees and James Severns.

In the little Plainfield cemetery, a mile and a half from the church, the Rev. Mr. Tanquist spoke a few final words as the casket was lowered into the grave.

Mrs. Worden's survivors are a son, Frank, Plainfield; a daughter, Mrs. Miriam Walker, Lincoln, Neb.; three brothers, Lloyd Conover, Leola, Wis.; Lester Conover, Almond, Wis., and Burrel Conover, Aurora, Ill., a sister, Mrs. Clifton Johnson, Leola, and four grandchildren.

# Gein Admits 2nd Slaying

A saw found along with portions of human bodies on the rural Plainfield farm of confessed slayer Ed Gein is taken into the State Crime Laboratory at Madison. Lab workers brought in a truck load of evidence from the Gein farm, with the unloading watched by University of Wisconsin students. — Sentinel photo.

November 21, 1957 Milwaukee Sentinel

# 'Robbed' Grave Ordered Open

## Findings May Clear Gein Story

*By Sentinel Staff Writer*

WAUTOMA, Nov. 22 — Waushara County Inst. Atty. Earl F. Kileen said Friday afternoon that several graves in Plainfield cemetery would be opened early next week to check Edward Gein's story that the grisly human remains found in his home were obtained by grave looting.

The announcement came after a conference of county and township officials. Kileen said the conference was called as a favor to him to help answer the questions of local citizens.

### STORY NOT BELIEVED

Asked if the calling of the conference indicated that local officials as well as enraged citizens didn't believe Gein's tales of grave robbing, Kileen answered "Yes."

The cemetery sexton and helpers will open one or two graves Monday to begin the investigation, Kileen said. He told reporters that as far as he knows "four or five" graves are all that Gein has indicated as robbed. He said one of the graves that will probably be opened is that of Mrs. Eleanore Adams. The grave of Gein's mother, Mrs. Augusta Gein, on a plot adjoining the Adams grave, would not be opened as her casket is in a concrete vault. He said he would not identify any of the other graves to be inspected besides Mrs. Adams'.

The Rev. Kenneth Engelman of the Wautoma Methodist Church, talking to reporters in the county jail in Wautoma after he visited Edward Gein of Plainfield, the confessed slayer of two women.

"We will try to do this in a painless way," Kileen said.

He indicated that ancestors of persons whose remains are to be exhumed would be contacted and consent sought, but that if necessary, the graves would be opened by his authority alone. The district attorney reported that if the bodies in the first two graves opened show no signs of mutilation, no more graves will be opened.

### COMPLAINS OF COST

Those participating in the conference besides Kileen were Joe Niemer, Waushara County treasurer; Earl Simensen, chairman of the county board of supervisors; Harold J. Collins, Plainfield village president; Sheriff Arthur Schley, and Gein's attorney, William Belter.

Kileen said he had also conferred with Belter as to how long county deputies would have to guard the Gein property.

### FEEL GUARDS NEEDED

Belter said later that none of Gein's distant relatives have contacted him regarding the property, but he felt that until it was disposed of, guards would be necessary to avert raids by curiosity seekers.

Belter also said after the conference that he had been informed that Gein dug up some graves but refilled them without mutilating the bodies.

He added "I assume the crime lab will want graves confirmed until they finish sorting the contents at the house."

FRIDAY, NOVEMBER 22, 1957

# 'Butcher' Faces Sanity Test

## Not Guilty Plea Slated By Lawyer

*Sentinel Staff Writer*

WAUTOMA, Wis., Nov. 21 — Defense and prosecuting attorneys agreed here Thursday to seek an immediate determination of the sanity of Edward Gein when the confessed slayer of two women goes to trial before Circuit Judge Herbert A. Bunde.

This development came to light as the 51-year-old bachelor handyman was bound over to the Circuit Court for trial on a first degree murder charge stemming from one of the killings, that of Mrs. Bernice Worden, 58, of Plainfield.

**PLEADS NOT GUILTY**

Gein's attorney, William N. Belter, entered a plea of not guilty and not guilty by reason of insanity, during the brief arraignment before County Judge Boyd Clark.

Judge Bunde, contacted at Wisconsin Rapids, said he would confer again Friday with Waushara County authorities and that the trial might begin "at any time thereafter."

If the hearing is a brief one, Judge Bunde indicated, it might be possible to schedule it before the judge is due to return to Waukesha Sunday in preparation for the arraignment Monday of former Waukesha County Sheriff Michael Lombardi on malfeasance and misconduct charges.

**JUDGE HAS CHOICES**

If the defense moves for a sanity test, the judge may either appoint a panel of three psychiatrists to conduct it, or he may order Gein committed to the Central State Hospital at Waupun, where staff psychiatrists will report on the man's mental condition.

Belter said he will move for such a test at the start of the hearing and added "I understand and have been informed that the district attorney will join in my request."

Kileen said Wisconsin law specifically permits such a defense action and that "under the circumstances, it wouldn't make much difference what I'd have to say."

Kileen added that although he is prepared to prosecute the case on the first degree murder charge, if necessary, "I'd hate to see an insane man stand trial."

**REMAIN ADAMANT**

Waushara County authorities, meanwhile, remained adamant in the face of mounting pressure from citizens of the area, that they press a complete investigation, on the local level, of Gein's story that he robbed graves for most of the human relics found on his farm Saturday.

Sheriff Art Schley said that the State Crime Laboratory is

Friday, November 22, 1957

Slayer Edward Gein stood before Judge Boyd Clark Thursday during his arraignment in Waushara county court at Wautoma. He pleaded innocent by reason of insanity to a first degree murder charge. Gein stood between his attorney, William Belter (left), and Sheriff Art Schley. —AP Wirephoto

## Findings May Clear Gein Story

*By Sentinel Staff Writer*

WAUTOMA, Nov. 22—Waushara County Dist. Atty. Earl F. Kileen said Friday afternoon that several graves in Plainfield cemetery would be opened early next week to check Edward Gein's story that the grisly human remains found in his home were obtained by grave looting.

The announcement came after a conference of county and township officials. Kileen said the conference was called as a favor to him to help answer the questions of local citizens.

### STORY NOT BELIEVED

Asked if the calling of the conference indicated that local officials as well as enraged citizens didn't believe Gein's tales of grave robbing, Kileen answered "Yes."

The cemetery sexton and helpers will open one or two graves Monday to begin the investigation, Kileen said. He told reporters that as far as he knows "four or five" graves are all that Gein has indicated he robbed. He said one of the graves that will probably be opened is that of Mrs. Eleanore Adams. The grave of Gein's mother, Mrs. Augusta Gein, on a plot adjoining the Adams grave, would not be opened as her casket is in a concrete vault. He said he would not identify any of the other graves to be inspected besides Mrs. Adams'.

"We will try to do this in a painless way," Kileen said.

He indicated that survivors of persons whose remains are to be exhumed would be contacted and consent sought, but that if necessary, the graves would be opened by his authority alone. The district attorney reported that if the bodies in the first two graves opened show no signs of mutilation, no more graves will be opened.

### COMPLAINS OF COST

Those participating in the conference besides Kileen were Joe Niemer, Waushara County treasurer; Earl Simensen, chairman of the county board of supervisors; Harold J. Collins, Plainfield village president; Sheriff Arthur Schley, and Gein's attorney, William N. Belter.

Kileen said he was going to try to find whether a way can be found to stop the State Crime Laboratory from continuing its investigation of the Gein case as it "is costing the county too much money."

(*The county pays one-half of the crime laboratory expense, which in the Gein case has amounted to $1,000 a day thus far.*)

"We are a poor county," Kileen said. "Our assessed valuation is only 15 million dollars."

Kileen said he had also conferred with Belter as to how long county deputies would have to guard the Gein property.

### FEEL GUARDS NEEDED

Belter said later that none of Gein's distant relatives have contacted him regarding the property, but he felt that until it was disposed of, guards would be necessary to avert raids by curiosity seekers.

Belter also said after the conference that he had been informed that Gein dug up some graves but refilled them without mutilating the bodies.

He added "I assume the crime lab will want guards continued until they finish sorting the contents at the house."

## Regular Treatment If Gein Behaves

*By Sentinel Staff Writer*

WAUPUN, Wis., Nov. 22 — If he behaves himself, confessed slayer Edward Gein will be treated like any other patient during his 30 days at the Central State Hospital for the criminally insane here.

In his free time, he will be allowed to watch television, read magazines, play games and take part in other recreational and occupational pursuits for inmates.

Dr. Edward F. Schubert, director of the state's only maximum security mental hospital, said homicidal cases, such as Gein, pose no special problem for the institution.

"It's been my experience usually that such cases certainly are no more of a problem than any other," Dr. Schubert said.

Much of Gein's time in the institution will be devoted to interviews with staff psychologists, psychiatrists and social workers, and any psychiatric tests that may be needed to unlock the secrets of his behavior.

## Rush Tests For Clues To Graves

MADISON, Nov. 22 (JP) Particles of dirt gathered at the home of Ed Gein, 51, should indicate within a few days whether the mild-mannered bachelor ever dug in Plainfield area cemeteries.

Criminologists who have studied similar cases said Friday it would be relatively easy to determine in a laboratory whether the particles came from a cemetery. These criminologists asked that they not be identified.

Gein insists that 10 skulls and other human evidence found in the rural home where he lived alone were taken from graves in the Plainfield area. He has admitted murdering two women but has denied that he killed others.

Crime laboratory technicians gathered dirt particles along with other evidence during their 36-hour investigation of the crime scene. These particles, key identification tools in criminal investigation, have been known to cling to clothing, tools and even bones for many years. Even a small particle in a bone cavity should provide an important clue.

A list of graves which Gein said he robbed also offers another identification possibility. The dirt and dust particles from Gein's home can be compared with those in the homes of persons whose graves were reportedly robbed.

In Plainfield, Dist. Atty. Earl Kileen of Waushara County said he would ask Charles Wilson, director of the State Crime Laboratory, to push the dirt particle phase of the investigation. He said he is under considerable pressure from local residents to determine whether the human parts came from graves in two Plainfield cemeteries.

Sheriff Arthur Schley of Waushara County has said he would notify relatives of persons whose graves Gein has admitted violating only in case the crime laboratory tests are not conclusive.

# Gein 'Remorseful,' Cries in Cell—Pastor

Special to The Chicago American.

WAUTOMA, Wis., Nov. 22 — Edward Gein is "truly remorseful," according to a pastor who prayed with the weeping slayer in his jail cell here.

The Rev. Kenneth Engelman, 33, pastor of the Wautoma Methodist Church since his graduation from Garrett Biblical Institute in Evanston, Ill., four years ago, said he sought out Gein because the slayer "is a citizen of God."

Whether he had meant to or not, the Rev. Mr. Engelman after his interview with Gein, almost immediately succeeded in getting his name in the papers by commenting to reporters about his visit.

### 'DEFINITE REMORSE'

Gein showed "definite remorse," the Rev. Mr. Engelman told the reporters in the jail lobby. He continued:

Gein showed "definite remorse," the Rev. Mr. Engelman told reporters in the jail lobby later. He continued:

"I returned here to correct an erroneous impression the newspapers have been printing about this fellow. He is truly remorseful. He cried while I was talking to him."

The pastor, who did not know Gein, said he called on him because "I am a Christian minister, and here is a man who needs help."

For the same reason, he went into court yesterday with Gein after the jail visit, waited for him during his arraignment, and walked out of court beside him.

Describing his conversation with Gein in jail, the clergyman said the prisoner broke into tears when his visitor walked into the cell saying:

### WEPT AGAIN

"Mr. Gein, I am here to give you spiritual help. This is a difficult day for you."

Gein wept again convulsively during the interview, the Rev. Mr. Engelman said, "and expressed concern about those who have been disturbed by his actions." The pastor said he assumed Gein meant the relatives and home communities of his victims. Gein told the clergyman:

**THE REV. MR. ENGELMAN**
Gein's spiritual advisor.

**MINISTER TALKS OF GEIN**
The Rev. Kenneth Engelman, Edward Gein's spiritual adviser, talks with reporters at the sheriff's office Thursday night after a visit with Gein. Engelman said Gein wept twice before his arraignment on a first degree murder charge in the death of Mrs. Bernice Worden of Plainfield. (AP Wirephoto)

November 22, 1957
Chicago

"I am sorry and I have asked forgiveness."

The Rev. Mr. Engelman said that he and the confessed murderer then knelt together beside the bunk bed in the cell "and prayed for his forgiveness and comfort."

He said Gein and he discussed no details of the occurrences in the prisoner's Plainfield, Wis., farmhouse because the pastoral visit "was strictly a matter of religion."

He said Gein thanked him for coming, and showed by his manner that the visit was welcome.

The Rev. Mr. Engelman added:

"He asked me to pray for him."

**ON WAY TO HEARING**
Edward Gein, 51, center, walks with Sheriff Art Schley, left, and Deputy Arnold Fritz, to his preliminary hearing Thursday on the death of Mrs. Bernice Worden, of Plainfield. (AP Wirephoto)

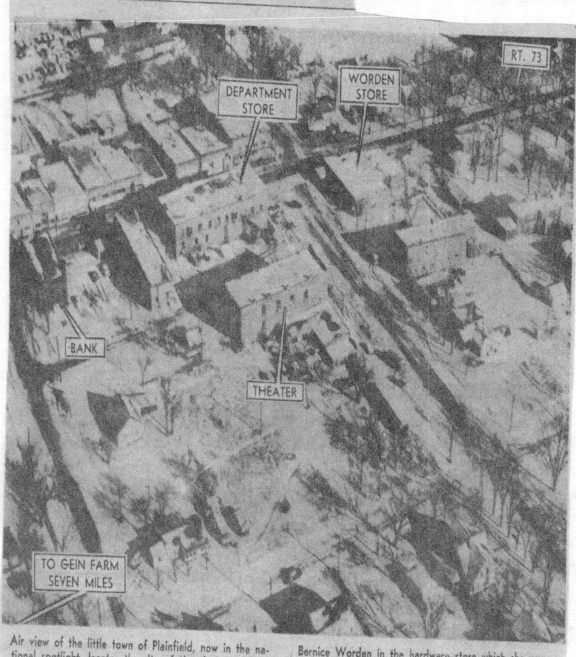

FRIDAY, NOVEMBER 22, 1957

Air view of the little town of Plainfield, now in the national spotlight, locates the site of the slaying of Mrs. Bernice Worden in the hardware store which she operated. Ed Gein has admitted the killing.

—Associated Press Wirephoto.

FRIDAY, NOVEMBER 22, 1957 — Milwaukee Sentinel

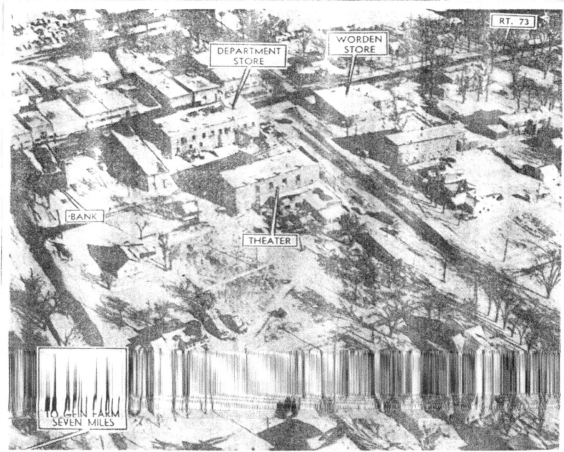

Air view of the little town of Plainfield, now in the national spotlight, locates the site of the slaying of Mrs. Bernice Worden in the hardware store which she operated. Ed Gein has admitted the killing.

*Associated Press Wirephoto.*

## Sex Mania Drove Gein To Murder

*By Sentinel Staff Writer*

MADISON, Nov. 21—Farmer Ed Gein murdered two women because he developed feminine tendencies arising out of an unnatural attachment for his mother, it was confirmed Thursday by Charles Wilson, director of the State Crime Laboratory.

Wilson said the bachelor farmer admitted in questioning at the crime laboratory that he killed and butchered Mrs. Bernice Worden, Plainfield hardware dealer, and Mrs. Mary Hogan, Portage County tavern operator, be-

### OEDIPUS COMPLEX

Gein's sexual abnormality is known medically as an Oedipus complex, an unnatural attachment for the mother on the part of the son.

The Plainfield murderer revealed he became disconsolate after the death of his mother whom he nursed after two paralytic strokes.

After his mother's death, Gein said he felt an urge to visit cemeteries and later to dig into new graves. Outside of one instance in which he dug up an entire body, Gein said he usually only took heads and parts of bodies of women.

### CUT, BURNED BODY

Gein said he disposed of Mrs. Hogan's body by cutting it up into small pieces and burning them in a stove. He said he saved the head and parts of her body.

Authorities discovered at least 10 skulls or death masks in the sadist's lonely house, located six miles outside of Plainfield on a narrow dirt road.

Gein said he stripped the facial skin and hair from the skulls, stuffed the face masks with newspapers and kept them preserved by rubbing oil on them.

The farmer said he noticed that Mrs. Hogan resembled his mother when he first saw her in her tavern when he stopped there to have coffee with a man who had employed him for an odd job.

# May Search Graves To Verify Gein's Story

## Sheriff States Slayer Told Where He Gathered Ghastly Human Remains

BY JACK GLASNER
Post-Crescent Staff Writer

(From Press Dispatches)

Examination of graves reputedly opened and desecrated by confessed butcher-murderer Edward Gein, 51, probably is imminent.

Waushara County Sheriff Arthur Schley, notably silent in the strange case of the bachelor recluse who murdered two women and kept a ghastly collection of human remains in his isolated farm home, said Thursday a county supervisor had demanded details on the grave robbing reports.

Supv. Ralph Wing, also chairman of the Plainfield town board, told Schley about reports that the body of his sister-in-law, Mrs. Eleanore M. Adams, had been disinterred. Mrs. Adams died at 51 of a heart ailment in 1951.

Wing said after the conference with Schley that he was satisfied, although neither man commented on details.

### List of Graves

Schley admitted authorities had a list of graves which Gein said he had opened and stolen parts of eight bodies and one entire corpse.

Gein awaits trial or sanity hearing on a first degree murder charge naming him as the slayer of Mrs. Bernice Worden, 58, Plainfield hardware merchant, whose butchered decapitated body was found Saturday hanging by its heels in the summer kitchen of Gein's littered farm home.

Gein also has admitted the murder and butchering of Mrs. Mary Hogan, 54, in her Portage county tavern nearly three years ago. The tavern is about six miles from Gein's home.

Dist. Atty. John Hake, Jr., of adjacent Portage county, where Mrs. Hogan lived, said Thursday he was not considering any charges in Mrs. Hogan's slaying until the state crime laboratory finishes its analysis of the horrendous physical evidence found in the Gein farmhouse.

The defense moved today to get an independent medical opinion on Gein's sanity.

### Examination Today

Counsel for Gein already has agreed with the prosecution on a mental examination before Gein goes to trial.

Atty. William Belter said, however, that he planned to have Gein examined by a Milwaukee psychiatrist today—before the mild-appearing little killer makes another court appearance.

Circuit Judge Herbert A. Bunde said he would confer with Dist. Atty. Earl Killeen today and might call the first degree murder trial "at any time thereafter."

Belter said he planned to obtain the private opinion on Gein's sanity, because in the event the court commits the prisoner now, on the grounds that he is presently incompetent to stand trial, he might later reestablish his sanity.

### Key Question

Under those circumstances, he could be ordered to trial and then would have to prove to a jury's satisfaction that he was insane at the time of the crimes.

"The important question is whether Ed Gein is insane now — not 3, 5 or 10 years from now," Belter said.

Gein wept and prayed Thursday when the same minister who preached the funeral service for Mrs. Worden Wednesday visited his cell.

The Rev. Kenneth Engelman, 33 pastor of the Wautoma Methodist church, told newsmen how Gein sobbed and prayed.

The young minister visited Gein in jail as "a citizen of God."

The Rev. Mr. Engelman said, "I walked in and said, 'Mr. Gein, I am here to give you spiritual help,' and we talked for awhile.

"After breaking down, he collected himself and then started to talk about it and then cried again. Gein sought forgiveness. I think he was referring to God."

He said he and the accused slayer knelt together beside the bunk in the cell "and prayed for his comfort and forgiveness."

### Pain of Others

The clergyman said Gein told him his concern was not solely for himself, but also for the pain he had inflicted on others.

After the minister left, Gein told Sheriff Schley, "I hope he comes again."

The clergyman's visit followed four days of official questioning during which the middle-aged handyman told how an unnatural attachment to his mother developed into a sex obsession and led to violation of graves and finally to the two slayings.

He said he watched death notices in newspapers and then opened the graves of women who had just been buried. He said that from some graves he took only the heads, while from others he took the heads and other portions of the corpses. He took a whole body from one grave.

### Await Crime Lab

Commenting on the list of graves which Gein has admitted opening, Sheriff Schley said, "We have this list. It is our plan to wait until we get a report from the state crime laboratory concerning scientific findings on examination of the heads. We will then notify the nearest relatives in each case.

"The relatives will be the ones, and the only ones, to decide whether any particular graves should be opened," the sheriff said. "They have that right."

Records of the Plainfield Cemetery association showed that Mrs. Adams was buried in a wooden casket encased in a wooden box. This gave a measure of credibility to Gein's grave robbing story, since officials have insisted that no one man in a single night could break into a grave protected by a concrete vault.

Patrick Danna, sexton of the Plainfield cemetery since 1953, conducted an inspection trip thru the cemetery. He pointed to the headstone marking the grave of Mrs. Adams. He was as much surprised as those with him to notice that the adjoining cemetery lot was that owned by the Gein family.

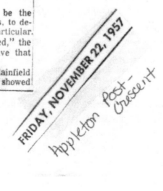
FRIDAY, NOVEMBER 22, 1957
Appleton Post-Crescent

Edward Gein (right) walks with Sheriff Art Schley to the preliminary hearing Thursday in Wautoma in the death of Mrs. Bernice Worden last Saturday.

*Associated Press Wirephoto.*

November 22, 1957
Milwaukee Sentinel

# Weeping Gein Prays in Cell With Minister

*By Sentinel Staff Writer*

WAUTOMA, Wis., Nov. 21—Edward Gein, the Plainfield, Wis., "butcher," wept and prayed in his jail cell in Wautoma Thursday afternoon with a young minister who had never seen him before but sought him out as "a citizen of God."

The Rev. Kenneth Engelman, 33, pastor of the Wautoma Methodist Church for the past four years, told newsmen who clustered around him in the jail lobby that Gein had shown "definite remorse" in the half hour interview.

## BREAKS INTO TEARS

He said Gein broke into tears when the clergyman walked into the cell remarking, "This is a difficult day for you." Gein wept again convulsively during the interview, the Rev. Mr. Engelman said, and expressed concern about those who have been troubled by his actions. The clergyman said he assumed Gein meant the relatives and home communities of his victims.

Gein told him he had already prayed for forgiveness, the clergyman said, adding that he and the accused murderer knelt together beside the bunk in the cell "and prayed for his comfort and forgiveness."

The Rev. Mr. Engelman said he had decided to make the call because "I am a Christian minister and here is a man who needs help."

## THANKED FOR COMING

He said Gein had thanked him for coming, and showed by his manner that the visit was welcome."

"He asked me to pray for him," said the clergyman.

After the clergymen had left, Gein told Sheriff Arthur Schley, "I hope he comes again."

The Rev. Mr. Engelman told reporters he intended to repeat the visit, possibly Thursday night.

NOVEMBER 23, 1957

# 'Robbed' Graves Ordered Opened

The Rev. Kenneth Engelman of the Wautoma Methodist Church, talking to reporters in the county jail in Wautoma after he visited Edward Gein of Plainfield, the confessed slayer of two women.

**ED GEIN,** (right) then 51, pauses for a photographer as he is escorted into the Central State Hospital for the Criminally Insane at Waupun Nov. 23, 1957, to undergo a 30-day mental examination. Gein had admitted slaying two women and dismembering their bodies. He also described robbing graves. With Gein is Waushara County Sheriff Art Schley.

*June 20 2001 paper*

## Gein's headstone makes Seattle rock scene

**By Patricia Wolff**
For The Post-Crescent

PLAINFIELD — The stolen grave marker for Ed Gein, Wisconsin's infamous grave robber and murderer from the 1950s, has been found in Seattle, Wash., but police aren't sure what to do with it.

The grave marker was taken, along with some grave dirt, about a year ago from Gein's grave in Plainfield Cemetery in northwestern Waushara County.

"We could bring it back and put it back in the cemetery, but it would only get stolen again," said Waushara County Sheriff Patrick Fox.

Gein

Members of the Waushara County Historical Society are considering placing it in the old jail museum on S. St. Marie Street near the courthouse in downtown Wautoma. Gein was in the jail briefly in the late 1950s after his grisly crimes came to light.

When Gein's grave marker was stolen last June, Fox and others expected to find it for sale on the online auction site eBay. That never happened. Instead, about a month ago Fox got a phone call from a woman who suggested a connection between the missing marker and the Seattle promoter of the rock band Angry White Males.

Police found the marker when they questioned the promoter. He had been selling rubbings of the stone for $50 each on his Internet site.

He said the marker he had was a reproduction of the original stone. Police did not buy his story, Fox said.

"It was the same granite stone, the graffiti was the same, and it was chipped in the same way," Fox said.

Patricia Wolff writes for the Oshkosh Northwestern.

## State Sets All-Out Gein Probe

*Sentinel Madison Bureau*

MADISON, Nov. 25 — Charles Wilson, director of the State Crime Laboratory, was directed Monday by Atty. Gen. Stewart G. Honeck "to continue with all steps necessary" to assure a complete investigation of the Gein murder case.

Honeck entered the bizarre case of the 51-year-old Waushara County murderer and grave robber upon orders of Gov. Thomson earlier in the day.

### SEEK OTHER CRIMES

Thomson also directed Honeck to determine whether any other crimes were committed by the Plainfield bachelor-handyman.

Gein, now being examined at Central State Hospital for the criminally insane at Waupun, has admitted killing two women and snatching the bodies of nine others from their graves.

Two of the grave robberies were verified Monday when two graves in Plainfield were opened and found empty.

Thomson explained that the crime laboratory's authority to act "is grounded on the request of local authorities."

### WILSON RESPONSIBLE

"If at any time, due to mounting costs of investigation, local authorities should withdraw their request for continued work by the laboratory, much valuable information respecting the crimes committed or possibly yet to be discovered would be lost," he said.

Honeck said he informed Wilson "the state will be responsible for investigations that local authorities feel they cannot undertake because of lack of funds or other reasons."

Wilson was told by Honeck to "continue with all steps necessary in your judgment to complete the analysis of all physical evidence" in possession of the laboratory.

### STATE STATUTES

"The state's entrance in this case will not supplant local officials in any way," Honeck told reporters.

"Each local official has continuing authority in actual or potential cases (arising from the Gein investigation) in their respective counties," he said.

Honeck explained that state statutes "clothe the attorney general with powers of a district attorney."

"But it is our intention merely to pass along to local officials any evidence discovered that may involve a crime with the expectation that they will then take over."

### STATEWIDE CONCERN

Waushara County officials previously explained the county could not even afford prorated costs of the crime laboratory's investigation.

Thomson noted that the Gein case was of "statewide concern" and that "possibilities of additional homicide" should be exhausted.

He said responsibility for the over-all investigation "should reside in one person." He told Honeck that the attorney general, as chairman of the State Crime Laboratory Board, is "the logical person to assume this responsibility."

## GHOUL
### Gein Interest 'Statewide'

NOVEMBER 23, 195[?]

# 'Butcher' Sent to Waupun

## Order Ghoul Graves Opened

### 30-Day Mental Check May Block Gein's Trial

*By Sentinel Staff Writer*

# MILWAUKEE SENTINEL

NOVEMBER 23, 1957

## Biggest Share of Gein Case Costs May Be State Burden

MADISON, Nov. 22 — Atty. Gen. Honeck said Friday that the state may have to bear the major share of the cost of investigating the Gein multi-murder case.

This developed from a conference between Charles M. Wilson, superintendent of the State Crime Laboratory, and Honeck.

The Gein case apparently has torn a large hole in the state law that outlines relations of the crime lab with county law enforcement officials.

It has raised the question of who is going to pay for the weeks of work that will be necessary to sift and evaluate the mountain of evidence gathered. Lab technicians still have not finished cataloging it.

Wilson has been aware of the difficulty from the beginning of the case and Friday sought a definite answer from Honeck.

The situation is created by a 1955 law, Honeck said, that requires the crime lab to "meter" time spent on each case. After eliminating administrative costs, the balance is paid by the state and locality involved on a 50-50 basis.

The simple formula is bound to break down in the Gein case, Wilson says, because there are four counties now involved and in all likelihood will be more. If he is to spend time figuring out how much each county should pay the laboratory work never will get done.

It has been determined, Honeck said, that in ordinary cases, over the past year, laboratory costs figure out at $9.55 an hour. On this basis, Milwaukee County paid $11,000 last year for work done. Dane County paid $7,000. Costs for work for all the counties this year is estimated at $47,000.

Waushara County District Atty. Earl F. Kileen suggested stopping the probe because "it is costing the county too much money."

## Regular Treatment If Gein Behaves

By Sentinel Staff Writer

WAUPUN, Wis., Nov. 22 — If he behaves himself, confessed slayer Edward Gein will be treated like any other patient during his 30 days at the Central State Hospital for the criminally insane here.

In his free time, he will be allowed to watch television, read magazines, play games and take part in other recreational and occupational pursuits for inmates.

Dr. Edward F. Schubert, director of the state's only maximum security mental hospital, said homicidal cases, such as Gein, pose no special problem for the institution.

"It's been my experience usually that such cases certainly are no more of a problem than any other," Dr. Schubert said.

Much of Gein's time in the institution will be devoted to interviews with staff psychologists, psychiatrists and social workers, and any psychiatric tests that may be needed to unlock the secrets of his behavior.

**PRIORITY PROBABL**

"In all probability, he will be given priority here," Dr. Schubert said.

"We will do our best to give him the necessary tests and conferences to facilitate his return to court."

Dr. Schubert said that "unless we run into unforseen difficulties" the report should be completed within the required 30 days. Then the report will be submitted in writing to Circuit Judge Herbert A. Bunde.

If the judge desires in the subsequent hearing, he may call experts from the staff here for direct testimony on the case, Dr. Schubert said.

When Gein arrives, he will be given an initial coursory physical examination, to determine whether he has any communicable diseases. Then, probably on Monday, intensive testing beginning with a complete physical, will begin.

Use of the hospital's recreational and occupational therapy facilities depends primarily on the patient's attitude, Dr. Schubert said.

"If a patient is unusually disturbed, it wouldn't be possible for him. But if he is cooperative, he would have that opportunity."

**CAN MOVE FREELY**

Dr. Schubert said patients are allowed to move freely within the hospital, although special care is taken to prevent any escapes. Windows of the hospital are barred and doors to the wards are kept locked, he said.

The hospital, which has a maximum capacity of 320 patients, presently has 307 inmates.

# THE CHICAGO AMERICAN

MONDAY—NOVEMBER 25—1957

# Graves to Be Opened

## Gein Story of Thefts Faces Test

WAUTOMA, Wis., Nov. 24 (INS)—Waushara County officials prepared for a series of exhumations which could settle the question of whether Wisconsin's "mad butcher," Edward Gein, murdered two persons—or many more.

The first grave probably could not be opened until Tuesday.

District Attorney Earl Kileen said mounting pressure by the public definitely precludes any further delay in testing Gein's assertion that nine skulls and various other human parts found in his home were trophies of moonlight grave-robbing forays.

A 30-day mental examination of the 51-year-old hermit-farmer at the state hospital at Waupun for the criminally insane has interrupted legal action on the murder of Mrs. Bernice Worden, whose mutilated body was found hanging a week ago in Gein's home near Plainfield.

### CITIZENS STUNNED

Gein also confessed the murder of Mrs. Mary Hogan, 54, a tavern operator in neighboring Portage County. Last night, shortly before he was taken to the state hospital, Gein took Portage County officials along the route he drove with Mrs. Hogan's body Dec. 9, 1954.

The townspeople of Plainfield, stunned by day after day of grisly disclosures, have demanded that Kileen open the graves Gein said he plundered. A county board official, Floyd Wing, led those who insisted on knowing the whole story of their neighbor's depradations.

Kileen, who estimated that "four, perhaps five" graves be opened, overruled urging by Charles Wilson, head of the state's crime laboratory at Madison, that the exhumations be delayed "a week or two" while the laboratory completes examination of the skulls.

### FIRST GRAVE CHOSEN

The district attorney said the first grave to be opened will be that of Mrs. Eleanor Adams, 51, Wing's sister-in-law, whose body Gein said he disturbed. She died in 1951.

District Attorney John J. Haka of Portage County said s will obtain a warrant charging Gein with the Hogan slaying, but that warrant may never be used.

If doctors at the state hospital pronounce Gein insane, he probably would be committed to the hospital until he died or recovered. And if he is declared competent to stand trial, Kileen explained, Gein faces a maximum life sentence for the murder of Mrs. Worden.

Wisconsin has no death penalty.

Waushara Circuit Judge Herbert A. Bunde already has heard a plea of not guilty by reason of insanity in the Worden case.

## Central State Hospital Has Slight Prison Atmosphere

Waupun, Wis. – (AP) – Wisconsin's central state hospital for the criminally insane, the all-male mental institution where slayer Ed Gein of Plainfield was committed Saturday for observation, is a hospital with a slight prison atmosphere.

The institution was built on a acre site next to the state prison here in 1913. It has 307 inmates who represent the state's dangerous and criminal-insane. The hospital is not connected with the state prison in any way.

Waupun is about 60 miles northeast of Madison and about the same distance northwest of Milwaukee.

### Cure Is Possible

In the past, the hospital has been considered the place for persons whose mental illnesses were beyond the knowledge of present day medicine. Today, however, that is not the case.

Wilbur J. Schmidt, director of the state department of public welfare, which operates the institution, said its aim was for eventual cure and release of its inmates, just as at any other state welfare institution.

A few persons eventually respond to treatment there and are released. Most, however, spend their lives there. In nearly every case, a court order is necessary before a patient can be released.

### Painted in Pastels

The hospital is a maximum security institution with about nine acres inside its two story walls. Inside is a baseball diamond, eight wards for inmates, a dining room and an administration area.

The locked and barred rooms, some holding up to five men, are painted in pastel colors to take away some of the prison atmosphere.

During the day, the men are permitted to move about freely. During their free time, inmates are permitted to watch television, read magazines, play games and take part in other recreational and occupational pursuits. Beginning next year, they will have their first full time teacher.

### Has Stock Farm

Persons admitted for observation usually are not permitted to join in hospital activities until their behavior and attitude has been observed. In their period of observation, they take personality and intelligence tests and are interviewed by staff psychiatrists.

The institution maintains a 150 acre stock farm with chickens and hogs. Thirty or more of the inmates carry on this activity outside the walls. Gardening provides fresh vegetables during summer months.

About 100 persons are on the staff.

## Confession by Butcher Confirmed

WAUTOMA, Wis., Nov. 25 (AP) — A small pinch bar, lying among violated bones on a looted casket, testified today to the truth of Edward Gein's statement to authorities that the portions of nine female bodies found at his lonely farmhouse had been carried home from graves.

District Attorney Earl Kileen said the evidence of the empty graves "appears to substantiate Gein's statement."

Gein, now committed to Wisconsin's central state hospital for the criminal insane for observation, also admitted killing and butchering two women of the neighborhood.

### 2 GRAVES OPENED

Kileen said this afternoon that two graves in the Plainfield Cemetery were opened today and were found empty, except for a few bones and the pinch bar that "apparently had been used to open" one of the caskets.

November 25, 1957

### GRAVE OF MRS. ELEANOR ADAMS

The grave of Mrs. Eleanor Adams, who died in 1951, was reopened Monday by Waushara County authorities to verify or refute Edward Gein's claim that he got his collection of human skulls and anatomies from cemeteries. When this grave was opened, diggers and observers found an empty casket. Later the crew moved just a short distance and dug up the grave of Mrs. Mabel Everson, who also died in 1951, and found substantially the same result. Reporters were barred from the cemetery during the digging, but were permitted to enter later. Looking at the overturned marker of Mrs. Adams are two of the many newspaper men sent here to cover the Gein case. (Northwestern Photo)

The graves were those of Mrs. Eleanore Adams and Mrs. Mabel Everson, both buried in 1951.

Mrs. Adams' casket was empty. The other casket also was empty, but Kileen said there were bones and the small prying device on top of the looted casket. Kileen said:

"At present I do not see any need to open any more graves."

### GOVERNOR INTERVENES

However, he added, if Wisconsin's Attorney General Stewart Honeck "believes that opening the others is necessary, we will open them all."

Honeck today was asked by Gov. Vernon Thomson to move into the case because of the possibility that additional crimes in other counties might be involved.

## Sift Evidence for Bones of Gein Victim

Nov 25, 1957

*By Sentinel Staff Writer*

STEVENS POINT, Wis., Nov. 24—When he receives a report from the State Crime Laboratory on 10 barrels of evidence taken from slayer-butcher Edward Gein's farmyard, Portage County Dist. Atty. John J. Haka expects to issue a second murder warrant charging Gein with the slaying of Mrs. Mary Hogan, Pine Grove tavernkeeper.

Haka Sunday repeated his desire to authorize the warrant on physical facts rather than just the confession of the 51-year-old Plainfield bachelor handyman whose secluded home held a grotesque collection of human remains.

Saturday, during a partial re-enactment of his shooting and butchering of Mrs. Hogan, Gein directed Haka and other Portage and Waushara County officials to a spot where he said the remains of the 54-year-old woman were buried.

Gein is already charged with the murder of Mrs. Bernice Worden, Plainfield hardware store owner, in a warrant issued in Waushara County.

Haka indicated that the barrels held ashes, blood-clotted soil, some clothing, "and what I imagine are bones."

The evidence was sent to the crime lab for checking and evaluation, Haka said.

The district attorney reported no intentions of exhuming graves in Spiritland Cemetery in the Town of Almond, a second graveyard which Gein has named in his tales of body-poaching.

Their has been no pressure from survivors of persons buried there to initiate the uncovering of caskets, he added.

Haka expressed a desire to be in on any further lie detector tests administered to Gein, "to clear up some questions on the Hogan case."

Waushara County District Attorney Earl F. Kileen has stated that crime lab officials want the additional tests to help in confirming the ghoulish excursions described by Gein, now at Central State Hospital for the criminal insane at

## GEIN
### 'House of Horrors' Still Under Guard

(Continued From Page 1)

Waupun for a 30-day observation session.

**WILSON UNAVAILABLE**

Crime lab superintendent Charles Wilson could not be contacted for comment on such tests.

An aid said that if they were to be made, the sensitivity of the detector equipment and the lack of proper facilities at the hospital would almost make it mandatory that Gein be transferred to Madison for testing.

Gein's attorney, former assemblyman William N. Belter, said he had no opposition to crime lab officials' intentions of such a temporary transfer.

Belter said deputies were still guarding the now boarded-up "house of horrors" at Gein's farm to discourage curio seekers, but that county officials want to drop the guard as soon as possible.

**NO REQUESTS**

The attorney said that neither the crime lab or law enforcement officials have made any requests to him to delay disposal of the house and its surrounding 190-acre property until they finish their investigations.

Belter, who obtained the power of attorney from Gein Saturday, said he hasn't yet been contacted by any of Gein's relatives and hasn't asked his client the names of distant kin in La Crosse, reportedly his only relatives still alive.

TUESDAY, NOVEMBER 26, 1957

# Find 2 'Gein Graves' Empty

## Butcher's Ghoul Story Called True By Investigators

*By Sentinel Staff Writer*

WAUTOMA, Nov. 25 — Dist. Atty. Earl Kileen said Monday he is confident Edward Gein did actually collect parts of nine bodies found in his Plainfield farm home by robbing graves, as he claimed he did.

The Waushara County prosecutor's comment came after law enforcement officers opened two graves Gein said he robbed in Plainfield Cemetery. The investigators found them empty "except for a few bones on top of one casket."

**AWAITS MIND TEST**

Gein, now undergoing 30 days of psychiatric observation at Waupun State Prison, hospital for the criminal insane, has confessed slaying Mrs. Bernice Worden of Plainfield and Mrs. Mary Hogan of Pine Grove.

Parts of their remains were found in his home, but Gein claimed the rest of his grisly collection of skulls and other anatomical parts was gathered in moonlight visits to Plainfield and Spirit Land cemeteries where he dug into and robbed fresh graves.

There had been speculation that the slight, 51-year-old bachelor could not have opened and closed a grave in the space of a single night, and might have actually committed other slayings.

Kileen said, however, that two men working with shovels opened the two graves in Plainfield Cemetery in an hour.

**OTHER GRAVES**

The district attorney said "as far as I am concerned, the opening of these two graves verifies Gein's story."

As to six other graves Gein listed, Kileen said "I won't open any more if I can help it."

Any further excavations will be "a state matter," Kileen said, and he will not order them unless Gov. Thomson provides funds to pay for the work.

The graves opened Monday were those of Mrs. Eleanore Adams and Mrs. Mabel Everson, both buried in 1951.

Kileen headed the group which entered the cemetery Monday morning, barring reporters and others from the grounds during the excavations.

**LAB AIDS THERE**

Officials with Kileen included Sheriff Arthur Schley, Deputy Arnie Fritz; Plainfield Village President Harold Collins; Ray Goult, an undertaker; some other deputies and representatives of the State Crime Laboratory, which has been analyzing evidence in the case.

Also present was Floyd Adams, husband of Eleanore.

Both Collins and Goult, who had urged the grave examination to check Gein's story, said they now felt he had been telling the truth.

## Sheriff Cites Co-operation As Key Factor in Arrest

Nov 27, 1957

The important role played by law officers from neighboring counties and local Plainfield residents in the apprehension of Ed Gein less than two hours after evidence of the crime had been made known, was recognized Wednesday by Sheriff Arthur Schley in a letter to the co-operating agencies.

The sheriff's office at Wautoma received the call from Plainfield at 5:10 p.m. Saturday. Gein had been arrested by 7 p.m. and was housed in a jail cell at Wautoma by 7:40 p.m.

The letter from the sheriff read as follows:

"Gentlemen:

"We wish to sincerely thank all persons who assisted in any manner in the recent investigation at Plainfield.

"All neighboring sheriff's departments which were contacted responded promptly and gave us their utmost co-operation.

"We also wish to thank the crime laboratory for their quick response and expert handling of their phase of the investigation.

"It is also true, that without the help and assistance of the volunteers in and around Plainfield, our investigation would not have been successful.

"To each and every one who assisted in any way we wish to repeat our thanks.

Waushara Co. Sheriff's Dept.
Arthur Schley, Sheriff"

Sheriff Schley told The Argus Wednesday morning that if even a few hours had elapsed allowing Gein time to completely dispose of the body, it would have been much more difficult to have solved the crime.

What took place in those first few hours, according to the sheriff, was essentially as follows:

Sheriff Schley and Deputy Arnold Fritz went directly to the Worden Store after receiving the call.

At the store there was obvious evidence of foul play with blood found on the floor, the fact that Mrs. Worden was missing, the truck belonging to the store was nowhere in the area, the cash register in the store was missing.

After a hurried conference, sheriff's offices in adjoining counties were called and the state crime laboratory notified.

The first search was for the truck, which was found just east of the village on a "lover's lane" road. Village residents went with officers from other areas to help guide them to possible hiding places.

A pattern of tires from the Worden truck was obtained from the place where the tires had been purchased.

Also, at the outset, there were at least "three or four" suspects, who for one reason or another there was cause to check. Gein was one of these.

The suspect was found and taken into custody at Hill's Grocery. While he was being questioned by Traffic Officer Dan Chase, Sheriff Schley and Captain Lloyd Schoephoester of the Green Lake County Traffic Department went to the Gein farm.

While Capt. Schoepnoester searched another part of the house, Sheriff Schley opened the door to the summer kitchen and found the mutilated body.

He radioed Officer Chase to bring Gein in.

## Grave Findings Touch Off Mass Exodus of Press

The findings on opening two graves in the Plainfield cemetery Monday morning has cleared the air on the truth of at least some of confessed murderer Ed Gein's story.

In the two graves opened, no body was found in the grave of Mrs. Eleanore Adams and only a few bones on the casket of the other, that of Mrs. Mabel Everson.

Both Sheriff Arthur Schley and District Attorney Earl Kileen have stated that no more graves will be opened unless relatives of persons on the Gein list request that it be done.

Whether or not other graves will be opened will also depend on the findings of the state crime laboratory and what their investigators deem necessary.

The state attorney general's office has assumed some of the responsibility in the case and have been directed by the governor to examine facts as to whether Gein might have committed other crimes.

Gein was taken to the state hospital at Waupun for 30 days of mental observation Saturday by Sheriff Schley and Deputy Arnold Fritz.

The findings at Plainfield Monday touched off a mass exodus of reporters and photographers from the area and as of Wednesday morning Sheriff Sohley, who has been pursued by the press since the first news of the murder broke, stated that there were only a few Chicago reporters still in the city.

The sheriff told the Argus Wednesday morning that reporters had been kept from the Plainfield cemetery as a protection to the relatives of deceased persons whose graves Gein has said that he entered.

He said that one photograper attempted to take pictures from a top a ladder at the edge of the cemetery and others were taken from an airplane hovering over the scene.

TUESDAY, NOVEMBER 26, 1957

# Find 2 'Gein Graves' Empty

## Butcher's Ghoul Story Called True By Investigators

*By Sentinel Staff Writer*

WAUTOMA, Nov. 25 — Dist. Atty. Earl Kileen said Monday he is confident Edward Gein did actually collect parts of nine bodies found in his Plainfield farm home by robbing graves, as he claimed he did.

The Waushara County prosecutor's comment came after law enforcement officers opened two graves Gein said he robbed in Plainfield Cemetery. The investigators found them empty "except for a few bones on top of one casket."

**AWAITS MIND TEST**

Gein, now undergoing 30 days of psychiatric observation at Waupun State Prison, hospital for the criminal insane, has confessed slaying Mrs. Bernice Worden of Plainfield and Mrs. Mary Hogan of Pine Grove.

Parts of their remains were found in his home, but Gein claimed the rest of his grisly collection of skulls and other anatomical parts was gathered in moonlight visits to Plainfield and Spirit Land cemeteries where he dug into and robbed fresh graves.

There had been speculation that the slight, 51-year-old bachelor could not have opened and closed a grave in the space of a single night, and might have actually committed other slayings.

Kileen said, however, that two men working with shovels opened the two graves in Plainfield Cemetery in an hour.

**OTHER GRAVES**

The district attorney said "as far as I am concerned, the opening of these two graves verifies Gein's story."

As to six other graves Gein listed, Kileen said "I won't open any more if I can help it."

Any further excavations will be "a state matter," Kileen said, and he will not order them unless Gov. Thomson provides funds to pay for the work.

The graves opened Monday were those of Mrs. Eleanore Adams and Mrs. Mabel Everson, both buried in 1951.

Kileen headed the group which entered the cemetery Monday morning, barring reporters and others from the grounds during the excavations.

**LAB AIDS THERE**

Officials with Kileen included Sheriff Arthur Schley, Deputy Arnie Fritz; Plainfield Village President Harold Collins; Ray Goult, an undertaker; some other deputies and representatives of the State Crime Laboratory, which has been analyzing evidence in the case.

Also present was Floyd Adams, husband of Eleanore.

Both Collins and Goult, who had urged the grave examination to check Gein's story, said they now felt he had been telling the truth.

## Sheriff Cites Co-operation As Key Factor in Arrest

*Nov 27, 1957*

The important role played by law officers from neighboring counties and local Plainfield residents in the apprehension of Ed Gein less than two hours after evidence of the crime had been made known, was recognized Wednesday by Sheriff Arthur Schley in a letter to the co-operating agencies.

The sheriff's office at Wautoma received the call from Plainfield at 5:10 p.m. Saturday. Gein had been arrested by 7 p.m. and was housed in a jail cell at Wautoma by 7:40 p.m.

The letter from the sheriff read as follows:

"Gentlemen:

"We wish to sincerely thank all persons who assisted in any manner in the recent investigation at Plainfield.

"All neighboring sheriff's departments which were contacted responded promptly and gave us their utmost co-operation.

"We also wish to thank the crime laboratory for their quick response and expert handling of their phase of the investigation.

"It is also true, that without the help and assistance of the volunteers in and around Plainfield, our investigation would not have been successful.

"To each and every one who assisted in any way we wish to repeat our thanks.

Waushara Co. Sheriff's Dept.
Arthur Schley, Sheriff"

Sheriff Schley told The Argus Wednesday morning that if even a few hours had elapsed allowing Gein time to completely dispose of the body, it would have been much more difficult to have solved the crime.

What took place in those first few hours, according to the sheriff, was essentially as follows:

Sheriff Schley and Deputy Arnold Fritz went directly to the Worden Store after receiving the call.

At the store there was obvious evidence of foul play with blood found on the floor, the fact that Mrs. Worden was missing, the truck belonging to the store was nowhere in the area, the cash register in the store was missing.

After a hurried conference, sheriff's offices in adjoining counties were called and the state crime laboratory notified.

The first search was for the truck, which was found just east of the village on a "lover's lane" road. Village residents went with officers from other areas to help guide them to possible hiding places.

A pattern of tires from the Worden truck was obtained from the place where the tires had been purchased.

Also, at the outset, there were at least "three or four" suspects, who for one reason or another there was cause to check. Gein was one of these.

The suspect was found and taken into custody at Hill's Grocery. While he was being questioned by Traffic Officer Dan Chase, Sheriff Schley and Captain Lloyd Schoephoester of the Green Lake County Traffic Department went to the Gein farm.

While Capt. Schoephoester searched another part of the house, Sheriff Schley opened the door to the summer kitchen and found the mutilated body.

He radioed Officer Chase to bring Gein in.

## Grave Findings Touch Off Mass Exodus of Press

The findings on opening two graves in the Plainfield cemetery Monday morning has cleared the air on the truth of at least some of confessed murderer Ed Gein's story.

In the two graves opened, no body was found in the grave of Mrs. Eleanore Adams and only a few bones on the casket of the other, that of Mrs. Mabel Everson.

Both Sheriff Arthur Schley and District Attorney Earl Kileen have stated that no more graves will be opened unless relatives of persons on the Gein list request that it be done.

Whether or not other graves will be opened will also depend on the findings of the state crime laboratory and what their investigators deem necessary.

The state attorney general's office has assumed some of the responsibility in the case and have been directed by the governor to examine facts as to whether Gein might have committed other crimes.

Gein was taken to the state hospital at Waupun for 30 days of mental observation Saturday by Sheriff Schley and Deputy Arnold Fritz.

The findings at Plainfield Monday touched off a mass exodus of reporters and photographers from the area and as of Wednesday morning Sheriff Schley, who has been pursued by the press since the first news of the murder broke, stated that there were only a few Chicago reporters still in the city.

The sheriff told the Argus Wednesday morning that reporters had been kept from the Plainfield cemetery as a protection to the relatives of deceased persons whose graves Gein has said that he entered.

He said that one photograper attempted to take pictures from a top a ladder at the edge of the cemetery and others were taken from an airplane hovering over the scene.

# THE MILWAUKEE JOURNAL

# Butcher' Tells of Robbing Graves

Slayer Ed Gein stood bareheaded as he was arraigned Monday before County Judge Boyd Clark at Wautoma.

## Gein at Crime Lab For More Lie Tests

MADISON (AP) — Killer-ghoul Edward Gein was taken to the state Crime Laboratory here for additional lie detector tests today. The 51-year-old admitted slayer of two women was brought here from the Central State Hospital the Criminal Insane in Waupun.

Attorney General Stewart Honeck said today, after a conference with Waushara and Portage County officials, that a decision on opening additional graves in the Edward Gein case would be deferred for at least a week or 10 days.

Honeck emerged from a meeting attended by Dist. Attys. Edward Kileen of Waushara County and John J. Haka of Portage County and State Crime Laboratory Director Charles Wilson and told newsmen what had been discussed this morning.

Honeck said:

"The question of further opening of graves was discussed and the decision deferred until such time as is determined by Mr. Wilson.

"Mr. Wilson advises that if his investigation continues as he expects it will be unnecessary to open further graves. But the decision will remain unsettled until a later date."

Asked how long this might be, Honeck said it would be a week to 10 days at the least.

Honeck added that the primary purpose of the meeting was "to block out plans and courses of action for either or both murder prosecutions on the assumption that the accused is found sane and able to stand trial."

Honeck also announced that another lie detector test would be given Gein, 51-year-old bachelor of rural Plainfield who has admitted killing two middle-aged women and robbing the graves of nine others.

Honeck said the purpose of the additional tests was to determine whether Gein was involved in other killings. Gein is undergoing 30 days of mental observation.

Gein's attorney, William Belter of Wautoma, said he had no objection to more lie tests for Gein but that he would doubt their reliability if Gein is judged insane.

"Gein is apparently trying to tell people honestly what happened," Belter said. "But perhaps he doesn't remember some things, and other facts may be perverted in his mind. If that is so, what value is a lie detector test?"

Two graves in Plainfield Cemetery were opened Monday and the caskets were found empty. Kileen said the opening of the graves verified Gein's story and added, "I won't open any more if I can help it."

Honeck has been directed by Gov. Vernon Thomson to investigate all phases of Gein's case.

Gein had pleaded innocent by reason of insanity to a charge of first-degree murder in the death of Mrs. Bernice Worden, 58-year-old Plainfield hardware store operator, Nov. 16. He also admitted killing Mrs. Mary Hogan, 54, who disappeared from her rural tavern in Portage County in December 1954.

## Gein Will Get New Lie Test
12-27-57
### Honeck Holds Parley With DA's to Talk Over Possible Trial

*Journal Madison Bureau*

Madison, Wis.—Ed Gein, the 51 year old Waushara county slayer and grave robber, will be given an additional lie test some time this week, Atty. Gen. Stewart Honeck said Tuesday.

Honeck said that this was being done at the suggestion of Charles Wilson, director of the state crime laboratory. Honeck said new evidence gained from the opening of two graves by Waushara county officials could be used in further tests and might produce valuable evidence. He said the test would be either at Waupun or Madison, whichever was more convenient.

Gein has been sent to the central state hospital for the criminally insane at Waupun to determine if he is sane enough to stand trial for murder.

### Sanity Is Presumed

Honeck said that the state was proceeding on the assumption that Gein would be declared sane and would have to stand trial.

[At Wautoma, Gein's attorney, William Belter, said he had no objection to the lie tests, although he doubted their value if Gein was proved insane.

["Gein is apparently trying to tell people honestly what happened," Belter said. "But perhaps he doesn't remember some things and other facts may be perverted in his mind. If that is so, what value is a lie detector test?"]

Honeck was meeting Wednesday with Dist. Attys. Earl Kileen of Waushara county and John J. Haka of Portage county. The attorney general said the conference would cover legal aspects of Gein's trial. Gein has confessed a murder in each county.

Honeck said that the state would do everything it could to determine scientifically whether there had been additional homicides.

"If it can't be determined without digging up more graves, rest assured that they will be dug," he added. However, all other sources would be exhausted first, he said.

### Thomson Enters Case

Monday, Gov. Thomson ordered Honeck to investigate all facts and circumstances involved in the case. Honeck said that the state's position was to co-operate with local authorities on all aspects of the case and to see that investigations started by the state crime laboratory were continued if county officials felt they could not afford to carry them on.

Dist. Atty. Kileen, in whose county Gein has been charged with murder and armed robbery, has said that he was interested in cleaning up only one murder, but would co-operate with other counties. However, he made it clear that Waushara county has only limited funds for such an investigation.

"I'll be guided by what the researchers at the state crime lab are able to find out with the evidence at their disposal," Honeck said.

### Won't Permit House Sale

On another point, Honeck noted that a newspaper had indicated interest in possible purchase of the ramshackle Gein farm southwest of Plainfield. He said that the state would object to such a sale because it did not want the premises disturbed until the investigation was completed.

## Feeling High In Plainfield

PLAINFIELD, Wis. (UP)—Recluse farmer Ed Gein was the only topic of conversation along the main street of this village of 700 today.

Most of the residents either knew Gein or had seen and heard about him.

"The town is stunned and angry," said Ed Marolla, editor of the Plainfield Sun. "No one is talking about anything else."

Feelings of some citizens were reported "high" in this shopping center for farms in this area.

"If the town got hold of that guy, the town'd know what to do about him all right," said one man who didn't want to be identified.

However, Marolla said "nothing violent was in the wind. No crowds are gathering."

Marolla said he had known Gein for several years.

"He was one of those fellows who's not too bright, but he was considered harmless. He liked to play with the kids, and even did some babysitting."

"He had no criminal record of any kind. He was kind of unimposing," said Marolla.

"As far as I know, he never pestered any women," said Marolla.

## Bones Discovered In Garbage Trench

11-30-57

STEVENS POINT (AP) — Portage County Sheriff Herb Wanserski said today he and a deputy have dug up another human skeleton on the Waushara County farm of Edward Gein, who already has admitted killing two women and looting nine graves.

Wanserski said he and Deputy Sheriff George Cummings dug up the bones, including a "complete skull, with its teeth and several gold crowns," in what appeared to be a garbage trench about a quarter mile from Gein's farm house.

The sheriff said he and Cummings located the trench after neighbors told him that Gein used to bury garbage in the woods, and found the bones after about a half-hour's digging Friday.

The sheriff said additional digging would be done today.

### Skull Appears Larger

He declined to say formally whether the skeleton appeared to be male or female, but other sources said that the skull was larger than any of the heads found in Gein's grisly collection.

All the other human remnants previously found were in the isolated farmhouse where the 51-year-old handyman lived alone, and all have been tentatively identified as female.

Wanserski has been pressing an investigation independently of Waushara County authorities because one of the women Gein has admitted killing was from Bancroft, across the county line in Portage County.

Still listed as missing in the area is Victor "Bunk" Travis, a resident of Adams County, which joins the other two counties near Gein's farm. Travis, who was 43, last was seen about 7 p.m. on November 1, 1952, while hunting near the Gein farm.

Authorities investigating Travis' disappearance at the time said he had decided to hunt with another man, but the other hunter never was located.

### Denied by Gein

Gein has denied having any knowledge of the Travis disappearance. He was committed to Wisconsin's Central State Hospital for the Criminal Insane at Waupun a week ago for determination of whether he is sane enough to stand trial for first degree murder in the slaying and butchering of 58-year-old Mrs. Bernice Worden of Plainfield on Nov. 16. He also has admitted killing and similarly mutilating Mrs. Mary Hogan, 54, of Bancroft, December 8, 1954.

Last Monday, Waushara County and State Crime Laboratory officials opened two of the Plainfield graves Gein claimed he robbed and found both empty. At that time, Waushara County Dist. Atty. Earl Kileen said that he thought finding the graves empty "substantiated" Gein's story that the other human relics in Gein's home came, as the frail-appearing little man insisted, from violated graves.

**BOARD UP HORROR HOUSE**—A workman finishes task of boarding up the windows and doors of the farm home near Plainfield, Wis., where "Butcher" Ed Gein, confessed slayer of two women, lived. Skulls and other human bones were found in the home after Gein's arrest.

## Will Quiz Gein About Possible Accomplice in Grave Pillaging

11-29-57

WAUPUN, Wis. (UP)—Confessed butcher-killer Edward Gein spent a quiet Thanksgiving Day in his isolated room at the Central State Hospital here.

The frail appearing, 51-year-old rural Plainfield farmer, whose "house of horrors" shocked the nation, was served the institution's traditional turkey dinner in his maximum security room near a ward.

Hospital Superintendent Dr. Edward Schubert said psychiatrists will continue to test Gein to determine if he will stand trial for the brutal slaying of Mrs. Bernice Worden, 58, a Plainfield storekeeper, and Mrs. Mary Hogan, 58, a Pine Grove tavernkeeper.

The doctor said there were no plans to take Gein to the State Crime Laboratory at Madison before completion of the sanity tests which got underway a week ago. Gein had undergone a second lie detector test at the capital Wednesday in which he disclosed he had robbed the graves of nine women—two more than a previous admission. However, one skull found in Gein's grisly collection at his farm home still was unexplained.

Atty. Gen. Stewart Honeck said Thursday Gein would be given another round of questioning when his tests here are completed to further probe the possibility of an accomplice on his moonlight forays to rob graves. The state officials also said Gein would be asked to disclose where the body of the unexplained skull was hidden.

Dr. Schubert said Gein would continue to be locked alone at the institution until it could be determined if he would fit in with a ward at the hospital for the criminally insane.

Officials have agreed not to exhume any more graves on Gein's list, at least for another 10 days, awaiting detailed reports from the crime laboratory.

*Post-Crescent Appleton November 23, 1957*

# Butcher-Slayer Edward Gein Faces 30-Day Mental Test

## Four Graves May be Opened to Verify Story of Body Thefts

Edward Gein, 51-year-old admitted butcher-slayer of two women, is in Waushara county jail awaiting days mental examination.

He was arraigned Friday afternoon, on a first degree murder charge before Circuit Judge Herbert A. Bunde, who ordered the examination.

Judge Bunde

Gein has identified eight of the cemetery plots he looted, Dist. Atty. Earl Kileen said today.

This morning Sheriff Art Schley told newsmen that "if they'd leave us alone until noon" for a final trip by auto to cemeteries in the area and to the Gein farm, the self-admitted killer and ghoul might be taken by tonight to a mental hospital.

### Missing Persons

Meanwhile, authorities said they plan to open as many as four graves to see if Gein was telling the truth when he said one of the skulls and most of the human remains found in his isolated farmhouse near Plainfield came from graves.

Gein will be sent to the Central State hospital for the criminally insane to determine whether he is competent to stand trial on a first degree murder charge.

The hospital staff psychiatrists also will seek to determine whether Gein was sane Nov. 16, the date of the mutilation slaying of Mrs. Bernice Worden. The 58-year-old Plainfield widow was one of two women the bachelor said he killed after observing they resembled his late mother.

Kileen said Gein would remain in the Waushara county jail three or four more days

## Sheriffs Differ on Gein Action
*12-4-57*

Journal Special Correspondence
Plainfield, Wis. — The Waushara and Portage county sheriffs disagreed Wednesday on the value of continued digging around the Edward Gein home southwest of here.

Gein, 51, a bachelor who lived on a rundown farm, has admitted killing one woman from each county and robbing the graves of several others. After his arrest, parts of the women's bodies were found in Gein's home and bones were found buried on the farm.

Sheriff Arthur Schley of Waushara county says he does not see any sense in digging unless he knows what he is digging for. Sheriff Herbert Wanserski says he has been pursuing a tip as to a possible burial site of more bones.

Schley said that several places were dug up Tuesday with no result. He said the tip was based on someone having seen some freshly dug earth on the farm several years ago.

Schley said, "Wanserski's hot tip turned out to be cold." He added that Wanserski had been giving information to the press "before he knows what he is talking about." He referred to bones found last week end which Wanserski thought might be male, but which were later identified as female.

*Oshkosh Northwestern 12-2-57*

# Deputies Digging For Truck on Gein Farm

(By Northwestern Staff Writer)
PLAINFIELD — Reports circulated here this morning that deputies were digging on the Ed Gein farm for a truck belonging to a hunter who disapeared in 1952 while hunting near the farm. The reports could not be confirmed by newsmen, who were rebuffed at the farm by two hard-eyed and unyielding deputies who had a standard answer for all inquiries:

"We don't know."

Victor (Bunk) Travis, who was 43 and a resident of nearby Adams County, disappeared on Nov. 1, 1952, while hunting near the Gein farm. Investigation of his disappearance at the time revealed Travis had decided to hunt with another man, but the other hunter never was located. Gein has denied having any knowledge of Travis' disappearance.

Reporters, confined to the road leading past the Gein farm, could see no digging activity or signs of it.

Visitors continued to badger the guards who are posted at the farm around the clock, but no one was being allowed on the place. Atty. William Belter, Gein's attorney and the court-appointed guardian of the property, who was refused admittance to the farm Sunday, planned to return to the farm and defy the deputies to arrest him. Belter was confined by illness to his home this morning.

The deputies are acting under orders of the Portage County sheriff, who told them that "no one" was to enter the farm. It was not explained immediately why the sheriff of Portage County was issuing orders involving a Waushara County farm, but one of the deputies said he assumed the Portage County sheriff was getting his orders from the attorney general at Madison.

At Wautoma, there was considerable skepticism over reports from Stevens Point Saturday that another skull found buried on the farm was that of Travis. Wautoma authorities said they were inclined to believe that all of Gein's victims were females.

# Incredibly Dirty House Was Home of Slayer

## Grave Robber Saved Everything — Books, Gum, Magazines — Amid Filth

By ROBERT W. WELLS
Of The Journal Staff

Plainfield, Wis.—Until Saturday, when he was arrested following the murder and decapitation of Mrs. Bernice Worden, this is the way the small, inoffensive village handyman named Ed Gein lived.

When he came home at night —perhaps from an odd job, perhaps from sitting with a child as a favor to a mother—he stood on the sagging rear porch and opened the back door into the room where the widow's butchered body was found Saturday, hanging from one of two blocks and tackles.

There was no electricity, no telephone—no sign, in fact, that this was 1957 instead of the 1917 of Gein's boyhood on the bleak farm. So when the little man came home, blinking his watery blue eyes against the gathering darkness, he must have lit one of the old lanterns or dusty kerosene lamps.

### Piles of Debris

Stepping inside the rude summer kitchen, he stepped over and around the piles upon piles of debris that filled four of the 10 rooms in the decaying house. This was home to Ed Gein, so he would not have noticed the cobwebs festooned from the ceiling or the mice peering from the rafters.

Judging from a tour of the house the reporter made Tuesday morning, Gein would have gone from the summer kitchen into the regular kitchen. At his left, as he moved through the door, was a chair with a bottom made of human skin. On a table was the top half of a human skull, turned over so that it formed a grisly bowl.

Near a window, partially covered by a curtain so old it was hanging in shreds, was an old-fashioned cook stove. Gein did not use it, though, except to store some of his accumulations —everything from used chewing gum saved in a neat but dusty collection to fine sets of hand tools.

### Mostly Pork and Beans

He apparently did his rudimentary cooking on top of the pot bellied stove in the living room. Next to it was an iron bedstead with an incredibly dirty mattress and coverings. Near the bed was the only object in the entire house that investigators found not covered by dust and dirt that had accumulated for months or perhaps years.

This was a table, covered with fresh newspapers, where Gein ate. Judging from the empty cans scattered on the floor, pork and beans and canned fruit formed the mainstays of his diet.

Next to the table was an old couch. On it was a violin with two strings, one broken; a small accordion, and a collection of books that included "Dorothy Dale, a Girl of Today" and "A Little Girl in Old Detroit."

Presumably, these children's books of a bygone day were not read but only saved. Gein saved literally everything he laid his hands on, judging from his house. His own reading tastes, presumably, were better reflected by the men's cheap magazines, some with lurid pictures, that were scattered about. One, showing an American soldier about to stab a Japanese, also armed with a long knife, was on the bed.

### Pieces of Skin Found

Some of the magazines were in boxes. Below them, investigators found pieces of human skin. Deputy Dave Sharkey of the Wood county sheriff's department said that these mementoes included a pair of macabre puttees made from the skin of the lower half of two human legs.

On the wall of the kitchen were pictures, including several pinups. Calendars, some of them from bygone years, helped hide the dirty wallpaper and the bare spots of plaster from which the wallpaper had been stripped.

It was in this shedlike wing of the Gein farm that the decapitated body of Mrs. Worden was found. The trailer (right), belonging to the Wood county sheriff's department, contains a portable generator used to supply electricity during the investigation of the house. The Gein home has no lights or telephone. —Journal Staff

# Lured to Graves by Moon—Farmer

Special to The Chicago American.

MADISON, Wis., Nov. 20—Edward Gein, hermit farmer who confessed butchering a woman neighbor, said last night he believes he robbed graves "by the light of a full moon."

The 51-year-old bachelor, who remained on his 190-acre farm near Plainfield after the deaths of his mother and brother, told Earl F. Kileen, district attorney, he had opened graves in at least two cemeteries. Ten skulls were found scattered around Gein's delapidated frame house, and he said all the skulls belonged to women.

Kileen said Gein has pointed out one grave in the Plainfield Cemetery from which he removed the head of a 60-year-old woman who died in 1949.

Kileen said Gein told him he began opening graves in the Plainfield area "about 1949 and quit it about three years ago."

Gein told the prosecutor he was "interested only in the bodies of women," Kileen said. He added:

"He said he opened the graves at night, removed the heads and other parts of the bodies, then refilled the graves.

"He said he always was in a daze while robbing the graves, but thought he had dug by the light of a full moon."

Kileen said Gein admitted he "always went to fresh graves after reading about burials of women in the papers." Kileen added:

"I am interested only in prosecuting this man for the murder of Mrs. Worden of Plainfield. The grave-robbing penalty is a term of one to three years. To press that charge would necessitate the opening of graves, and I want no part of that. Think how the poor relatives would feel."

Kileen said a woman neighbor who has known Gein all her life told him she "would not be surprised if one of the 10 skulls was his mother's, or that another was that of his brother."

The neighbor told the prosecutor that the mother, Augusta, a widow who died in 1945, ruled her sons with an iron hand. The elder brother, Henry, died in 1944, apparently after a heart attack that followed exertion at a brush fire, which Edward helped him extinguish. Henry was planning to marry at the time, Kileen said.

Kileen said other neighbors have told how Mrs. Gein frequently lectured her sons about the "dangers of meeting up with women who curl their hair or wear corsets."

Plainfield residents have described the Geins as very clannish people "who never attended church but often were heard mouthing references to God and the Bible."

This is a corner of the kitchen at the Ed Gein farm home near Plainfield. Deputy Sheriff Dave Sharkey, of Wood County, is looking at the many items which were scattered about the kitchen. Many of the knives owned by Gein were found in the drawer of the small table and in the old unused stove at the right.

Members of the State Crime Laboratory staff from Madison collected sacks filled with possible evidence from the Gein home. Here is James E. Halligan, a crime lab official, carrying out several paper bags with items collected from the littered home.

Tuesday, November 19, 1957 — THE MILWAUKEE JOURNAL

Gein talked with Sheriff Art Schley (left) as the slayer was led from the farm Monday after a visit to the place with law officers. Later, Gein was arraigned before Judge Boyd Clark (right). — United Press Telephoto

—Journal Staff by Fred L. Tonne
Gein covered his face with his gloved hands as authorities prepared to take him to his farm Monday.

# Woman Almost Married Him

PLAINFIELD, Wis., Nov. 20 (AP)—Edward Gein, bachelor recluse who has admitted butchering a Plainfield woman, was "good and kind and sweet" to the woman who said she almost married him, the Minneapolis Tribune reported in a copyrighted interview.

Adeline Watkins, 50, who lives with her mother in a small apartment here, said that during a 20-year romance with Gein he "was so nice about doing things I wanted to do, that sometimes I felt I was taking advantage of him."

## LAST DATE IN '55

A Tribune reporter quoted her as saying she had her last date with Gein Feb. 6, 1955. She said:

"That night he proposed to me. Not in so many words, but I knew what he meant."

Miss Watkins, described as a plain woman with graying bangs and horn-rimmed glasses, said:

"I turned him down, but not because there was anything wrong with him. It was something wrong with me. I guess I was afraid I wouldn't be able to live up to what he expected of me."

## POLITE MAN

The Tribune quoted Miss Watkins' widowed mother as saying Gein was a "sweet, polite man," and that she told him to have her daughter in from dates by 10 p. m. and "he never failed me once."

Miss Watkins, the story related, said she and Gein used to discuss books. She related:

"We never read the same ones, but we liked to talk about them anyway. Eddie liked books about lions and tigers and Africa and India. I never read that kind of books.

"I guess we discussed every murder we ever heard about. Eddie told how the murderer did wrong, what mistakes he had made. I thought it was interesting."

# Gein Case Reaches 'Crucial' Stage, Attorney Believes

A session at the Waushara county courthouse Tuesday, for the purpose of motions in the Edward Gein case, has promoted that case to a stage that attorney for the defense, William Belter, called "crucial."

Associate attorney for the defense, Dominic Frinzi, appealed to circuit court judge, Robert Gollmar, to dismiss the case on the grounds that the complaint issued by the late Earl Kileen at the time of the crime was defective. He cited the case of White vs. Simpson as precedent for the motion.

After calling an adjournment to give him time to study the matter, Gollmar returned to deny the motion.

Judge Gollmar stated that this was a unique issue, in so far as he could ascertain, the first time such a question had been raised in Wisconsin. He said that in view of these special circumstances he felt that it was proper for him to deny the motion.

The counsel for the defense will appeal his decision to the supreme court, he said.

Three other motions were brought before the court. The first requested dismissal on grounds of insufficient evidence.

The second asked the court to compel the state to furnish the defense with copies of any confessions or statements they possess, as well as allow them to examine any physical evidence they might have in their possession.

The third motion asked for supression of any physical evidence acquired in an unconstitutional manner.

Using the famous Miranda verdict as precedent this could include supression of any confessions or statements given at the time of the crime, officials said.

Judge Gollmar will hold these motions under advisement until a hearing set for 9:30 a.m., Wednesday, April 24, at the courthouse. At that time the court will hear testimony from both sides to determine whether the motions should be accepted or denied.

A number of witnesses had been subpoenaed for the Tuesday session, but they were dismissed because of lack of time. They will be recalled for the April 24 hearing.

Belter said that one of the witnesses, Captain Lloyd Schoespheoster, captain of Green Lake county traffic control, has been subpoenaed by both the defense and the state. Another witness will be Dr. Schubert, the phychiatrist from Central State, Waupun, who determined that Gein was capable of standing trial for the murder of Bernice Worden in 1957.

The April 24 hearing will be the first time that actual evidence and materials will be introduced into the court in the Gein case. It will at that time be the task of the court to determine what evidence could be submitted legally in case of a jury trial.

## Plainfield Sets Hunt For Eggs

The Plainfield Lion's club will hold their annual Easter egg hunt on Saturday, April 13.

Max Harrington, newly elected president of the group said that pre-school to second grade children will meet at the village park.

Children from third to sixth grade will meet for their egg hunt at the high school.

Both egg hunts will begin at 1 p.m.

## Services Set For Friday

On Friday, April 12, at 1 p.m., at the Wautoma Assembly of God, 640 South Water Street, a Union Good Friday service will be held. The theme for the service will be, "View of The Cross."

The Rev. Charles Starkweather of the Oxford Street United Methodist church will be speaking on, "The World's View of The Cross." The Rev. Lester Thiel of the Elm Street United Methodist church will speak upon, "The Believer's View of The Cross," and the host pastor, Rev. John Wibley of the Assembly of God, will speak on, "God's View of The Cross."

## Courthouse To be Closed

The Waushara county courthouse will be closed April 12, Good Friday, in the afternoon.

**MINISTERS ARE TOLD . . .**

# Judge Bunde Rules Gein Legally Insane

*January 6, 1958*

### Says 51-Year-Old Plainfield Killer Not Likely to See Liberty Again

(Pictures, Stories on Pages 13 and 20)

WISCONSIN RAPIDS (AP)—Slayer Edward Gein was back in the Central State Hospital for the Criminal Insane today for what could be the rest of his life.

Gein, the mutilation killer of two women and grave robber from Plainfield, was adjudged insane by Circuit Judge Herbert Bunde following a hearing here Monday.

Authorities searched Gein's cluttered living quarters and turned up an assortment of women's heads and objects made from human skin.

Waushara County investigators unearthed two Plainfield caskets to check Gein's story of plundering women's graves. They found both caskets empty.

"It is unlikely he ever will be at liberty again," Judge Bunde said in announcing the court's decision.

Judge Bunde said, "I must rely on the opinions of the experts who ... without equivocation declared Gein to be legally insane."

Testimony to Gein's insanity came during the hearing from Dr. Edward Schubert, superintendent of the hospital, and Dr. Milton Miller, who reported on a 60-day observation period of Gein.

**Charged With Slaying**

The 51-year-old bachelor specifically was charged with the Nov. 16 slaying of Mrs. Bernice Worden, a 58-year-old Plainfield widow who operated a hardware store. He later admitted slaying Mrs. Mary Hogan, 54, a Portage County tavern operator, in December, 1954.

Throughout the sanity hearing Gein remained silent and impassive. The proceedings were halted for two short periods in the afternoon because Gein had a slight stomach upset.

In testimony, Dr. Schubert said Gein was withdrawn, had insufficient ego, was immature, lived a rather expansive fantasy life centered about himself and had little faith in people. He also said that Gein was legally insane and incompetent to stand trial.

**Found Gein Schizophrenic**

Dr. Miller said he examined Gein twice and found Gein was "a long-standing schizophrenic." He said Gein's defects of judgment, inappropriate emotional responses and distorted view of reality led to the conclusion that he was insane.

**GEIN FOUND LEGALLY INSANE**

Edward Gein, 51-year-old Plainfield handyman, leaves Wisconsin Rapids Circuit court where Monday he was ruled legally insane and incompetent to stand trial. Gein, butcher-slayer of two women and who also looted the graves of a dozen other women, will return to the Wisconsin State Hospital for Criminally Insane. (AP Wirephoto)

Miller said that subsequent to the death of Gein's mother in 1945, the man led two lives. One consisted of reading books, Miller said, and carrying out fantasies with lurid undertones. He said the other was his odd behavior brought on by periods of extreme loneliness and the belief that no woman was available to him.

Atty. Gen. Stewart Honeck, who wanted Gein tried for first degree murder, called Dr. Edward M. Burns, assistant professor of psychiatry at the University of Wisconsin, as a witness for the state.

Burns said he did not feel that Gein was feeble minded or mentally deficient but was chronically mentally ill.

"I feel that he is conscious of the predicament that he is in and aware of the subsequent penalty," Dr. Burns said.

Dr. Burns was the only psychiatrist to testify that he thought Gein was legally sane and competent to stand trial.

The tale of Gein's admitted slayings and grave lootings unfolded after he was arrested for the Nov. 16 slaying of Mrs. Worden. Her body was found hanging in a shed at the rear of his home. He admitted butchering both women.

## Funeral Fund' For Gein Is Set By County Court

7-29-58

WAUTOMA, Wis. (UPI)—A $300 "funeral fund" has been set aside for butcher-ghoul Ed Gein, 51.

Waushara County Judge Boyd Clark Monday ruled that $300 from a homestead fund now held in guardianship for Gein be placed in the county treasury to pay his burial expenses.

Clark said the remainder of the $800 homestead fund be used to pay the state for its care of Gein, who is confined to the Central State Hospital at Waupun.

The homestead fund was relatively small because Gein's "house of horrors" farm home was burned a short time before a public auction. The fund represented only the sale of the small plot where the house stood.

Judge Clark said the $5,375.52 general guardianship fund, which came from the sale of all of Gein's property and possessions, should be distributed on a prorated basis between persons having filed claims on his estate and also to the state for its care of the bachelor farmer.

## Barred Door Swings Behind Shy Ghoul, Most Likely for the Last Time

1-17-58

By HARRY S. PEASE
Of The Journal Staff

Waupun, Wis.—Ed Gein—lunatic, murderer, ghoul—left the world the rest of us know at 8:02 p.m. Monday.

A khaki clad guard in the central state hospital for the criminally insane inserted a big brass key in the lock of a steel barred door and swung it back. Norman Topham, hospital supervisor, took Gein by the elbow and steered him briskly down a corridor and made a sharp turn to the right.

According to testimony of three psychiatrists at his sanity hearing, it is unlikely that Gein will pass through that barred door again while he lives. There could be little doubt that the world will be a better place for his absence.

Even the lawmen who brought him to the hospital from the Wood county courthouse in Wisconsin Rapids seemed eager to be rid of him.

Waushara county's sheriff, Arthur Schley, provided his own 1957 Plymouth for the chore. It was the nicest car Gein ever rode in.

—Journal Staff by Fred L. Tonne
Barred doors of the central state hospital for the criminally insane at Waupun opened for Ed Gein Monday. The Plainfield killer was admitted to the hospital, where he may spend the rest of his life, after he was found insane.

Tuesday, January 7, 1958
Milwaukee Journal

## Funds Okayed To Go on With Gein Case Quiz

4-8-58

MADISON (UP)—Funds to continue investigation of the case of slayer-ghoul Ed Gein were approved Monday by the State Emergency Board which left the amount of expenditures up to Atty. Gen. Stewart Honeck.

Earlier costs in the probe of the State Crime Laboratory were shared on a 50-50 basis by the state and counties involved. The counties dropped out after they got the information they needed but Honeck was ordered by Gov. Vernon Thomson to continue the investigation until it has been determined that no more murders were committed by Gein.

Crime Lab Director Charles Wilson said 295 man-hours of work remains to complete examination of human remains and other items in the case. Wilson estimated this would cost about $2,817.

Gein, who was committed for mental treatment, admitted murdering two women and robbing the graves of a number of other women.

At Wausau Monday, Deputy State Fire Marshal John Hassler reported his investigation of a fire that destroyed Gein's farm home near Plainfield is still underway.

Hassler said he has spent three full days at the farm, but has not been able to determine if the fire was arson or accident. He plans to go to the farm again this week to "check out several more leads."

# Gein Returned To Waupun for Indefinite Stay

Jan 8, 1958

What may well be the final chapter in the Ed Gein case was written Monday with a sanity hearing in the court of Judge Herbert Bunde at Wisconsin Rapids.

Gein was taken to Wisconsin Rapids early Monday morning by Sheriff Art Schley and deputies Arnold Fritz, Arthur Schwandt and "Buck" Batterman.

Judge Bunde heard testimony from three psychiatrists, who all agreed that he was medically insane, but only two of the three thought he was also legally insane and unable to stand trial.

On the findings of the three and other testimony, the judge ruled that the confessed slayer was legally insane and ordered him committed to central state hospital for the criminally insane at Waupun for an indeterminate term.

The judge commented, "I think it is adequate to say that he will never be at liberty again".

Shortly after 8 p.m. Monday night, Gein was delivered to the tsate hospital by county authorities

And unless something unforeseen occurs, there he will stay until the end of his life.

# Ed Gein Is Ruled Insane, Committed to State Hospital

1-17-58

## Judge Decides His Fate After Hearing Three Psychiatrists Give Views on Slayer

By RICHARD C. KIENITZ
Of The Journal Staff

Wisconsin Rapids, Wis.—After listening to day long testimony by three psychiatrists Monday, Circuit Judge Herbert A. Bunde declared that Ed Gein, confessed slayer and grave robber, was legally insane.

He ordered the 51 year old Plainfield handy man recommitted for an indeterminate term to central state hospital for the criminally insane at Waupun, where he has spent the last six weeks under observation.

"I think it is adequate to say that he will never be at liberty again," the judge commented as he concluded the sanity hearing he had called in order to obtain expert advice as to whether Gein was mentally competent to stand trial for first degree murder.

All the psychiatrists who testified agreed that Gein was medically insane. Two of the three also said that he was legally insane. The third declared that while he believed Gein was competent to stand trial, he believed that the man who robbed at least 12 graves was "close to the border" of legal insanity.

The judge indicated that this "borderline" view made his decision easier, although it was the toughest he ever had to make. He said the question of legal sanity was a "sore point" in the law and required further legislation.

The legal questions to be answered were whether Gein was capable of conferring with counsel and assisting in his own defense, and whether he could distinguish the difference between right and wrong.

### State Questioning Detailed

Atty. Gen. Stewart Honeck, who entered the case at the direction of Gov. Thomson, admitted that Gein was mentally ill, but his detailed cross-examination of the witnesses was directed toward establishing that Gein might be able to face trial.

"If this matter were an appeal," he said in a brief closing statement, "there would be credible evidence to sustain a finding in either direction. We have attempted to bring testimony that would be of assistance." He pointed out that it was a legal matter that the judge must decide.

Judge Bunde said, "In a matter of this kind, I must rely on the opinion of experts.... I have no illusions, delusions or hallucinations of the criticism of the court's decision no matter what it would be."

### Admits Slayings

Gein has been charged with first degree murder in the death of Mrs. Bernice Worden, 58. He admits shooting her in her Plainfield hardware store and butchering her body Nov. 16. He also admits slaying Mrs. Mary Hogan, 54, a Portage county tavern keeper, in 1954, as well as robbing graves to get parts of women's bodies with which he decorated his farm home near Plainfield.

Judge Bunde's decision means that he will be kept at the state hospital for life unless it is determined later that he is competent to stand trial.

However, Dr. Edward M. Burns, the Madison psychiatrist who was reluctant to say that Gein was legally insane, said there was a "very poor chance of the patient ever recovering." The other doctors agreed.

Burns, an assistant professor of clinical psychiatry at the University of Wisconsin, was called to testify by Honeck. He said that Gein was neither feeble minded nor mentally deficient, but mentally ill.

"I believe he knows that society disapproves of murder and that it is punishable," Burns said. "I believe he does have delusions that somehow or an other his role was predestined," he added later.

All three psychiatrists said that Gein was living in a dream world privately while acting normally publicly, and that he blamed other things and other people for his actions.

Dr. Edward L. Schubert, superintendent of the Waupun state mental hospital, said that most of Gein's fantasy or dream world had to do with the death of his mother in 1945 and a desire that his mother return to him.

### Put Faith in Will Power

"After her death," Schubert said, "he had ideas he could arouse the dead by an act of will power and tried to do this with his mother. He also tried to arouse some of the bodies he dug up by an act of will power."

Schubert explained that Gein underwent a week long series of tests at the hospital. These indicated that Gein was usually withdrawn; felt that his own self-sufficiency was questioned; blamed his actions on other people and other things; had illogical thought processes; had odd religious beliefs; had little trust in people; was aggressive beneath the surface, and was confused and had difficulty looking at situations realistically.

Schubert added that Gein had rather rigid moral concepts which he expected others to follow.

### Felt Compelled to Act

The patient, he said, attempted to make no distinction between right or wrong at the time of his crimes, but felt that he was merely doing "what was ordained to be done" by "some outside force—God," that impelled him.

His hospital staff agreed, Schubert said, that Gein was legally insane and has been mentally ill at least since the death of his mother, and probably would not recover.

William Belter, Gein's counsel, called a psychiatrist he had hired to testify. He was Dr. Milton Miller, assistant professor of psychiatry at the University of Wisconsin, who said he interrogated Gein for six hours.

Miller said some things about Gein were beyond his comprehension, but others "fit together like a puzzle."

### Lived Two Lives

After Gein's mother died, Dr. Miller said, he lived two lives—one apparently normal, and one of fantasy at home where he read books of Nazi atrocities and other lurid things.

"Subsequently he carried out these atrocities," Dr. Miller continued, stating that the grave robberies began in the loneliness that he felt when he felt that his neighbors had deserted him and other women, "available to him, at least," were not acceptable to him.

Gein might be able to stand trial on a personal traffic or hunting law violation, and that he might be able to testify accurately about a traffic accident he might witness, but not about a murder, where human emotions were concerned.

Twice Monday afternoon, the trial was interrupted when Gein became ill. The first time, a sickly look spread over his face and a 15 minute recess was called while he was taken to a washroom, where he vomited. Later, a 10 minute recess was called when he looked ill and said he wanted to go to the toilet.

During the noon recess, the three psychiatrists heard tape recordings of questioning of Gein at the state crime laboratory at Madison. This was at the request of Atty. Gen. Honeck, who also suggested that the judge hear them. The judge declined, stating that he might have to preside at a murder trial in the case and did not want to hear testimony beforehand.

When the hearing resumed, the psychiatrists reported that the recorded questions were not the type they would ask and tended to be suggestive. They said the answers had no effect on their opinions.

Honeck also had subpenaed three Plainfield area residents to testify on their impressions of Gein's outward behavior. However, he excused them late in the afternoon, saying that the testimony already heard had brought this out.

## Gein's Car Now Is Used as Side Show

*7-24-58*

PORTAGE, Wis. (UPI) — A Rockford, Ill., concession operator purchased a car which belonged to butcher-ghoul Ed Gein has turned it into a "gruesome" sideshow exhibit at 25 cents a look, a carnival operator confirmed Wednesday night.

Michael Stark, Mount Sterling, who operates the Gold Bond shows, said the car, an old Ford sedan, was purchased and is being shown at Wisconsin fairs by Sonny Gibbons, Rockford, Ill.

Stark said the car, which was sold at auction a few months ago for $150, was displayed as part of the Gold Bond show at the Outamie County fair for three days but was not being shown at the Columbia County fair which opened here Wednesday. Gold Bond is operating a show here.

### More Appearances

"I believe Gibbons took the car to a different fair at Slinger this week," Stark said. "But he's going to rejoin our show with the car for the Brown County Fair at De Pere next week, the Door County Fair at Sturgeon Bay the following week and the Sheboygan County Fair at Plymouth the week after that."

Stark said he thought Gibbons missed up the Portage County fair because "it's too close to the scene" of Gein's crimes and he was "afraid he might stir up the people in the area."

Although Stark said he hasn't seen the exhibit himself, he said he understands "it's quite a gruesome thing."

### Wax Figures

"It's the same car Gein used to carry bodies of his grave robberies and murders to his farm," Stark said. "Gibbons has it fixed up with wax figures inside the car, depicting the mutilated bodies and parts of bodies, all hacked up. He's even got blood streaming from the bodies."

Gein is the 51-year-old bachelor farmer who admitted murdering two women and robbing graves of others for parts which he kept in his rundown farm home near Plainfield. He was committed indefinitely to the State Hospital for the criminally insane at Waupun after admitting the crimes last November.

## One Year Ago Tomorrow, Gein Had His Last Baby-Sitting Job

*Sat, Nov. 15, 1958*

PLAINFIELD, Wis. (AP)—Just a year ago tomorrow, Ed Gein had his last baby-sitting job.

They weren't really babies any more, though. Les Hill's two children walked down the town road from their parents' crossroads store to visit their 51-year-old friend at his rickety old farmhouse, and invited him to supper.

Ed Gein came out of his woodshed and said he'd be ready as soon as he finished dressing his deer.

The children laughed at another of Ed's jokes. The deer season had opened that day, all right, but they knew there couldn't be a deer in the woodshed because Ed didn't go deer hunting

And they were right. It wasn't a deer. It was the butchered body of a middleaged businesswoman, Mrs. Bernice Worden, who had vanished that morning from her main street hardware store.

That was on Nov. 16, 1957. Mrs. Worden's body was discovered just after dark, by a deputy sheriff who walked into the woodshed looking for Gein. Later other officers and the State Crime Laboratory, sifting through the ghastly contents of the secluded farmhouse, found the remains of one other murdered woman and of 14 cadavers dug from neighborhood graves.

The Gein farm, seven miles from the village, has changed too. Nothing but fire blackened debris is left where the peeling old house stood. The flames that destroyed it last winter — when there was talk that outsiders might buy it and set it up as a bizarre museum—never were explained.

Today Ed Gein is occupied doing what authorities call "ordinary menial tasks" in a sick ward of Central State Hospital for the Criminal Insane. Dr Edward Schubert, superintendent of the institution, says that the reticent little bachelor whose career as part-time handyman and part-time ghoul covered nearly two decades, has made "a satisfactory adjustment."

He has not been out of the maximum security institution. He has had no visitors, except official callers. He has, says Dr. Schubert, "shown no change that would indicate he could be returned to court for possible reexamination and trial on the two first degree murder chages held against him in the slayings of Mrs. Worden and his other admitted victim, tavernkeeper Mary Hogan.

During the proceedings in which Gein was sent to Central State last year, Dist. Atty. Earl Killeen said that the action undoubtedly meant "that Ed Gein never will walk the streets of Plainfield again."

And that, said Circuit Judge Herbert A Bunde in his commitment comment, would be "the desirable conclusion."

Plainfield Village President Harold Collins said that "it seems to be the general feeling that the fire was no accident."

With the house gone and with it the basis for any such exploitation, the farm sold at auction for a few dollars an acre. Its new owner knocked down the remaining outbuildings and has begun planting the sandy marginal soil to small evergreen trees, a common crop for otherwise unproductive lands in this central Wisconsin area.

There is little discussion nowadays in Plainfield of the story that touched all the literate world with horror. They did not even open all the graves Ed Gein said he robbed. In a community of fewer than 700 persons there are things better not known.

And some things known too well already.

# Gein's Estate Is Being Sued

*3-10-58*

### Widower Files $5,000 Claim; 'House of Horror' to Be Opened

WAUTOMA — A farmer filed a $5,000 claim against the estate of Edward Gein today, claiming the confessed killer-ghoul "wantonly disturbed" his wife's grave.

The claim, received by Irene Drew, Waushara County register of probate, was made by Floyd Adams, Rt. 2, Wisconsin Rapids.

He is the widower of Mrs. Eleanor Adams, one of two women whose graves were opened by authorities during the Gein investigation and found to be empty. Later, her remains were found at Gein's ramshackle Plainfield farm house and positively identified.

Gein was committed to the Central State Hospital for the Criminal Insane at Waupun last January by Judge Herbert A. Bunde after the 51-year-old recluse was found insane by two psychiatrists. Gein had admitted killing and butchering two women and looting the graves of at least nine others.

Adams, who is represented by Attorney T. W. McLean of Nekoosa, accused Gein of trespassing on his wife's grave and removing her body. He also said that Gein's actions caused him "mental suffering ... in the amount of $5,000."

Adams moved to Wisconsin Rapids after his wife's death in Plainfield in 1951.

Ironically, Mrs. Adams' plot was adjacent to that of Gein's mother.

WAUTOMA — The dilapidated farm home of Edward Gein, which was boarded up last fall and a court order issued barring visitors from the premises, will be opened for inspection March 23.

The inspection will be exactly one week prior to the public auction which will be held Sunday afternoon, March 30. The inspection and auction were arranged by Harvey Polzin, Plainfield, guardian for Gein, who is under an indefinite commitment at the Central Wisconsin Hospital for the Criminally Insane at Waupun.

Gein had confessed killing Mrs. Bernice Worden, Plainfield businesswoman, and mutilating her body. He has been charged with her murder but medical authorities have advised Circuit Court that Gein is unable to stand trial. Gein has also admitted killing Mrs. Mary Hogan, Portage County tavern owner, and robbing several graves in Plainfield Cemetery.

### Property Listed

The property to be sold includes a farm in the Town of Plainfield just east of the Adams County line, certain household goods, and various pieces of farm machinery and equipment. Gein, who is unmarried, lived on the farm since coming to Waushara County as a youth.

The filthy, debris-laden house has become known the country over as the "house of horrors" because it allegedly contained, in addition to the mutilated body of Mrs. Worden, a number of other human skulls and parts of human anatomies.

Meanwhile, there were reports here that a son and daughter of Mrs. Worden were instituting suits against Gein and his guardian totaling $57,800. Although notices of claims have been filed against the guardian and answers made to the suits, none have been filed officially with the clerk of circuit court here.

### May File Suit

It was understood that Frank Worden, Plainfield, son of the dead woman, and his sister, Mrs. Miriam E. Walker, Nebraska, were to file one suit for $12,000 claiming wrongful death of their mother; another suit for $20,000 claiming pecuniary loss to themselves and loss of expectancy; a third suit for $800 for goods allegedly stolen by Gein prior to the murder, and $25,000 for injured feelings and mutilation of the body of Mrs. Worden.

In each suit Gein would be named as principal defendant and Polzin as a representative of the incarcerated man. It was understood that Polzin, through his attorney, has filed his answers to the suits. In general, the claims were denied although some of the denials were qualified.

# Gein Property Will Be Sold In Auction March 30

*3-5-58*

WAUTOMA — The personal property of confessed slayer-ghoul Edward Gein of Plainfield will be sold at a public auction at his farm March 30.

Harvey Polzin, general guardian of Gein's estate, has been authorized by Waushara County Judge Boyd Clark to sell property, 195 acres of real estate, Gein's home, barn, out buildings, furniture, car, truck, and personal effects.

The auction will be handled by Reedsburg Farm's Sale Service.

Arrangements will be made for persons interested in buying property to inspect the premises prior to the sale.

Gein was arrested last Nov. 16 after the disappearance of Mrs. Bernice Worden, Plainfield storekeeper. Her butchered body was found hanging in a shed on the Gein farm and subsequent investigation revealed several parts of human bodies in the Gein home. Gein later confessed the killing of Mrs. Worden and Mrs. Mary Hogan in 1954, but maintained he had obtained the other human remains through grave-robbings. He was found not mentally fit to stand trial and committed to a state mental hospital at Waupun.

# Gein Auction Due to Start At Noon Sunday

*3-29-58*

PLAINFIELD — What may be the final chapter in the "Gein case" will be written Sunday when a public auction is held on the farm of the man confined to Central State Hospital as an insane confessed murderer and ghoul.

With pleasant weather a good possibility, thousands of people are expected to gather at the rundown Town of Plainfield farm to witness the auction which will be conducted by a Reedsville Sales Company.

The auction will be less spectacular than first anticipated. The biggest attraction, the infamous "House of Horrors," was destroyed by fire 10 days ago. But sale of the sub-marginal farm land, a few pieces of rusty farm machinery, some personal effects and house furnishings will go on as scheduled.

The personal effects of Gein, confessed murdered of two women and robber of a dozen graves, and some of the household goods escaped the fire as they had been removed earlier by authorities. They will be returned to the farm for the auction.

Presumably, the sale will start as scheduled at noon, but there were reports actual selling may be delayed slightly as there will be fewer articles to sell than originally planned.

# Ed Gein's Farm Home Is Destroyed by Flames

3-20-58

PLAINFIELD — The House of Horrors is no more. Exactly four months and four days after the ramshackle building was steeped in infamy by Edward Gein, flames leveled it to the ground, destroying the filthy interior with its heaps of rubbish and other mementoes of a ghastly crime.

The conflagration was not unexpected; destruction of the house had been predicted freely during the investigation of the Gein case last fall. With arson a distinct possibility, Deputy State Fire Marshall John Hassler, Wausau, was called to the scene by Sheriff Arthur Schley. Intense heat of the charred ruins and poor weather conditions prevented an immediate probing of the debris. Hundreds of spectators gathered at the farm in the early forenoon as news spread that the "house was gone."

The eerie scene — it was snowing hard — was reminiscent of the macabre atmosphere there in November when visitors by the thousands crowded around the house in which the body of Mrs. Bernice Worden was found, mutilated and dressed out, animal-style.

The fire was noticed about 2 a.m. by Burt Carlson, Plainfield night marshal, who saw flames in the distant sky. He notified the Hancock police officer who drove toward the fire and found it was the Gein house. The Plainfield fire department was called, reaching the scene about 2:30.

The first fireman to arrive at the farm was the chief of the Plainfield department, Frank Worden, son of the woman Gein has admitted murdering.

Firemen reported that the house was just about leveled when they arrived. Early reports were that the fire apparently started at the west end of the building, but no one would venture a guess on its

## STATE IN CASE

MADISON (AP) — State Fire Marshall Rossiter said today his office had officially moved into an investigation of a fire that early today destroyed the home of Edward Gein near Plainfield.

"We had to assume that the fire was set," Rossiter said.

origin. Other small buildings in the farm yard were saved.

At Wautoma, William Belter, attorney for Harvey Polzin, guardian of Gein's property, said the scheduled sale of the Gein place "would go on."

A public auction is scheduled for March 30. The sale became the center of a local controversy earlier this week when several Plainfield clergymen protested holding the public sale on Palm Sunday. Ed Marolla, editor of the Plainfield Sun, who often has been considered a spokesman for the community, had said there was "rising public sentiment" against "commercializing Gein's crime" by holding a public auction.

The nation was shocked last November when it was revealed that Gein, a 51-year-old bachelor, kept a "house of horrors" at his farm, consisting of parts of human bodies.

Gein later confessed the butcher slaying of two Plainfield area women and stealing female bodies from a dozen area graves to add to his grisly collection.

He was charged with first degree murder and committed to Waupun State Hospital as criminally insane.

"Surprisingly enough, in view of the spectacular nature of the fire," Marolla said, "only a few people turned out to watch the flames." He said the only neighbor who showed up was Milton Johnson, who said he was awakened by a passing fire truck. He said he hadn't seen the fire before the truck went by.

### "Nothing Left of Interest"

MADISON (UP)—State Crime Lab Director Charles Wilson said today "there was nothing left of interest to us" in Ed Gein's "house of horrors" which was destroyed by fire early today.

"We completed our processing of material in the house several months ago and have all the evidence in the lab here for study," Wilson said.

Wilson said all the evidence in the lab hasn't been processed because of lack of funds. But Wilson said he will go before the State Emergency Board in a few weeks to request additional money.

The governor has approved a state investigation of the case because Waushara County, where Gein committed his crimes, could not afford the cost of a complete inquiry.

SMOLDERING RUINS OF ED GEIN FARM HOME

## Gein House Gone; Auction to Go On
*3-21-58*

### Five Outbuildings, 195 Acres of Land Will Be Sold by Bids on Palm Sunday

PLAINFIELD, Wis. (UP)—Deputy State Fire Marshal John Hassler today searched the charred ruins of killer-ghoul Ed Gein's "house of horrors" to determine whether Thursday's fire was set by a villager or accidentally.

Meanwhile, the guardian of the property and the 195 acres of land owned by the insane butcher of two women and robber of a dozen graves said there still will be an open house of the area Sunday and a public auction Palm Sunday.

But the pre-dawn fire, which quickly consumed the rambling two story building where authorities last November found the dressed out body of a woman and a grisly collection of human remains, dispelled all fears of Plainfield residents the place might become a "museum for the morbid."

**Auction Sacrilegious**

Left now for the public auction, which some villagers said hinted at being sacrilegious because of the church day it is falling on, are five sagging outbuildings and the land that has been uncultivated for some time. The total estate of Gein had been valued at $4,700 before the fire.

Hassler said after day-long probing through the ruins Thursday he couldn't decide immediately on the cause of the fire. He said a spark from a bonfire of rags and paper 75 feet from the house Wednesday could have started the blaze.

Ed Marolla, editor of the weekly Plainfield Sun, said the villagers had a belief the fire was set. He would not call it arson, however, and indicated it could have been a "righteous act."

"At least we know it won't be turned into a museum," he said. "Now some neighbor might buy the land. Farms are expanding here like everywhere else."

## Women Object, So Gein's Car Display Closed
*7-26-58*

SLINGER (AP)—A display of an auto which once belonged to ghoul-slayer Ed Gein was closed Friday for the duration of the Washington County Fair after a group of women objected to the side show.

Sheriff Alvin Schmidt said Bunny Gibbons, a concessionaire from Rockford, Ill., was cooperative in closing the display.

The car contains mannikins supposed to depict Gein and one of his female victims. Gibbons bought the car at the recent auction of the Gein estate.

Gein has been committed to the Central State Hospital for the Criminal Insane.

## Attorney General in Gein Case Says Appeal Can't Be Made
*3-7-58*

MADISON (AP)—Atty. Gen. Honeck said he did not believe an appeal could be made to the Wisconsin Supreme Court on a Circuit Court finding that Edward Gein of Plainfield, an admitted killer, was insane and not incompetent to stand trial.

Gein was committed to Central State Hospital for the Criminal Insane by Judge Herbert A. Bunde early in January after the 51-year-old recluse farmer had been found insane by two psychiatrists.

John J. Haka, district attorney of Portage County, in a letter to Honeck said that several citizens of the Plainfield and Bancroft area, where Gein lived, told him that they thought Gein was sane. He asked Honeck if the judge's decision could be appealed to the Supreme Court.

Honeck replied:

"The order in question was made before jeopardy, but it did not result in a final disposition of the case.

"The order merely holds that defendant Gein is not competent to stand trial at the present time. Upon his recovery, if that should occur, the defendant may still be brought to trial. In other words, the present order merely delays the trial and in that respect is similar to an order granting a continuance, which I do not believe would be appealable.

"In the second place an appeal would quite obviously be futile if the Supreme Court should determine that the order was appealable and it could consider the case on the merits.

"You will recall that the court's finding of fact was supported by the testimony of two qualified psychiatrists at the hearing. In addition it was made to appear that the opinion expressed by Dr. Edward Schubert, superintendent fo the Central State Hospital, was concurred in by a number of other psychiatrists who gave the matter careful consideration at a staff meeting at the institution.

"Under such circumstances the decision of the trial court will not be upset by an appeal. Indeed, if the weight of the evidence be determined by counting the witnesses, then the court's finding would appear to be supported by the preponderance of evidence.

Gein has admitted killing and butchering two women and looting the graves of several others

## Gein Farm Is Scene Of Tree Project
*5-21-58*

PLAINFIELD (AP)—The planting of 60,000 trees is under way on the 195-acre farm formerly owned by Edward Gein, admitted slayer and grave robber.

The trees are being planted as a reforestation project by William A. Welch, who operates a tree nursery at Red Granite.

Welch is doing the planting for Emden Schey and Allen Little, Sun Prairie real estate men who bought the farm at auction last March 30.

Gein, who was arrested last November after discovery of a murdered woman's body at his farmhouse, is confined to the Central State Hospital for the Criminal Insane at Waupun.

## Ed Gein's Farm to Be Auctioned
*3-2-58*

Wautoma, Wis.—(AP)—The farm which held the hidden horrors of madman Ed Gein will be sold at public auction Mar. 30, along with remaining personal property of the 51 year old murderer and grave robber.

The Waushara county judge, Boyd Clark, authorized the sale by Harvey Polzyn, who was appointed general guardian of the property after Gein was committed to central state hospital for the criminal insane earlier this year.

The auction list includes the 195 acre farm a few miles from Plainfield, the farm buildings where authorities found grisly remains of more than a dozen women last fall, an automobile and a few personal effects.

The sensational series of crimes came to light last November when Gein shot and killed Mrs. Bernice Worden, Plainfield businesswoman, and hung her mutilated body in his woodshed. He later admitted the similar killing of Mrs. Mary Hogan, a woman tavern operator, several years earlier, and the looting of a still undetermined number of graves.

## 20,000 Curious Visit Gein Farm

**By QUINCY DADISMAN**
*Sentinel Staff Writer*

PLAINFIELD, Wis., March 23 — An estimated 20,000 people drove out to killer-grave robber Ed Gein's farm Sunday afternoon.

But this reporter couldn't find one who was interested in actually buying the place.

Muddy roads leading to the 195-acre farm — appraised at $4,700 before a fire of suspected incendiary origin burned the "house of horrors" to the ground last Thursday — didn't deter the curious from driving past the place in steady streams all afternoon.

### TRAFFIC JAMS

Deputies from Waushara and Adams Counties had their hands full untangling traffic jams that probably wouldn't have developed had the weather not been perfect for a Sunday drive.

Sunday was "inspection day" at the Gein property. Next Sunday at an auction the land, several unpainted sheds and some rusty pieces of farm machinery will be sold for Gein's estate by Harvey Polzin, court-appointed guardian.

Gein, whose dismemberment of two women and stealing of body parts from 12 graves of women shocked the nation last November, is confined at the Central State Hospital for the Criminal Insane, Waupun.

### FEW INTERESTED

Farmers who got out of their autos Sunday saw possibilities in the land, uncultivated for many years. "A fellow could make a neat profit by planting trees, cucumbers, corn or potatoes," several said, pointing out, however, that they themselves aren't interested in buying.

So antiquated was the machinery that one farm youth said to his father:

"What are these things?"

The father confessed that he hadn't seen such equipment in 20 years.

## Gein Estate Split Settlement Reached

WISCONSIN RAPIDS, June 27 (Special) Out-of-court settlement of $64,190 in claims against the small estate of Ed Gein, Plainfield butcher-slayer and grave robber, was announced Friday by Thomas McLean of Nekoosa.

McLean is the attorney for Floyd Adams of Wisconsin Rapids, who claimed $5,000 from the estate after Gein admitted one of the dozen graves he robbed was that of Adams' wife, Eleanor.

McLean said division of the estate was agreed upon with Atty. James Murat of Stevens Point and William Belter, counsel for Gein, who now is in Central State Hospital for the Criminal Insane at Waupun.

Murat represents a son and daughter of Mrs. Bernice Worden, Plainfield storekeeper whose body was found in Gein's farm home last November.

Frank Worden, Plainfield, and his sister, Mrs. Miriam Walker, Lincoln, Neb., sought $57,800, while Belter claimed $1,390 was due him.

Gein's estate, after his property was auctioned, was listed at $5,000 in Waushara County Court, but McLean said it had been reduced to "less than $3,000" by administrative expenses and costs incurred for Gein's care at the hospital.

The amount claimants will receive was not announced.

## $66,700 in Claims Against Gein Estate

WAUTOMA, April 29 (AP) — Claims totaling $66,700 have been filed against the modest $5,000 estate of Edward Gein, admitted Plainfield slayer and grave robber who is confined to Central State Hospital for the Criminal Insane.

The deadline for filing such claims was passed Monday. A probate hearing set for Tuesday before Waushara County Judge Boyd Clark was postponed at the request of William Boelter, attorney for the Gein estate.

The Gein farm property brought $5,000 at public sale.

County Register in Probate Irene Drew said the biggest claim, amounting to $57,800, was filed by Frank E. Worden, Plainfield, and Mrs. Miriam E. Walker, Lincoln, Neb., children of Mrs. Bernice Worden, whom Gein admitted slaying last fall.

Floyd Adams, Rt. 2, Wisconsin Rapids, filed a $5,000 claim. Authorities say the grave of Adams' wife, Mrs. Eleanor Adams, was one of the several graves Gein admitted violating.

Waushara Country seeks $1,355 and Portage County $1,237, representing the costs of Gein's sanity hearings and the expense of maintaining guards at the Gein farmhouse.

Atty. Boelter, himself, filed a $1,390 claim.

## Gein 'Relics' To Be Buried

Madison, Wis—UPI—The state crime laboratory was authorized Friday by the board on government operation to spend $125 to dispose of the remains in the Ed Gein case.

Director Charles Wilson of the lab told the board the money would be used to acquire a cemetery lot to bury the remains of victims rather than to burn them in an incinerator because of requests from Bishop William P. O'Connor of the Madison archdiocese.

"I think this is the final wind-up of the Gein case," Wilson said.

The state crime laboratory had collected the remains at Gein's home near Plainfield when the bizarre episode became disclosed in Nov., 1957. Gein was committed to the Central State hospital for the criminally insane where he now polishes stones.

The gruesome remains found in Gein's "house of horrors" represented a collection of various parts of dead bodies which he acquired in robbing the graves of about a dozen or more women. The identities of the victims have never been learned.

The Gein case, which rates as one of Wisconsin's most shocking crimes, was uncovered when authorities found the butchered body of Mrs. Bernice Worden, 58, hanging in Gein's farm home.

## Bonfire Cited In Gein Blaze

### Was Building Ignited By Spark? Marshal Probes Ruins

Plainfield, Wis.—Deputy Fire Marshal John E. Hassler of Wausau said Thursday night that sparks from a rubbish fire could have caused the blaze which destroyed the farm home of slayer and grave robber Ed Gein.

Hassler visited the farm after it burned to the ground Thursday morning to determine whether the fire was accidental or the work of an arsonist.

He said he found hot coals buried in the two foot high pile of ashes left by Wednesday's bonfire, which was started by a crew assigned to dispose of trash at the farm in anticipation of an open house Sunday.

### Open House Still On

The fire was about 75 feet from the house, Hassler said that the fire was a large one, but that the flames did not travel along the ground.

Meanwhile, Harvey Polzin, guardian of the 195 acre Gein farm, said there still would be an open house there Sunday and a public auction on Palm Sunday.

But the predawn fire, which quickly consumed the rambling two story building where authorities last November found the body of a woman, dispelled the fears of Plainfield residents that the place might become a "museum for the morbid."

### Outbuildings Left

Left now for the public auction, which some villagers contended would be sacrilegious because of the church day on which it falls, are five sagging outbuildings and the land that has been uncultivated for some time. The total Gein estate had been valued at $4,700 before the fire.

Gein has been committed to central state hospital for the criminally insane at Waupun.

Flames destroyed the farm home of slayer and grave robber Ed Gein early Thursday. No one has lived in the frame house near Plainfield since Gein was arrested in November for the murder of Mrs. Bernice Worden. Gein has been committed to the central state hospital for the criminally insane. The ruins are shown above.
—Charles Webster

## 20,000 Jam Roads To See Gein's Farm

PLAINFIELD, Wis. (AP)—About 20,000 persons drove out to look over the burned out ruins of slayer-ghoul Ed Gein's farmhouse Sunday.

Gein, now in the Central State Hospital for the Criminal Insane, is the 51-year-old bachelor who butchered his two murder victims and robbed at least a dozen graves.

Deputies from Waushara and Adams counties were busy untangling traffic jams as the cars continued to roll into the area until sundown.

Sunday was inspection day at the farm, in preparation for an auction of the property next Sunday. The farmhouse burned to the ground early Tuesday. All that remains are several sheds and rusty pieces of farm equipment.

The entire property—195 acres of unworked land—was appraised at $4,700 before the fire destroyed the house.

Reporters said it was difficult to find any prospective buyers among the curious throngs who packed the muddy roads leading to the property.

Authorities said that some of the curiosity seekers came 70 miles to view the farm.

1958

### 2,000 View Auction; $3,883 Bid for Farm; Old Car Brings Surprising $760

*Journal Special Correspondence*

Plainfield, Wis. — All that slayer-ghoul Ed Gein owned was sold Sunday for little more than $5,000.

The money will be held in trust for the little bachelor handyman, who was committed last January to Central State hospital as criminally insane after he confessed two murders and several grave robberies.

Emden A. Schey, a Sun Prairie real estate and insurance broker, bid $3,883 for Gein's ramshackle, scrub pine and sandy soil farm and five weatherbeaten outbuildings. But the real surprise was $760 bid for Gein's 1949 maroon Ford car.

A representative of the buyers, who outbid 14 others for the car, would not comment on what the buyers — whom he identified as Koch Brothers of Rothschild—planned to do with it. The car was last used by Gein in November to haul the body of one of his murder victims, Mrs. Marie Worden, to his farm from her hardware store in Plainfield. He was arrested shortly after that.

[No one named Koch living in Rothschild is listed in the Wausau telephone directory, which includes Rothschild.]

A 1938 Chevrolet pickup truck, used by Gein to haul to the farm the body of Marie Hogan, a tavern keeper whom he murdered in 1954, was sold for $215. The buyer, Chet Scales, of Chet's Auto Wreckers, Highland (Iowa county), said he needed the truck to haul scrap iron and eight old wagon wheels he bought at the auction.

### 2,000 Attend Auction

Although only a few persons bid, a crowd of about 2,000 assembled at the farmstead west of here for the auction. It was scheduled to start at noon, but the cars started coming much earlier. The cars still were lined bumper to bumper along the narrow clay roads that intersect near the farm as the buyers were leaving after the sale was ended.

A flurry of excitement surged through the crowd when a mound was found about 200 feet into the woods behind the ruins of the house. Deputy sheriffs blocked off the area and said it would be investigated.

### Judge Must OK Sales

James and Harold Gavin of Reedsburg, who were the auctioneers, explained that all of the major purchases would have to be approved by County Judge Boyd Clark of Waushara county. It also was explained that Harvey Polzin, Plainfield, court appointed guardian of the estate, had paid this year's taxes on the property. The tax bill totaled $161, the Gavins said.

Walter Golla, Plainfield junk dealer, bought most of the miscellaneous items sold for approximately $171. His purchases included two plows, two plow shares, a drag, disk, mower, cultivator, wagon, rake, manure spreader and sleigh. The prices ranged from $2.50 for the plow shares to $35 for the manure spreader.

### Odds and Ends Sold

Also sold were the eight wagon wheels to Scales for $7; a pile of junk, $11; a pile of used lumber, $10; an old iron range, $15.50, a keg of nails, $7; keg of spikes, $6.50, and an old violin, $7.50.

The land was separated into three parcels for bidding purposes, but an over-all bid also was accepted. It will be up to Judge Clark to decide how the sale is to be made.

In the separate bidding, Schey bid $775 for the homestead site, outbuildings and 40 acres. There is no home on the farm. It was destroyed by fire Mar. 20 and officials theorized it could have been arson in protest to scheduling the auction on Palm Sunday.

A crowd of about 2,000 attended the auction sale Sunday at the Plainfield farm of Ed Gein, confessed slayer and grave robber. The site of the burned out homestead is in the right foreground. Emden A. Schey (lower), Sun Prairie real estate broker, was high bidder for the farm and outbuildings. The sale brought approximately $5,000.
—Journal Staff (top); United Press Telephoto

## All Ed Gein Owned Is Sold for $5,000

March 31, 1958

# Grisly Evidence From Plainfield Murder

After 5½ hours of questioning at the State Crime Laboratory here Tuesday, Edward Gein, 11, Plainfield butcher-slayer, was taken to the Madison City Jail for the night. In the picture at the left, Gein (right) is shown in handcuffs as he was escorted from the Crime Lab building by Deputy Sheriff Leon Murty, of Waushara County. The Crime Lab's truck arrived in Madison Tuesday with a load of items collected from

3-31-58

## 2,000 View Gein Farm at Auction

A crowd estimated at about 2,000 gathered at killer-ghoul Ed Gein's farm near Plainfield Sunday to watch the farm and Gein's other possessions auctioned off. A Sun Prairie man who bought the 195-acre farm said he planned to put it in trees. The crowd here is standing south of the burned out farmhouse in front of the row of outbuildings which escaped the fire. Some of Gein's antiquated farm machinery is at the left. (Story on Page 1.)

Howard Clark photo

# Publicity's Spotlight Enjoyed by Wautoma

## Sheriff Schley, Weary of Whole Gein Case, Slams Door on Interview at Jail

By ROBERT W. WELLS
Of The Journal Staff

Wautoma, Wis.—The glare of a national spotlight that has focused on this community and its still smaller neighbor, Plainfield, since the Ed Gein murder case began less than a week ago, has produced a mixed reaction among the townsfolk here.

Some are profoundly weary of the whole affair. Others, including the residents who have experienced for the first time the heady sensation of seeing themselves quoted in print, are rather enjoying it. To most of those not directly affected, the case has brought the not unpleasant feeling that they are bystanders at an event which the whole nation and parts of the rest of the world are watching.

### 30 Newsmen Here

More than 30 newsmen and photographers from 20 papers, magazines and news syndicates are in this county seat. Watching them roam the downtown streets in packs, keeping a wary eye on each other, townsfolk are tempted to believe that the number is even larger. Brock's motel, east of town, has been nearly full with the visitors all week, and local restaurants have also welcomed the increased business in a season when things are usually pretty slow in Wautoma.

Sheriff Art Schley, on the other hand, would doubtless be happy if he never saw another reporter. A newcomer to his job, faced with the most bizarre murder case in the state's history, Schley has a full time staff of exactly two deputies and an annual budget of a mere $11,500.

He and his wife and three daughters live in the front half of the county jail building. Gein is housed all by himself in the back. A couple of other prisoners were released promptly for good behavior when Gein arrived, and Schley is hoping he won't have to arrest anyone else until he gets Gein off his hands.

### Clamor for Interview

Thursday afternoon and well into the evening, from a dozen to more than two dozen newsmen were packed like sardines into the sheriff's small front reception room. They were clamoring for an interview with the prisoner, which his attorney, William Belter, had agreed to try to arrange.

For most of the afternoon, no one would tell the morose reporters even as simple a matter as where the sheriff was. The newsmen exchanged with each other their dark suspicions that Schley had spirited Gein away to point out in secret the burial places of some of the bones that are still missing. It finally developed, however, that the sheriff was in the jail basement helping repair the hot water pipes.

Belter couldn't reach Schley either for some time. Anyway, the defense attorney is also justice of the peace, so he was hearing game law violations.

But at last, a good eight hours after the newsmen had begun their vigil, Belter got Gein to agree to see six reporters, who would pool the information they got with the others.

### Six Are Chosen

The six chosen by Belter were from the three principal wire services, plus Time magazine, The Milwaukee Journal and the Oshkosh Daily Northwestern. The Chicago Tribune man put up a bitter beef at being excluded, but finally subsided. The six chosen went outside to the jail entrance with Belter, followed closely by a jostling mob of their colleagues, who hoped for a chance to eavesdrop.

Schley, it has been observed, is generally easy to get along with on a man to man basis. But crowds—especially crowds of reporters and photographers—seem to make him nervous. When he saw the mob of newsmen rushing around the jailhouse toward him, he immediately shouted that no more than three could go inside. This brought new cries of anguish and increased the confusion.

Belter, besieged on all sides, finally ruled that the Associated Press, the United Press and Time magazine would get the nod, which brought on a strong protest from International News Service. As the argument waxed heavy, Schley waxed wroth. He slammed the jail door, swore a few times and called the whole affair off. So the day's long wait was wasted.

### Cleaner Than Home

Of all the people most concerned with the case, perhaps the least inconvenienced so far is Gein. The little man, it is true, must spend his time in jail. But the Washara county jail, whatever its shortcomings, is far cleaner and less cluttered than his farm home. The food is better than the canned beans he used to warm on his pot bellied stove. And for the first time in Eddie Gein's life, people are paying attention to him.

A week ago there wasn't a person in the entire world who would have gone far out of his way to have a word with the little handy man with the twisted smile. But Thursday night, when the jail door clanged shut on the representatives of the nation's press and Schley stormed back into his living quarters, the cries of disappointment that went up over being unable to hear a few syllables from Gein's own lips were as heart rending as they were ironic.

## Thiensville Calls to Become Local

Telephone calls between Thiensville and the Milwaukee area will be on a local charge basis beginning Monday, the Wisconsin Telephone Co. announced Thursday.

Unlimited calls between Thiensville and a zone south of it will be allowed under the new system. The zone includes all Flagstone exchanges. Calls between Thiensville and the rest of the service area will be charged on a unit basis.

A spokesman for the telephone company said that the company hoped to install direct distance dialing for Thiensville by the spring of 1959. Until then, he said, residents will place their calls through the long distance operator but will be charged on a local call basis.

# Gein Quiz Ends Her Search for Mother

CARLINVILLE, Ill., Nov. 20 (AP)—A Wisconsin sheriff's recognition of a skull apparently was brought to a shocking end the search for a Carlinville woman for her mother.

Mrs. Christine Selvo, 37, who last saw her mother, Mrs. Mary Hogan, about 27 years ago in Carlinville, began to search again for her two years ago when she learned Mrs. Hogan was reported missing in Wisconsin.

One of the skulls has been identified by Wisconsin authorities as that of Mary Hogan.

Victor Selvo, husband of Christine, told a reporter today an administration of Mrs. Hogan's estate brought the first word in years to his wife of her mother's whereabouts in 1955.

Mrs. Hogan was a 54-year-old Portage County, Wis. divorcee who disappeared in December, 1954, from the rural tavern she operated at Bancroft, about six miles from the farm of Ed Gein.

Gein, a 51-year-old bachelor, is being held in connection with the slaying of a widow and the finding of 10 human skulls on his farm home near Plainfield, Wis.

# Gein, His Activities Seldom Mentioned

Gein said that he and another man stopped at a tavern in the town of Pine Grove in Portage county. It was operated by Mrs. Mary Hogan, 54.

Later that day, Gein confessed, he returned alone to the tavern, shot Mrs. Hogan and carried her body to his home. He kept some parts of it and burned or buried the rest. Her disappearance was investigated but no one suspected the mild mannered handyman from Plainfield who sometimes was hired as a baby sitter by his neighbors.

### Son Provided Tip

Gein's arrest 10 years ago was made on a tip from Mrs. Worden's son, Frank, a deputy sheriff who repaired farm equipment at his mother's hardware store in Plainfield. When he returned from hunting on the first day of deer season he found his mother missing. A cash register and delivery truck were gone. There was a trail of blood across the floor.

Worden recalled seeing Gein in the store earlier that week. The handyman had been looking at guns and talking about hunting. Worden mentioned his suspicions to Schley and Gein was arrested just after eating dinner at the home of a rural storekeeper.

Gein admitted having gone to Mrs. Worden's store on the morning of Nov. 16 and shooting her in the head. He used the truck to take her body to a nearby lovers' lane. Leaving it there, he walked two miles to his home, got his car, transferred the body to it and took it to his house.

He started dressing it out as a hunter would a deer, interrupting his task to put snow tires on his car and to play with the cash register — its printing tape intrigued him.

Reporters managed to dig out the macabre facts one by one. This piecemeal method, made necessary by attempts at secrecy, only succeeded in keeping Plainfield in the spotlight for a longer period of time.

The grudgingly unfolded chapters of Gein's life were spread across front pages in all parts of the country. They got three column headlines in Cambodia. A London newspaper flew in a reporter from Jamaica.

Schley, faced with unprecedented problems, feuded with the newsmen. They watched his every move with the sometimes accurate suspicion that he was hiding things from them.

Dozens of reporters waited for hours in the combination jail and sheriff's living quarters one day, certain that Schley had escaped their vigilance. It turned out that the sheriff had spent the afternoon in the basement, tinkering with the jail's heating plant.

After demands for an interview with Gein were finally taken all the way to the governor's office, Schley agreed to a pool arrangement where three reporters would talk to Gein and share their notes with the others. A long argument over which three would be selected was finally settled.

The man from The Milwaukee Journal and two others headed for the outside door to the jail, followed at a little distance by the other newsmen. The sheriff went inside and opened the door. As he did, a television cameraman leaped out of the shadows, fixing the sheriff in his lights and setting his camera whirring.

Startled, Schley slammed the door. The interview was canceled. None ever was held.

### Picture Unfolds

Still, the picture of Gein's life gradually emerged. A bachelor who had long since abandoned a boyhood dream of becoming a doctor, he was the son of a drunken, shiftless tannery worker who had moved his family to the Plainfield farm from La Crosse when Ed was 8 years old.

The father died in 1940. Gein's brother, Henry, died fighting a marsh fire in 1944. That left only Ed and his ailing mother on the lonely farm.

Mrs. Gein filled her son with the belief that morality in the region was low and that an "unworthy" woman had somehow been responsible for Henry's death. He nursed her through a series of strokes. When she died, he sealed off her favorite room as a sort of shrine.

Reporters saw the room. In a house filled with litter and dirt, it was immaculate. It was as if Gein, in his twisted imaginings, expected his mother to return at anytime.

### Began in 1945

Psychiatrists who examined Gein said that his mental illness began about 1945, shortly after his mother's death. They said he lived in a fantasy world, believing that he could restore his mother to life.

It was in this period when he began to steal into the cemetery, late at night, and dig up bodies of women about his mother's age. He learned of the burials by reading newspaper obituaries.

Gein say he prayed that he could resist this compulsion and that he stopped his grave robberies in 1952, five years before they were discovered. In December, 1954, he turned to murder.

Townspeople could hardly believe the details that came out about Gein's activities. The man was regarded as odd, but harmless.

Mrs. Donald Foster said she had once pointed to a closed door in Gein's home and asked him, as a joke, whether that was where he kept his shrunken heads. He gave her a funny look, she recalled.

Police from as far away as Chicago tried to tie Gein's activities to unsolved murder cases. It turned out that the only time he had been as far away from home as Milwaukee was during World War II, when he had gone there to be examined for the draft and been rejected.

Gein's attorney entered a plea of not guilty by reason of insanity in Mrs. Worden's death. Gein was committed to the central state hospital. The doors swung shut behind him Jan. 6, 1958, after a sanity hearing at Wisconsin Rapids.

In the weeks after Gein's arrest, throngs drove past his home and there was talk of converting it into a privately operated museum for the morbidly curious. To the satisfaction of most local residents, the house burned to the ground a few days before it was to be sold at auction.

A Sun Prairie real estate dealer bought the land and planted 60,000 pine trees. Gein's total estate amounted to $5,000, more than half of it in the land.

Gein's 1949 Ford sold for $760. It turned up as an attraction at the Washington county youth fair at Slinger. The sheriff ordered the exhibit closed.

Dr. Pyle said Gein's condition is evaluated each six months to determine whether he can stand trial. He sees no chance that he will ever be set free.

# Two Years Later, Trees Now Grow at 'House of Horrors' Site

11-17-59

PLAINFIELD (AP)—Just two years ago today, Wisconsin residents saw in their Sunday morning newspapers a brief but conspicuously displayed item about the finding of a Plainfield woman's body on a nearby farm.

It was almost a day later that they learned the reason for that strange contradiction: in its shocking first stages, the story of Ed Gein's long carnival of death was almost too ghastly to believe.

Horrified investigators found first the body of the Plainfield businesswoman, 58-year-old Mrs. Bernice Worden, who had been shot to death, spirited from her hardware store in broad daylight, then hung in the woodshed of the rambling old farmhouse where Gein lived alone and butchered his victim.

"I thought I was dressing out a deer," was one of the Gein comments reported by shocked authorities.

Searching through the debris of years at the farmstead where the shy, 51-year-old Gein frequently had been visited by neighbor children, state Crime Lab crews began to find grisly remnants of other bodies, all female. They identified one other murder victim of Gein's, a long-missing tavern keeper named Mrs. Mary Hogan.

The other remains came from a dozen or more graves which Gein finally admitted he had opened and despoiled.

Gein himself was committed to Central State Hospital as insane. His farm went up for public auction, but before plans to preserve the site of his ghoulish capering materialized, the building was destroyed by a mysterious fire. Since then the remaining buildings have been razed and the area planted to young trees by its new owner.

A. J. Little, Lake Delton, bid $2,400 for a 115 acre tract, and George Mulder, 3602 W. Ohio av., Milwaukee, bid $710 for a 40 acre tract across the road from the main farm.

Schey's over-all bid of $3,883 was higher by $25.

Claims totaling $6,537.15 have been filed in Waushara county court against Gein's estate and lawsuits totaling $57,800 have been started against him in circuit court as a result of his crimes.

### Adams Asks $5,000

Floyd Adams, route 2, Wisconsin Rapids, is asking $5,000 in damages because Gein removed the body of Adams' wife from her grave in the Plainfield cemetery.

Waushara county has filed a $1,355.15 claim for the expense of guarding Gein's property and conducting his hearing. The state public welfare department has entered a $182 claim for Gein's keep in the state hospital during January.

The lawsuits were filed in circuit court by Frank Worden, Plainfield, and Mrs. Miriam Walker, Lincoln, Neb., son and daughter of one of Gein's murder victims. They also plan to file a $57,800 claim in county court.

Gein has one heir, an elderly uncle who lives in Grantsburg.

**GEIN FARM, THEN AND NOW** 11-59

Just two years ago today, a newsman talked to a deputy sheriff in the driveway of the lonely Ed Gein farm near Plainfield while investigators from the State Crime Laboratory searched the dilapidated house for remnants of some 16 female bodies. Now (lower) only the driveway remains at the site of one of history's most grisly crimes, as brush and young trees reclaim the clearing where the house stood. Gein, who confessed to killing and grave-robbing, was committed as insane. (AP Wirephoto)

# Gein 'Relics' To Be Buried

Madison, Wis—UPI—The state crime laboratory was authorized Friday by the board on government operation to spend $125 to dispose of the remains in the Ed Gein case.

Director Charles Wilson of the lab told the board the money would be used to acquire a cemetery lot to bury the remains of victims rather than to burn them in an incinerator because of requests from Bishop William P. O'Connor of the Madison archdiocese.

"I think this is the final windup of the Gein case," Wilson said.

The state crime laboratory had collected the remains at Gein's home near Plainfield when the bizarre episode became disclosed in Nov., 1957. Gein was committed to the Central State hospital for the criminally insane where he now polishes stones.

The gruesome remains found in Gein's "house of horrors" represented a collection of various parts of dead bodies which he acquired in robbing the graves of about a dozen or more women. The identities of the victims have never been learned.

The Gein case, which rates as one of Wisconsin's most shocking crimes, was uncovered when authorities found the butchered body of Mrs. Bernice Worden, 58, hanging in Gein's farm home.

## Bill Knutson

## The end of a ghastly murder tale

"His hands shaking, the small, gray-haired man in the too-large, rumpled suit picked up the rifle and in a soft, slow voice, told how it fired the bullet that killed the woman he is accused of murdering."

Gein in 1957

So began the story I telephoned to The Post-Crescent from the Waushara County Courthouse Nov. 13, 1968.

A madman sat in the witness stand in the crammed, hushed courtroom.

A helpless, pitiful, bewildered madman named Ed Gein, whose ghastly killings and grave looting in and around his native Plainfield turned a nation's stomach.

Gein died quietly Thursday in a Madison mental hospital at the age of 77. He had been institutionalized since shortly after police found the decapitated and dressed-out body of Bernice Worden hanging by the heels in a woodshed behind his ramshackle house Nov. 16, 1957.

At the same time, police who searched Gein's house found parts of more than a dozen mutilated bodies of other women, along with death masks and other items made from female body parts.

I was a senior in high school when the Gein story struck.

I was a fledgling court reporter for this newspaper when, 11 years later, Gein was deemed fit to stand trial for the slaying of Worden, a widowed Plainfield hardware store owner.

I saved every word I wrote about the Gein trial, maybe because a reporter does that when he covers his first murder trial. More likely it was because it was Ed Gein on trial.

Saturday, July 28, 1984 The Post-Crescent, Appleton-Neenah-Menasha, Wis. A-2

## The end of Gein...

Continued from page 1

The newspapers that chronicle the trial look and smell old, I found when I located them in their dusty hiding place.

They reminded me of some things I had forgotten about the grisly yet captivating case; interesting and significant things that have gone unreported in this week's "last chapter" media coverage following Gein's death.

● While Gein, then a patient at the old Central State Hospital for the criminally insane, was anxious to stand trial and go free, he actually had confessed to killing Worden with a rifle from a rack in her store, and stealing her cash register.

He was convinced he was "chosen as an instrument of God in carrying out what fate had ordained should happen" to Worden, a psychiatrist quoted Gein as saying.

Gein also had confessed to killing Mary Hogan, a Bancroft (Portage County) tavern owner in December of 1954. He said he butchered her, as he had Worden.

Although police said a head found in Gein's house appeared to be Hogan's, and experts testified that Gein's fingerprint and a spent cartridge that came from a pistol found in his house were discovered in Hogan's blood-spattered tavern, Gein was never charged with the divorcee's death, which remains officially unsolved.

During Gein's trial, he testified he accidentally shot Worden as he was handling a jammed .22 caliber rifle in her store. He had no idea how her body wound up at his residence, he said as he looked at the pictures of her hanging in his woodshed.

● Gein was "brutally attacked" in his jail cell by Waushara County Sheriff Arthur Schley, who was a friend of Worden's and was distraught over her death.

Schley grabbed Gein and threw him against the cell wall about 2 a.m. Nov. 17, 1957, shortly after Gein was arrested. Three of Schley's deputies pulled the sheriff off Gein, who was a much smaller and older man.

In part because of the attack and authorities' use of what a judge called "third degree" methods of interrogation, Gein's confession to the Worden slaying was thrown out of court.

● Gein's grave pirating began as early as 1947, two years after his mother died, and lasted until 1952, according to a Madison psychiatrist who examined him. "With some regularity," the psychiatrist quoted Gein, freshly buried female bodies were removed from their graves and taken to Gein's home.

● Gein blamed the press for his failure to gain freedom. Had the press not "blown up" the case, he probably would have been released from the institution, he said. On the other hand, records at Central State Hospital indicated Gein "placed the ultimate blame for everything that occurred on an outside force, which is conceived by him to be God."

● During the trial, authorities feared that someone in the shocked and incensed farm community — particularly Mrs. Worden's son, Frank Worden Sr. — might try to harm Gein.

Police lodged Gein nights in the Winnebago County Jail in Oshkosh instead of in the Waushara County Jail in Wautoma.

●

There were threatening letters.

One day, before Gein entered the courtroom, a sheriff's deputy loudly announced, "If anybody's got any weapons, better get rid of them right away. If the sheriff catches you with them, you're in trouble."

Worden was searched before he took the witness stand, and Gein was moved to a courtroom doorway, within earshot but out of sight of the dead woman's son.

The judge was told that Worden "had tremendous hostility" toward Gein, and might not be able to control himself if he saw him in the courtroom.

Worden stayed calm on the stand.

● What ailed Gein?

A smorgasbord of mental maladies, according to a parade of psychiatrists at his court proceedings. He was a chronic schizophrenic. He had mixed and simple paranoid features. He was psychotic. He had sexual deviate symptoms.

"He was susceptible to suggestion," a doctor testified. "He tended to want to give you answers he felt would make you happy or satisfied."

Another psychiatrist described Gein as being "difficult and confusing to examine. There is no single word to characterize him."

● Gein was pictured at his trial as a lonely man following the death of his mother. He never married. His world was the home in which he was raised.

He could not relate to women. He was teased by other men in the community.

He read a great deal after his mother died. Subject matter included history, action stories and stories relating to Nazi atrocities and South Sea island ceremonies.

In the words of Judge Robert Gollmar, who sent Gein back to Central State Hospital in 1968 after finding him guilty of murdering Mrs. Worden, but then innocent by reason of insanity: Gein was "an unfortunate man" who "lived in some sort of a fantasy world..."

Gollmar recently wrote a book about the Gein case.

# Gein, His Activities Seldom Mentioned

Gein said that he and another man stopped at a tavern in the town of Pine Grove in Portage county. It was operated by Mrs. Mary Hogan, 54.

Later that day, Gein confessed, he returned alone to the tavern, shot Mrs. Hogan and carried her body to his home. He kept some parts of it and burned or buried the rest. Her disappearance was investigated but no one suspected the mild mannered handyman from Plainfield who sometimes was hired as a baby sitter by his neighbors.

### Son Provided Tip

Gein's arrest 10 years ago was made on a tip from Mrs. Worden's son, Frank, a deputy sheriff who repaired farm equipment at his mother's hardware store in Plainfield. When he returned from hunting on the first day of deer season he found his mother missing. A cash register and delivery truck were gone. There was a trail of blood across the floor.

Worden recalled seeing Gein in the store earlier that week. The handyman had been looking at guns and talking about hunting. Worden mentioned his suspicions to Schley and Gein was arrested just after eating dinner at the home of a rural storekeeper.

Gein admitted having gone to Mrs. Worden's store on the morning of Nov. 16 and shooting her in the head. He used the truck to take her body to a nearby lovers' lane. Leaving it there, he walked two miles to his home, got his car, transferred the body to it and took it to his house.

He started dressing it out as a hunter would a deer, interrupting his task to put snow tires on his car and to play with the cash register — its printing tape intrigued him.

Reporters managed to dig out the macabre facts one by one. This piecemeal method, made necessary by attempts at secrecy, only succeeded in keeping Plainfield in the spotlight for a longer period of time.

The grudgingly unfolded chapters of Gein's life were spread across front pages in all parts of the country. They got three column headlines in Cambodia. A London newspaper flew in a reporter from Jamaica.

Schley, faced with unprecedented problems, feuded with the newsmen. They watched his every move with the sometimes accurate suspicion that he was hiding things from them.

Dozens of reporters waited for hours in the combination jail and sheriff's living quarters one day, certain that Schley had escaped their vigilance. It turned out that the sheriff had spent the afternoon in the basement, tinkering with the jail's heating plant.

After demands for an interview with Gein were finally taken all the way to the governor's office, Schley agreed to a pool arrangement where three reporters would talk to Gein and share their notes with the others. A long argument over which three would be selected was finally settled.

The man from The Milwaukee Journal and two others headed for the outside door to the jail, followed at a little distance by the other newsmen. The sheriff went inside and opened the door. As he did, a television cameraman leaped out of the shadows, fixing the sheriff in his lights and setting his camera whirring.

Startled, Schley slammed the door. The interview was canceled. None ever was held.

### Picture Unfolds

Still, the picture of Gein's life gradually emerged. A bachelor who had long since abandoned a boyhood dream of becoming a doctor, he was the son of a drunken, shiftless tannery worker who had moved his family to the Plainfield farm from La Crosse when Ed was 8 years old.

The father died in 1940. Gein's brother, Henry, died fighting a marsh fire in 1944. That left only Ed and his ailing mother on the lonely farm.

Mrs. Gein filled her son with the belief that morality in the region was low and that an "unworthy" woman had somehow been responsible for Henry's death. He nursed her through a series of strokes. When she died, he sealed off her favorite room as a sort of shrine.

Reporters saw the room. In a house filled with litter and dirt, it was immaculate. It was as if Gein, in his twisted imaginings, expected his mother to return at anytime.

### Began in 1945

Psychiatrists who examined Gein said that his mental illness began about 1945, shortly after his mother's death. They said he lived in a fantasy world, believing that he could restore his mother to life.

It was in this period when he began to steal into the cemetery, late at night, and dig up bodies of women about his mother's age. He learned of the burials by reading newspaper obituaries.

Gein say he prayed that he could resist this compulsion and that he stopped his grave robberies in 1952, five years before they were discovered. In December, 1954, he turned to murder.

Townspeople could hardly believe the details that came out about Gein's activities. The man was regarded as odd, but harmless.

Mrs. Donald Foster said she had once pointed to a closed door in Gein's home and asked him, as a joke, whether that was where he kept his shrunken heads. He gave her a funny look, she recalled.

Police from as far away as Chicago tried to tie Gein's activities to unsolved murder cases. It turned out that the only time he had been as far away from home as Milwaukee was during World War II, when he had gone there to be examined for the draft and been rejected.

Gein's attorney entered a plea of not guilty by reason of insanity in Mrs. Worden's death. Gein was committed to the central state hospital. The doors swung shut behind him Jan. 6, 1958, after a sanity hearing at Wisconsin Rapids.

In the weeks after Gein's arrest, throngs drove past his home and there was talk of converting it into a privately operated museum for the morbidly curious. To the satisfaction of most local residents, the house burned to the ground a few days before it was to be sold at auction.

A Sun Prairie real estate dealer bought the land and planted 60,000 pine trees. Gein's total estate amounted to $5,000, more than half of it in the land.

Gein's 1949 Ford sold for $760. It turned up as an attraction at the Washington county youth fair at Slinger. The sheriff ordered the exhibit closed.

Dr. Pyle said Gein's condition is evaluated each six months to determine whether he can stand trial. He sees no chance that he will ever be set free.

..Continued

But, when legal fees are carried to the extreme that murder results in ridiculous reimbursements to those involved in the trials, it is time that the public stepped in and demanded a halt.

In England a labor government introduced socialized medicine because the party felt doctors were abusing their position of treating the nation's health. No one here is advocating socialized legal services, but this will be the logical result if the present system continues.

The legal profession has an abuse on its hands that it will have to cure itself......or the people will do it for them.

The bar association could certainly set ceilings for defense fees and court recording.....just as the state has set ceilings for counties to pay in holding the trials.

## Ed Gein Again

Ed Gein, Plainfield, who was committed to the state hospital for the criminal insane at Waupun 10 years ago, after discovery of mutilated bodies in his home, has been declared mentally competent to stand trial. We have the word of state psychiatrists that the man who enjoyed the quaint hobby of upholstering furniture with human skin taken from dead women, is now cured.

If he is tried, he will be charged with first degree murder of two women, but it will take the genius of a Clarence Darrow to make out a case with witnesses, lawyers and others who had anything to do with the case, now dead or missing.

Even Ed Gein has a right to his day in court, and he has a lot more going for him now than when he was arrested. His lawyer entered a plea of innocent because of insanity and he was put safely away.

The people of Plainfield will suffer again because of the revival of the case. They were in the international news spotlight for weeks. Nobody with a memory that goes back 10 years passes the Plainfield sign on Highway 51 without recalling the horrifying case. It has marked the community for life.

The only redeeming thing about bringing him into the spotlight again is that if the psychiatrists can cure Ed Gein there is definite hope for every person in mental institutions.

*Elkhorn Independent*

**The Waushara Argus**

that it may never revert to normal. After about 40 years of routine, of getting her husband off and getting him back at the same time every day and feeding him on schedule, of having him on hand only two days a week, she must be taught how to let her husband wiggle his way into the pattern and knock over a few sacred cows until he gets comfortable.

2 -- The personal confrontation. A second course should show the wife that a man and woman can't stare at each other 24 hours a day, seven days a week, then teach her ways to shoo him out of the house, preferably every day, preferably at the same time every day. Yard work, a basement workshop, a hobby might do it, but a regular civic duty or paying job that got him off the premises where he could see other people would be better. The wife could be taught how to find such jobs through her friends and

## Writer Objects to Funds Spent on Trial of Gein

The following letter to the editor appeared in the Milwaukee Journal. It is carried here because of its interest to residents of Waushara county.

'WHY TAXES GO UP'

To the Journal: Last year we paid taxes on several properties in our fair state. And every tax bill went up. We read with interest your article, "Aide Quits to Defend Gein."

It's true that every human being is innocent until proven guilty. Gein committed the most horrible crimes possible and all the evidence points to guilt. Yet one of our assistant district attorneys recently gave up his job to defend this man. But that's not the sad part of our woe.

It is Waushara county's business how they spend their taxpayers' money but it's every Wisconsinite's business how our state spend our money. Your article stated that the county will pay up to $10,000 to defend Gein and the state will pick up the tab for anything over $10,000. Well, we for two don't want our money spent like this.

Isn't it sad that one can commit such grotesque crimes and without a penny to his name have the state defend him and hand the bill to the taxpayers?

One should have a chance to be proven guilty or not guilty but it's simply beyond our comprehension why all this money is being wasted on a case where the facts and evidence say he is guilty, regardless if at the time the psychiatrists said he was insane. He was sane enough at the time to admit he had committed these crimes.

Mr. and Mrs. Roman Friess Route 4, Hartford, Wis.

BOOK Your '68 Weddings & Receptions

## *Insanity*
# Gein Case Illustrates Difficulties of Change

Gein   Frinzi

**Vagueness Feared**

Atty. William Belter, who represented Gein 10 years ago and was again assigned to the case, admitted that forgotten details could hamper the defense.

"A certain vagueness builds up after 10 years," he said. "And there were things I didn't put into my notes and records."

Belter said he believed that the time lapse would hurt the prosecution's case more. But Robert E. Sutton, an assistant attorney general and one of the prosecutors, said, "None of the competent evidence has been lost."

Thus far the prosecution has presented little evidence — a death certificate on autopsy report and testimony of the crime laboratory official that Gein confessed in 1957. The confessions have not been tested in court.

**Split Trial Possible**

Belter said that if an insanity plea was entered for Gein — no plea has been made yet — a split trial would be requested on the issues of guilt and insanity. The state then would have to prove Gein guilty before the insanity question would be considered by the court.

The split trial is a recent development in Wisconsin criminal law that has accompanied changes in the legal insanity test. The defense now has an option to use a broader insanity test than the long standing M'Naghten rule, considered restrictive by some lawyers and psychiatrists.

Frinzi said the Gein case could have been resolved in 1957, had the court then found him insane at the time of the crime. However, the law does not permit such a finding when a defendant is ruled mentally incompetent to stand trial.

The question remains: What will happen to Ed G

**"Function in Society"**

Schubret said that Gein was still mentally ill though much less severely so than in 1957 when admitted to central state hospital.

"I think he could function in society," Schubert said, "but he could not go back to Plainfield."

The doctor said Gein might adjust if he "could get lost in a large city, work every day and have interested people to provide a home life and recreation for him."

If Gein is acquitted by reason of insanity, the law requires that he be returned to central state hospital for an indefinite commitment.

**"Morally Ridiculous"**

Gein could later petition for his release. But the court would have to be shown that he was sane and that his illness would be unlikely to recur.

Schubert called the mandatory commitment "morally ridiculous."

"You find a person not responsible because of insanity, then you lock him up," he said.

He suggested that a hearing should be conducted after a trial to determine whether the acquitted defendant actually was dangerous, requiring commitment.

# LaFollet Expected in Wautoma for Gein Case Hearing

Feb 15 1968

The attorney general of the state, Bronson LaFollet, will come to Wautoma Wednesday, Feb. 21 in regard to the Edward Gein case, District Attorney Howard Dutcher told the county board Tuesday.

Dutcher explained that in 1957 the attorney general's office sequestered all evidence pertaining to the Gein case. Earl Kileen had requested assistance with the case and an attorney, Stewart Ponack, was appointed. He took all the evidence to Madison at that time.

As a result, Dutcher said, he does not have a file on Gein in Waushara county. LaFolette is expected to bring some of the necessary documents needed to proceed with the hearing to be held before Judge Andy Cotter of Marquette county in the Wautoma courthouse. Cotter was appointed after Judge Boyd Clark disqualified himself.

Dutcher said that two things must be proved at the hearing: has a crime been committed?; and is there reasonable cause to believe that the defendant committed the act?

Dutcher said that neither of these things may be easy to prove. This is due to a number of decisions that have been handed down by the supreme court in the ten ensuing years since the crime was committed. He said that there would be about eight counts that the defense could use against the state, beginning with the fact that law enforcers searched Gein's property without a search warrant, and that Gein was not informed of his rights to a defense counsel, etc. The Marinda law and other corrollary laws will be retroactive in the case, which may mean that much of the evidence will become inadmissable, he said.

If these two points are successfully proved at the hearing, the Gein case will then be transferred back to circuit court and there will be ten days for motions. Dutcher said there is no doubt in his mind that there will be a motion for a change of venue and that it will automatically be granted.

The case will probably be tried in Green Bay before Judge Gollmar. As set by the precedent of the McBrair trial, the Gein trial may be a bifurcated trial, meaning that two cases are tried before the same jury. The first question would be: "Did the defendant commit the crime?" and the second, "Was he insane or not insane at the time of committing the crime?"

# Decision Expected in Ma on Closing 3 Rural Scho

The chief business before the Wautoma school board at their meeting last week was to study various proposals concerning the possible closing of Spring Lake, Dakota and Mountain View schools.

Under one plan Spring Lake and Dakota schools would be closed, but Mountain View would remain open. A second plan would mean the closing of all three of the outlying schools, Mountain View included.

room and a special opportunity room.

Kindergarten children transported from the Dakota school occupy a fourth room. A main room upstairs is being used as a central library and two rooms in the basement formerly utilized as classrooms have been closed because of their unsuitability as teaching locations.

In addition next year the fifth grade class which has been taught at the county col-

facilities.

Hauer pointed out that the Wautoma school system is one of the few in the state left with seven separate elementary departments. Eight years ago, when most other school systems were being consolidated, the Wautoma area was able to continue outlying schools by updating buildings, but the board has become convinced that both economically and educationally a fully integrated district would prove most advantageous.

What would happen to the school buildings if Dakota and Spring Lake were closed? Hauer surmised that it might be possible to use them under Title I for something like migrant education in the fall. Over 200 temporary students each fall strain the local system until migrant families depart upon completion of the harvest. Hauer said he had been doing some checking to

## Are Murder Trials Now Too Expensive?

Feb 22 1968

A letter on this page objecting to the costs of defending persons involved in sensational murder trials probably represents the feeling of most taxpayers in the state.

District Attorney Howard Dutcher dwelt at length on the costs of defending James Mc Brair and Ed Gein in his appearance before the county board last week.

He said, among other things, that costs for a special defense counsel could run as high as $18,000 and court reporters could submit bills ranging from $6,000 to $12,000.

While Waushara county is reimbursed by the state for expenses above $10,000, the burden of paying the balance is nonetheless passed on to all taxpayers.......those living in Waushara county as well as in the rest of the state.

And, as a result of recent supreme court decisions, we are probably seeing just the beginning of many such cases which will be retried in the years to come.

Dutcher was explaining why the Waushara budget is showing a strain. But, while he may not have intended doing so, he was also pointing out a weakness in our present system of law.

No one objects to a persons being presumed innocent until proven guilty. No one objects to providing adequate legal counsel to those who do not have the funds to defend themselves.

But, when legal fees are carried to the extreme that murder results in ridiculous reimbursements to those involved in the trials, it is time that the public stepped in and demanded a halt.

In England a labor government introduced socialized medicine because the party felt doctors were abusing their position of treating the nation's health. No one here is advocating socialized legal services, but this will be the logical result if the present system continues.

The legal profession has an abuse on its hands that it will have to cure itself......or the people will do it for them.

The bar association could certainly set ceilings for defense fees and court recording.....just as the state has set ceilings for counties to pay in holding the trials.

## THE GOLDEN YEARS - - -

## What Husbands Need at 65 a Wife Retirement School

You are a husband who will be retiring soon.

You want no truck with any welfare or group programs that might advise you. You prefer even to sidestep any retirement counseling your employer may offer. You'll keep your affairs to yourself, thank you. You'll manage quite all right.

An industrial retirement expert, W. P. Grady, thinks you'll get by, but will drift into a dull and useless life as most retired husbands do. He says what you need is a retirement school for your wife.

"I learned this from a wife who foresaw her husband's retirement as a serious domestic problem," Grady explains. "She spent a year studying the factors involved and then guided her husband into the richest retirement life I've seen anywhere."

Out of this wife's exience, Grady has drawn a plan for what a retirement school for wives ought to teach. It follows:

1 -- The household. One course should teach the wife how to hold it in a state of suspended animation for about three months after the husband retires. And let her know that it may never revert to normal. After about 40 years of routine, of getting her husband off and getting him back at the same time every day and feeding him on schedule, of having him on hand only two days a week, she must be taught how to let her husband wiggle his way into the pattern and knock over a few sacred cows until he gets comfortable.

2 -- The personal confrontation. A second course should show the wife that a man and woman can't stare at each other 24 hours a day, seven days a week, then teach her ways to shoo him out of the house, preferably every day, preferably at the same time through the want ads and the news stories in the paper.

3 -- The tag-along. The wife should be taught how to cope with her husband when, after he has upset her tidy and tranquil household and balked at the outside jobs she finds for him, he slides into a role as "service attendant" to her. Good husbands, out of boredom, will do this, driving the wife everywhere, helping her do the marketing, joining her in conversations with neighbors, even going with her to call on her friends.

This can bore her to tears, but it can ruin him by sapping his spirit and making him look ridiculous. This course should teach the wife how to start an intensified social life, aimed directly at cultivating new daytime cronies for him -- men, of course. They would keep him from growing into a male housewife-type, give him activities of his own to do, give him something fresh and different in conversation to bring into the house.

4 -- The realities of life. This course should teach the wife exactly what her place in Social Security is, how to check her husband's retirement benefits, how to understand his life insurance and at least something about the investment of savings. It may be vital, at any time, for the wife of a retired man to know all this. But even without a tragedy, there is not one man in a hundred who can handle his retirement money matters alone as well as he can with a knowledgeable wife.

In this course, also, the wife should be taught how to choose a lawyer (young enough to outlive her, hungry enough to keep practicing and satisfied enough not to get into politics), how to sell her home if she ever must and where she would move if, when left alone, she

Tuesday, January 16, 1968

# State to Return Gein to Court

Journal Special Correspondence

**Wautoma, Wis.** — Ed Gein, committed to a mental institution 10 years ago after the discovery of mutilated bodies in his home, has been declared mentally competent to stand trial.

Waushara Dist. Atty. Howard Dutcher said he was notified by Circuit Judge Robert Gollmar Monday that a hearing would be held at 1 p.m. next Monday in circuit court.

Gollmar said E. F. Schubert, superintendent of the central state hospital at Waupun, no-

Ed Gein

tified him that the institution considered Gein to be sufficiently recovered to understand the proceedings against him and to aid in his defense.

Gein, now 61, was charged with murdering Mrs. Bernice Worden, a 58 year old widowed grandmother, in 1957 and Mrs. Mary Hogan, 54, in 1954. Authorities found Mrs. Worden's headless body, dressed out like a deer car-

cass, hanging from the heels in his kitchen. While searching the house they also found parts of bodies of 12 women he had taken from graves.

### Plea of Insanity

Gein was accused of having slain Mrs. Worden and Mrs. Hogan, a tavern operator. However, Gein's attorney, William M. Belter, Wautoma, entered a plea of not guilty by reason of insanity in Mrs. Worden's death and Gein was committed to the hospital after a sanity hearing at Wisconsin Rapids.

Dutcher said a new attorney would probably be named for Gein because Belter now is an assistant district attorney.

"It (the hospital's decision) hit us like a bombshell," Dutcher said. "Some of the docotrs who examined him have passed away. It will be hard to get witnesses back. Some of the evidence has disappeared."

Dutcher pointed out that the attorney general's office had most of the files because attorneys from that office had prosecuted the case. Dutcher said he was not familiar with all the details of the case because he was out of the state, serving in the navy at the time of the trials.

### Retest Often

Dr. Schubert said, "We retest and re-examine these patients periodically." He said doctors started "to take a closer look at him (Gein) about six months ago."

"He has expressed a desire to return and have his day in

*Turn to GEIN, page 3, col. 5*

## Gein

*From page 1*

court," Dr. Schubert said. "This is not unusual. In fact, it happens rather frequently."

In November, Dr. Richard Pyle, the hospital's clinical director, said he doubted that Gein ever would be set free. Dr. Schubert said Tuesday that Dr. Pyle did not mean that Gein would never be released from the hospital, only that it did not appear likely that he would be free in society.

Gein has been a model patient at the hospital, working in the lapidary section—cutting and cleaning stones.

"He seems content to live day by day," a spokesman said.

Dr. Schubert said Gollmar had the authority to order new mental tests for Gein by private doctors and then compare the reports with the hospital's judgment.

If the doctors appointed to make the new tests said Gein was unable to stand trial, Gollmar could accept their opinion and return Gein to central state hospital.

"The court must determine if an individual is ready to stand trial. We merely advise," Dr. Schubert added.

Dr. Schubert said he expected someone from the Waushara county sheriff's department to pick up Gein Monday morning and retain custody of him through the court proceedings. Usually, this would mean that Gein would be housed in the jail, but Dr. Schubert said sometimes the court allowed the prisoner to be housed in the hospital while the case was being heard.

## Letter Sent Journal on Gein Incident

*Jan 22 1958*

(Editor's note: In the past two weeks, at least two articles have appeared in The Milwaukee Journal relative to the trip made from Wisconsin Rapids to Waupun by Waushara County officers in which they returned Ed Gein to the State hospital. In reference to the letters, the following material was sent to The Journal this week from the Waushara County Sheriff's Office.)

"Mr. Wallace Lomoe,
Managing Editor
The Milwaukee Journal
Milwaukee, Wis.

Dear Sir:

Regarding the unfavorable publicity my department is receiving in the Editorial section of your newspaper, I wish to say that the facts as stated in your original news item are completely untrue. For example, in your column you stated, 'But Batterman kept the speedometer needle above 80 for most of the 95 mile trip'. I cannot understand how you arrived at this speed and thought you were so accurate in your statements when Mr. Batterman was not even driving the car.

In many instances I have noticed misconstrued and exaggerated facts in your paper, but I have disregarded them; however, this particular exaggeration directly concerns me and my department and I want the matter straightened out and the truth brought before your readers immediately. If you are unable to do this I will be very happy to give the true facts to the Milwaukee Sentinel and have them take care of it for me.

If your representative wishes to contact me regarding the facts of this incident, I will be very happy to sit in conference with him.

Very truly yours,
Arthur E. Schley
Sheriff, Waushara County

Oshkosh, Wis., Tuesday Evening, January 16, 1968

# Gein Competent, Able to Be Tried

## Alleged Plainfield Slayer

Ed Gein, the Plainfield farmer who 10 years and 10 days ago was committed to Central State Hospital in Waupun after a gruesome pair of murders, has been declared competent to stand trial.

This was announced late Monday by Waushara County District Atty. Howard Dutcher. Gein will be returned to Waushara County for a hearing scheduled for 1 p.m. next Monday at Wautoma.

Dutcher said he had been informed that Gein was competent to stand trial in a telephone call from Circuit Judge Robert Gollmar of Baraboo. Judge Gollmar was informed of Gein's competency by Dr. Edward F. Schubert, superintendent of Central State Hospital.

Dutcher said he had talked with Assistant Atty. General William Platz after the call from Judge Gollmar and will be reviewing the files on the Gein case prior to Monday's hearing.

Gein, who is now 61, was committed to the hospital on Jan. 6, 1958, by Judge Herbert A. Bunde. Judge Bunde made his ruling after testimony from psychiatrists from the hospital that Gein was not competent to stand trial.

The bizarre Gein murder case, which caused a nationwide sensation, began to unfold on Nov. 16, 1958, when Waushara County Sheriff Arthur Schley went to the Gein farmhouse to investigate the disappearance of Mrs. Bernice Worden, a Plainfield widow who operated a hardware store in Plainfield.

Inside the trash-littered Gein house, he found the dismembered body of Mrs. Worden hanging by the heels from the ceiling.

Authorities later found parts of 14 bodies in the house or buried nearby. Under questioning, Gein later admitted that one of the bodies was that of Mrs. Mary Hogan, a Bancroft tavern operator who disappeared Dec. 8, 1954. Gein admitted that he had also killed Mrs. Hogan, but said the other bodies had come from graves he robbed.

The authorities at first doubted Gein's story about the grave robberies, but changed their mind after opening two of the graves and finding the coffins empty.

Gein's attorney, William Belter of Plainfield, subsequently entered a plea of innocent by reason of insanity. Gein was ordered committed for tests at Central State Hospital on Nov. 22. A month later, the hospital psychiatrsits announced their finding that Gein was not mentally competent to stand trial.

At the time, Plainfield residents described Gein as a "not too bright" but harmless, mild-mannered man. He worked as a handyman and also did occasional baby-sitting.

The fixation which led to the murders and grave robberies was described by a psychiatrist at the court hearing as an attempt to "bring his mother back to life by an act of will." Gein reportedly had a strong emotional attachment for his mother, who he had lived with until her death 12 years earlier. Gein, a bachelor, lived alone after his mother's death.

Gein has reportedly been a model patient since he was committed. Officials at the Waupun institution reported last November that his health was good and that he worked daily in the hospital's occupational therapy division. He has been in charge of the hospital's lapidary section, cutting and cleaning stones.

"He seems content to live day by day," a hospital official had reported. "We've never had the least bit of trouble with him."

The "House of Horrors" where the bodies were found burned to the ground one night about four months later. There was a strong suspicion at the time that the fire was caused by an arsonist, since there had been widespread rumors around Plainfield that the Gein farmhouse would be burned.

Dutcher said the court would probably appoint an attorney to represent Gein. Belter is now an assistant district attorney and thus cannot represent Gein.

Waushara County Sheriff Virgil Batterman said he is not certain at this time when he will bring Gein back to Wautoma.

# 'Bifurcated' Trial Hinted for Ed Gein

1-17-68

WAUTOMA — Waushara County Dist. Atty. Howard Dutcher hinted today that Ed Gein, 61-year-old Plainfield farmer, may have a bifurcated (twin) trial.

Dutcher, who has had experience with bifurcated trials (one in which the defendant is adjudged guilty and sane or insane at two separate hearings before the same judge and jury) said today at a news conference here that "the Gein trial could be of the same nature."

Gein was committed to Central State Hospital in Waupun after he was declared incompetent to stand trial for murder.

The bizarre care gained national attention on Nov. 16, 1957, when law enforcement officers, in investigating the disappearance of a Plainfield widow, entered Gein's house and found the dismembered body of the woman hanging by the heels from the ceiling.

Later authorities found parts of 14 bodies in the house and buried nearby. Gein admitted he killed a Bancroft tavern operator and also that he had robbed the graves in the area.

The former farmer and handyman was declared competent to stand trial on Tuesday and will be returned to Waushara County for a hearing planned at 1 p.m. Monday at Wautoma.

Dutcher said that all the evidence on the Gein case are in the files of the attorney general's office this morning. However, the district attorney said that William Platz and Robert Sutton of the attorney general's office will be in Wautoma Monday to assist at the hearing. Platz helped the prosecution on the initial Gein case.

The hearing will be held before Judge Robert Gollmer, Baraboo, circuit judge for Sauk, Columbia and Waushara Counties.

Circuit Court Judge Herbert Bunde said it was likely that Gein would spend the remainder of his life at Central State Hospital. That was in 1958. However, Dr. Edward Schubert, Central State Hospital superintendent, said this week that the hospital recently found significant changes in the mental status of Gein which meet the criteria for his standing trial in Wisconsin.

Dutcher was prosecuting attorney for the state's first bifurcated trial involving James McBriar Jr., 27, Wautoma, former Plainfield resident who was found guilty of four counts of first degree murder on Aug. 21, 1967, in Sauk County Court before Judge Gollmer.

A jury of 10 men and two women also found McBrair sane in a separate hearing five days later. He was sentenced to serve four concurrent life terms in the state prison on Nov. 5.

McBrair was charged with murdering his estranged wife, father-in-law, his wife's stepsister and a babysitter on March 5, 1967, in a cottage on Fish Lake, three miles east of Wautoma.

# Woman Almost Married Him

PLAINFIELD, Wis., Nov. 20 (AP) — Edward Gein, bachelor recluse who has admitted butchering a Plainfield woman, was "good and kind and sweet" to the woman who said she almost married him, the Minneapolis Tribune reported in a copyrighted interview.

Adeline Watkins, 50, who lives with her mother in a small apartment here, said that during a 20-year romance with Gein he "was so nice about doing things I wanted to do, that sometimes I felt I was taking advantage of him."

**LAST DATE IN '55**

A Tribune reporter quoted her as saying she had her last date with Gein Feb. 6, 1955. She said:

"That night he proposed to me. Not in so many words, but I knew what he meant."

Miss Watkins, described as a plain woman with graying bangs and horn-rimmed glasses, said:

"I turned him down, but not because there was anything wrong with him. It was something wrong with me. I guess I was afraid I wouldn't be able to live up to what he expected of me."

**POLITE MAN**

The Tribune quoted Miss Watkins' widowed mother as saying Gein was a "sweet, polite man," and that she told him to have her daughter in from dates by 10 p.m. and "he never failed me once."

Miss Watkins, the story related, said she and Gein used to discuss books. She related:

"We never read the same ones, but we liked to talk about them anyway. Eddie liked books about lions and tigers and Africa and India. I never read that kind of books.

"I guess we discussed every murder we ever heard about. Eddie told how the murderer did wrong, what mistakes he had made. I thought it was interesting."

## Motion to Dismiss Gein Case Loses

**By QUINCY DADISMAN**
*Sentinel Staff Writer*

Wautoma, Wis. – A motion dismiss first degree murder theft charges against Ed in, 61, was turned down esday by Circuit Judge bert H. Gollmar, who then tered a preliminary hearing.

Gein, formerly of rural infield (Waushara county), accused in the Nov. 16, 57, death of Mrs. Bernice orden, 58, and in the theft a cash register from her rdware store in Plainfield. e discovery of her decapited body at Gein's home led a story of murder and ve robbery that became a ional sensation.

Waushara County Judge yd Clark later set the preinary hearing for 9 a.m. . 21.

**Back From Hospital**

Gein was returned Monday m the central state hospital Waupun, where he had en since Jan. 6, 1958. In a ter accompanying him, hosal authorities said that Gein s now mentally capable of operating with his attorney his defense.

His court appointed attor-, William Belter, Wauto- was given a co-defense nsel Tuesday when Milukee Atty. Dominic Frinzi s named to aid in the de-se.

Gollmar turned down a secution motion asking for ew mental examination af- Frinzi and Robert Sutton, assistant attorney general o is aiding District Atty. ward Dutcher, argued over etter.

The letter, which Gollmar id he did not want read in en court, was written by . Edward F. Schubert, surintendent of the central ate hospital.

### Argument Told

Sutton argued that Dr. Schubert's letter was contradictory to his testimony at the time of Gein's sanity hearing in 1958. The judge said that the intent of the law was to assure a speedy trial for a defendant and therefore rejected the motion for a new examination.

Gollmar said his ruling would not keep him from ordering another examination if it became apparent later that Gein was not competent to stand trial.

Frinzi then challenged the original complaint on the ground that it was signed on "information and belief" by then Dist. Atty. Earl F. Killeen. Frinzi argued unsuccessfully that Killeen has since died, and therefore the basis of his information and belief cannot be questioned.

### Reports Cited

Authorities reported in 1957 that they found the body of a woman "dressed out like a deer" hanging in a shack near Gein's farm home and also found human skulls, death masks and furniture made from human remains in the home.

News media and the public, however, never got a glimpse of the alleged handiwork at the time Gein was arrested.

Wilson confirmed that the items existed, but said they had since been disposed of. He said the lab could not continue to preserve the actual evidence indefinitely.

### Photographic Record

"It has been preserved photographically," he said.

Wilson said the evidence was disposed of by burial so that religious beliefs of the area's residents would not be offended.

"I made certain at the time nothing would be offensive to their faith," he said.

Wilson said the crime lab bought a cemetery plot to dispose of the remains because of possible objections to cremation.

He said the location of the plot was "classified," as were the records on the case.

*Milwaukee Sentinel*

ON WAY TO COURT...Ed Gein (left), flanked by Virgil Batterman, Waushara county sheriff, steps outside for his half block walk to the courthouse, June 27. Gein petitioned Circuit Court Judge Robert Gollmar to be released from Central State hospital, Waupun. Four psychiatrists testified Gein was still mentally ill, diagnosed as a schizophrenic. Gein was returned to Waupun where he has been since the 1957 first degree murder of Mrs. Bernice Worden, Plainfield.

## Gein Returns to Wautoma Jail

### Accused Murderer Appears Healthy, Smiles at Newsmen

WAUTOMA (AP) — Ed Gein, 61 arrived today in Wautoma after leaving Waupun State Hospital where he was admitted 10 years ago following the discovery of portions of the bodies of an estimated 14 women in his rural Plainfield home.

Gein, charged with slaying one of the women whose mutilated bodies were found in 1957, was in custody of Waushara County authorities pending a court hearing later in the day. He had been taken to Waupun before his murder trial could begin.

He appeared in good health, and weighed more than he did 10 years ago. He smiled and nodded to a group of about 15 newsmen waiting for his arrival.

He was discharged from the Waupun hospital after officials there announced he was mentally competent to stand trial.

Gein was charged with the slaying of Bernice Worden, a hardware store operator whose body was among those discovered during a search for the missing woman.

He also was accused of slaying one other woman. Officials said most of the bodies found at Gein's home had been dug from a cemetery over a period of several years.

*Appleton Post-Crescent Jan. 22, 1968*

January 23, 1968
Murder hearing

January 23, 1968

January 23, 1968
Ed walking out of
Wautoma jail for
this murder trial
hearing

**CROWD AWAITS GEIN HEARING**
Spectators nearly fill the courtroom of the Waushara County Courthouse as they await the start of the hearing in the Ed Gein murder and grave robbery case. The general mood of the crowd, which eventually overflowed the seating capacity of the courtroom, seemed to be curious rather than hostile.
—Northwestern photo

**GEIN WALKS TO COURTHOUSE**
Ed Gein, accompanied by a bevy of news cameramen, is shown as he enters the Waushara County Courthouse for his hearing before Circuit Judge Robert Gollmar Monday. Waushara County Sheriff Virgil Batterman is on Gein's right.

Jan. 1968 Oshkosh Northwestern

# Courtroom Jammed For Second Day of Gein Trial

The walls of the courtroom were lined with spectators and every seat was taken when the court convened for the second day of the Ed Gein trial Tuesday.

Dominic Frinzi of Milwaukee was appointed special counsel for the defense. He asked for a recess to be allowed to examine the warrant of arrest and original complaint made in 1957. The judge granted a ten minute recess.

As the ten minute recess stretched to a half hour the continued rumble of half-audible opinions and comments filled the air. A man read a newspaper. A girl pushed a pencil back and forth through her french twist. Someone opened a door at last as the atmosphere grew more oppressive.

Gein sat for the most part like a wax statue, unmoving, only the back of his head visible to the spectators. He displayed no sign of restveness, but he spoke with apparant animation to Sheriff Virgil Batterman when he was within range.

When the recess ended Frinzi asked for dismissal of both counts filed against Gein in 1957, robbery and murder, on the grounds that the complainant, Earl Kileen, was now deceased and that the warrant and complaint did not meet the minimal requirements under the law.

Judge Robert Gollmar ruled in favor of the prosecution's arguments and refused dismissal.

The attorneys for the defense then requested a preliminary hearing in the local court. Judge Gollmar granted the request remanding the case to Judge Boyd Clark. Gein was ordered into the custody of Sheriff Virgil Batterman without bond.

The preliminary hearing will be Wednesday, Feb. 21, at 9 a.m.

Vigourously chewing gum, his eyes mostly on the floor ahead of him, Gein was led from the court house.

A woman leaning against a wall of a corridor stared at him wide-eyed as he passed then shuddered.

Chief Deputy Don Losey said Gein would not be kept in the Waushara county jail but would be held at Winnebago.

On Monday a swarm of reporters converged on Gein as he was led from the Waushara county jail by officers to the Wautoma courthouse where he was scheduled to stand trial for the slaying of Bernice Worden in 1957.

Now, at 61, a small man with the bent shoulders of a laborer, silver haired, he blinked and winced at the flashbulbs and once half lifted his hand as if to fend off the human press, dangling cords and movie cameras.. all the paraphernalia seeking to record his every nuance.

The courtroom was packed with spectators but strangely hushed. As the court commenced there was no sound but the gurgle of water in one of the steam radiators and the quiet civilized voices of the judge and counselors.

Gein asked to be represented by Wautoma attorney William Belter who had represented him at a hearing before Judge Bunde in 1957.

District Attorney Howard Dutcher raised the question of the legality of representation by Attorney Belter, based partly on the fact that Belter was now assistant district attorney and partly on a previously ruling in regard to counselors taking on cases with which they have been connected before.

Robert Sutton, the associate representative for the state, spoke at length on the fact that Gein might later demand a retrial if the complete legality of Belter's being his counsel were not established.

Judge Gollmar said that as the ruling was written it would not be illegal for Belter to be counsel for Gein. He said further that he defined his own obligation as seeing that the defendant received the best possible counsel available.

Belter then rendered his resignation as assistant district attorney and accepted the appointment as Gein's counsel.

Regarding the question of whether Gein is mentally competent to stand trial at this time, Sutton asked that independent phychiatrists be brought into examine him to settle the question objectively before the trial.

Judge Gollmar did not rule out this possibility but suggested that the court for the time being accept the judgement of the staff at the Central State hospital that Gein is competent to stand trial.

Belter requested a preminary hearing and Judge Gollmar adjourned the court until the following day to allow Gein some time to counsel with his defense.

ATTORNEY FOR THE DEFENSE - William Belter resigned his position as assistant district attorney of Waushara county, Monday, so he could act as defense counsel for Edward Gein. Belter had previously represented Gein when he was brought into court in 1957 for the slaying of Bernice Worden.

FLANKED BY SHERIFF VIRGIL BATTERMAN and Deputy Richard Hotchkiss, with Deputy Chester Wegenke behind him, Gein returns to his home county to face charges of robbery and murder.

January 1968  Wautoma Argus

Thursday, November 14, 1968 — THE MILWAUKEE JOURNAL

## Ed Gein Guilty of Murder

By JOHN G. SHAVER
of The Journal Staff

Wautoma, Wis. – Circuit Judge Robert H. Gollmar Thursday found Ed Gein, 62, guilty of first degree murder in the slaying and mutilation of a Plainfield woman in 1957.

Gollmar rejected Gein's contention that he accidentally shot Mrs. Bernice Worden, 58, in her hardware store Nov. 16, 1957, while he was examining a .22 caliber rifle off a display rack.

A second trial opened Thursday before Gollmar on the question of Gein's sanity at the time of Mrs. Worden's death. The defense had requested a so-called bifurcated trial in which guilt is first determined, then the question of sanity.

Gollmar noted in his ruling Thursday that Gein had long been familiar with guns, probably was an expert marksman and "had the skill to place one bullet in her head."

In his closing argument Wednesday, Defense Atty. Dominic H. Frinzi of Milwaukee had made much of the fact that Gein had placed only one cartridge in the rifle while he looked at it in the store.

**Wanted Antifreeze**

Frinzi said that if Gein had intended to kill Mrs. Worden he would have placed more bullets in the rifle. Gein testified Tuesday that he had gone to the store to buy antifreeze and then asked Mrs. Worden if he could look at one of her rifles.

He testified that he found one or two cartridges in his pocket, left over from squirrel hunting the day before. After inserting one of the cartridges in the rifle, Gein said the gun jammed, then somehow discharged as he attempted to eject the shell.

Special prosecutor Robert E. Sutton, in his closing argument, maintained that Gein had fabricated the story.

**Behavior Analyzed**

The judge said that he found significant Gein's behavior immediately after the shooting.

"He did not check to see if she was dead or alive," Gollmar said. "He did not do what most people would have done if the shooting were accidental — run out in the street and seek the immediate aid of a doctor."

Instead, Gollmar said, Gein dragged the body to the store's service truck, later transferred it to his own car and took it to his home. Gein testified Tuesday that he "blacked out" and could not remember what happened after Mrs. Worden was shot.

Gein in 1957 confessed to killing Mrs. Worden and Mrs. Mary Hogan, 54, the tavern operator. The confession had been ruled inadmissible by Gollmar. Gein, who has not been charged with Mrs. Hogan's death, denied killing the woman in testimony Tuesday.

**Hardened Expression**

If Gein is found to have been insane at the time of the slaying, he would be acquitted of murder because of his mental condition and automatically committed to central state hospital, Waupun, until the court believes he is sane and would be unlikely to commit a crime.

Gein, in whose farm home Mrs. Worden's headless and mutilated body was found, spent the last 10 years in central state hospital because his mental condition made him unable to stand trial.

Throughout the final arguments Wednesday, Gein sat with his arms folded and his mouth drawn tight — his facial expression more hardened than in earlier portions of the trial.

Sutton relied in his argument on the testimony of a psychiatrist and psychologist that Gein unconsciously forgot unpleasant events in his life, a condition known as hysterical reaction.

**Lesser Charge Suggested**

Psychiatrist William Crowley and psychologist John D. Liccione said it would not be inconsistent with a hysterical reaction for Gein to have believed that he accidentally killed Mrs. Worden.

They said Gein was a schizophrenic with a history of hysterical reaction in which he forgot or distorted distasteful things in order to live with himself.

Crowley, clinical director of the Milwaukee county north division mental health center, and Liccione, the center's chief psychologist, were called as prosecution witnesses.

Asked by the judge whether Gein might have committed any lesser offense instead of first degree murder, Frinzi suggested homicide by reckless conduct or second degree murder. Gollmar is hearing the case without a jury.

In another development Wednesday, Sutton was unsuccessful in attempting to prove that Gein killed a Pine Grove woman tavern operator in 1954. Gollmar heard the testimony but refused to admit it as evidence.

Sutton called six investigators to testify Wednesday. Their testimony showed that a .32 caliber cartridge found in Mrs. Hogan's tavern in 1954 was fired from a German automatic pistol recovered from Gein's home in 1957.

Herbert Wansersky, 48, a Stevens Point papermill worker and former Portage county sheriff, testified that he found a head in Gein's home in 1957 that resembled that of Mrs. Hogan.

Frinzi repeatedly objected to introduction of the Hogan case as irrelevant to the Worden death. He accused Sutton of making a "grandstand play."

In refusing to admit the testimony, Gollmar said: "The court cannot feel there is sufficient proof here of a connecting link to a similar crime." He said there was no evidence to show that Gein intended to kill Mrs. Hogan.

Ed Gein

Dec - 1981

# Judge Gollmar thinks maybe Ed Gein wasn't so crazy . . .

**JOHN COMBELLICK**
*Northwestern staff writer*

On Nov. 14, 1968, Judge Robert H. Gollmar, acting as judge and jury, declared Edward Gein, the ghoulish Plainfield handyman, to be legally insane, and he ordered Gein to be recommitted to Central State Hospital.

But Gollmar, in his new book on the sensational Gein murder case, spends a lot of time building evidence that Gein wasn't so crazy after all.

Gollmar is currently on a tour of Wisconsin cities to promote his book. He was in Oshkosh Wednesday for an autograph-signing session at Robbins Restaurant, 1810 Omro Road.

Gollmar's book, despite the fact that it has had virtually no exposure outside of Wisconsin, appears to be a commercial success. Gollmar said the first printing of 5,000 copies has been virtually sold out, only a month after it came off the presses. A second printing by the publisher, Charles Hallberg & Co. of Delevan, is scheduled to begin Monday.

Gollmar wasn't involved in the original Gein murder case in November, 1957. He entered the Gein affair in 1968, when psychiatrists at Central State Hospital ruled Gein was now mentally competent to stand trial, and Gein was temporarily released from the Waupun state institution.

Gollmar     Gein

**Review, interview on Page 5**

I got to know Gollmar in 1968, too. I covered the Gein trial, and all of the preliminary hearings preceding the trial at the Waushara County Courthouse in Wautoma.

Gollmar, in his book, repeatedly cites evidence that Gein has a considerable amount of craftiness, and is fairly intelligent.

Gein, who is now 75, is presently an inmate at Mendota Mental Health Institute.

Gollmar notes that when Gein was arrested as a suspect in the murder of Bernice Worden of Plainfield in 1957, Gein readily acknowledged, as the investigation unfolded, his grave-robbing exploits and his practice of fashioning ghoulish and bizarre artifacts from parts of the bodies of his human "trophies."

But Gein refused to admit to any murders — at least that he had committed any murders when he was rational enough to know what he was doing.

Gein eventually confessed the murder of Mrs. Worden to a state crime laboratory investigator, Joseph Wilimovsky. But Gollmar, because of testimony by deputies who were present — that Gein had been violently manhandled during the November 1957 interrogation by Waushara County sheriff at that time, Arthur Schley — ruled that the Gein confession couldn't be entered as evidence in the 1968 trial.

Schley, who might have been subpoenaed to testify at the trial, died of a heart attack shortly before the trial.

The most damning evidence Gollmar submits that mild-mannered Ed Gein was also a cold-hearted killer is the circumstances that suggest that Gein also murdered his brother.

Gollmar thinks there is persuasive evidence that Gein murdered at least seven people — Mrs. Worden; his brother; Bancroft tavernkeeper Mary Hogan; two teenage girls from La Crosse and Jefferson who disappeared, and a man named Richard Travis and a friend of Travis who disappeared after they visited an Adams County bar.

Gollmar says, in a quote from a tape-recorded conversation he had with a Central State Hospital psychiatrist after Gollmar sent Gein back to the hospital, "Gein killed Mary Hogan and he admitted it. I am thoroughly convinced Gein also killed numerous other people. I believe that he killed his brother, whose death was never investigated, and who died mysteriously in a marsh fire. I think Gein did that because he was motivated, in part, by his desire for money. This was never stressed, but Mary Hogan had $1,500 that disappeared. There was $182 in the Worden cash register. And there was the matter of Dick Travis and his friend who disappeared mysteriously after flashing a large roll of bills in a local tavern frequented by Gein. All of these incidents indicate to me 'murder for money.'"

In an article on the 1968 trial which was intended to give some of the atmosphere of the courtroom and the trial, I noted that by the time of the trial, the community's attitude toward the trial and Gein seemed to have changed from hostility to moderate curiousity. I said, "The diminishing of the hostility toward Gein can be attributed partly to the passage of time and partly to the change in Gein himself. After 11 years, Gein just looks harmless and kind of grandfatherly."

I also described Gollmar and his handling of the frequent jibes exchanged by defense attorney Dominic Frinzi and state prosecutor Robert Sutton. I said, "Gollmar, a white-haired jurist from Baraboo with apparently indefatigable good humor, only chuckles at the sallies between Frinzi and Sutton. When he feels they are getting too far off the subject, he chides them to get back to the business at hand."

As a literary effort, the Gollmar book could use some work. There are incidents of conversations being described without adequate explanation of their significance, events and interviews being recounted without saying in which year they took place, and people interjecting comments in

# 'Bifurcated' Trial Hinted for Ed Gein

1-17-68

WAUTOMA — Waushara County Dist. Atty. Howard Dutcher hinted today that Ed Gein, 61-year-old Plainfield farmer, may have a bifurcated (twin) trial.

Dutcher, who has had experience with bifurcated trials (one in which the defendant is adjudged guilty and sane or insane at two separate hearings before the same judge and jury) said today at a news conference here that "the Gein trial could be of the same nature."

Gein was committed to Central State Hospital in Waupun after he was declared incompetent to stand trial for murder.

The bizarre care gained national attention on Nov. 16, 1957, when law enforcement officers, in investigating the disappearance of a Plainfield widow, entered Gein's house and found the dismembered body of the woman hanging by the heels from the ceiling.

Later authorities found parts of 14 bodies in the house and buried nearby. Gein admitted he killed a Bancroft tavern operator and also that he had robbed the graves in the area.

The former farmer and handyman was declared competent to stand trial on Tuesday and will be returned to Waushara County for a hearing planned at 1 p.m. Monday at Wautoma.

Dutcher said that all the evidence on the Gein case are in the files of the attorney general's office this morning. However, the district attorney said that William Platz and Robert Sutton of the attorney general's office will be in Wautoma Monday to assist at the hearing. Platz helped the prosecution on the initial Gein case.

The hearing will be held before Judge Robert Gollmer, Baraboo, circuit judge for Sauk, Columbia and Waushara Counties.

Circuit Court Judge Herbert Bunde said it was likely that Gein would spend the remainder of his life at Central State Hospital. That was in 1958. However, Dr. Edward Schubert, Central State Hospital superintendent, said this week that the hospital recently found significant changes in the mental status of Gein which meet the criteria for his standing trial in Wisconsin.

Dutcher was prosecuting attorney for the state's first bifurcated trial involving James McBriar Jr., 27, Wautoma, former Plainfield resident who was found guilty of four counts of first degree murder on Aug. 21, 1967, in Sauk County Court before Judge Gollmer.

A jury of 10 men and two women also found McBrair sane in a separate hearing five days later. He was sentenced to serve four concurrent life terms in the state prison on Nov. 5.

McBrair was charged with murdering his estranged wife, father-in-law, his wife's stepsister and a babysitter on March 5, 1967, in a cottage on Fish Lake, three miles east of Wautoma.

Monday, May 20, 1968 — THE MILWAUKEE JOURNAL

# Laws, World Are New as Ed Gein Faces Trial

By JOHN G. SHAVER
Of The Journal Staff

The little man with gray hair and a kindly face sat passively throughout the daylong court hearing.

To an observer he appeared to understand the proceedings, conferring occasionally with his lawyers.

The setting was a recent preliminary hearing in the tiny brick courthouse at Wautoma. The small courtroom was filled with spectators and sheriff's deputies.

### Never Proved in Court

The man was Ed Gein, 61, committed 10 years ago to a hospital for the criminally insane. He was accused of killing a widowed grandmother in one of Wisconsin's most notorious and bizarre murder cases.

The prosecution was never required to prove the evidence against Gein. The Plainfield handyman and occasional baby sitter was committed to central state hospital at Waupun after a sanity hearing in 1958 found him mentally incompetent to stand trial.

The Gein case illustrates the complications that can arise in a changing field of law.

No one expected that Gein ever would go to trial. At the sanity hearing the judge concluded: "I think it is adequate for me to say it does not appear he will ever be at liberty again."

However, Dr. E. F. Schubert, superintendent of central state hospital, notified Waushara county last fall that Gein had sufficiently recovered to stand trial.

Schubert, who examined Gein 10 years ago, said at the time that it was unlikely he would ever recover.

### "Has Mellowed"

But the doctor said recently that Gein had mellowed in his stay at the hospital and his symptoms had lessened. Gein has undergone a gradual change, developing a "better realization that the acts he allegedly committed were frowned upon by society," Schubert said.

Since Gein's commitment in 1958, the legal standard for determining mental fitness for trial has been changed from simply knowing right from wrong. The new standard says a defendant is unfit for trial if he is unable to understand the proceedings against him and to assist in his defense because of mental deficiency.

Using the new standard, Gein probably could have stood trial 10 years ago, Schubert said. Although Gein did not understand that his alleged acts were wrong, he could hold discussions with psychiatrists and presumably with his lawyer, the doctor said.

Gein was bound over for trial in circuit court after the preliminary hearing. The proceeding was to determine whether there was enough evidence to try him.

The prosecution still must prove beyond a reasonable doubt, that Gein murdered Mrs. Bernice Worden, the widowed grandmother, and stole a cash register from her Plainfield hardware store.

Her headless body was found Nov. 16, 1957, hanging by the heels in a shed attached to Gein's weathered farm home. Later, authorities found parts of other human bodies collected by Gein in nighttime grave robberies.

### Problems for Prosecution

The task of proving Gein guilty a decade after the crime may be difficult. Significant changes have occurred in criminal law. Restrictions on the use in court of confessions and evidence seized without a search warrant are much more rigid.

"I don't think anyone at the time could have anticipated these changes," said Atty. Stewart G. Honeck, then the prosecutor of the case.

He said there "might be trouble" with some of the evidence, but declined to elaborate because of Gein's pending trial.

A state crime laboratory official, Joseph C. Wilimovsky, obtained confessions from Gein in 1957 in Madison, where he was taken for a lie detector test.

Tape recordings of the confession have since disintegrated, but officials said written transcripts were kept. The defense is expected to challenge the accuracy and completeness of these transcripts.

Atty. Dominic H. Frinzi, who is assisting in Gein's defense, said he would attack the confessions at the trial on several grounds, including these:

Even though Gein may have been given warnings of his rights to silence and to a lawyer at the time of the interrogation, as is now required by law, he was incompetent to waive these rights because he was insane. Gein consented at the time to questioning without his lawyer present.

Psychiatrists have testified that Gein was extremely suggestible and would readily give answers sought by questioners. This testimony could cast doubt on the validity of Gein's 1957 confessions.

Frinzi unsuccessfully challenged the charges that were filed against Gein in 1957. The Wisconsin supreme court changed the procedure for issuing warrants in 1965. Frinzi claimed that this made the old warrants invalid but he was overruled Apr. 25 by the supreme court on an appeal.

The case is further complicated by the deaths of three key persons: The sheriff who conducted the initial investigation, the doctor who performed the autopsy on Mrs. Worden and the district attorney who issued the original charges. Memories also have faded.

continue.....

Thursday, November 14, 1968 — THE MILWAUKEE JOURNAL

## Ed Gein Guilty of Murder

By JOHN G. SHAVER
of The Journal Staff

Wautoma, Wis. — Circuit Judge Robert H. Gollmar Thursday found Ed Gein, 62, guilty of first degree murder in the slaying and mutilation of a Plainfield woman in 1957.

Gollmar rejected Gein's contention that he accidentally shot Mrs. Bernice Worden, 58, in her hardware store Nov. 16, 1957, while he was examining a .22 caliber rifle off a display rack.

A second trial opened Thursday before Gollmar on the question of Gein's sanity at the time of Mrs. Worden's death. The defense had requested a so-called bifurcated trial in which guilt is first determined, then the question of sanity.

Gollmar noted in his ruling Thursday that Gein had long been familiar with guns, probably was an expert marksman and "had the skill to place one bullet in her head."

In his closing argument Wednesday, Defense Atty. Dominic H. Frinzi of Milwaukee had made much of the fact that Gein had placed only one cartridge in the rifle while he looked at it in the store.

### Wanted Antifreeze

Frinzi said that if Gein had intended to kill Mrs. Worden he would have placed more bullets in the rifle. Gein testified Tuesday that he had gone to the store to buy antifreeze and then asked Mrs. Worden if he could look at one of her rifles.

He testified that he found one or two cartridges in his pocket, left over from squirrel hunting the day before. After inserting one of the cartridges in the rifle, Gein said the gun jammed, then somehow discharged as he attempted to eject the shell.

Special prosecutor Robert E. Sutton, in his closing argument, maintained that Gein had fabricated the story.

### Behavior Analyzed

The judge said that he found significant Gein's behavior immediately after the shooting.

"He did not check to see if she was dead or alive," Gollmar said. "He did not do what most people would have done if the shooting were accidental — run out in the street and seek the immediate aid of a doctor."

Instead, Gollmar said, Gein dragged the body to the store's service truck, later transferred it to his own car and took it to his home. Gein testified Tuesday that he "blacked out" and could not remember what happened after Mrs. Worden was shot.

Gein in 1957 confessed to killing Mrs. Worden and Mrs. Mary Hogan, 54, the tavern operator. The confession had been ruled inadmissible by Gollmar. Gein, who has not been charged with Mrs. Hogan's death, denied killing the woman in testimony Tuesday.

### Hardened Expression

If Gein is found to have been insane at the time of the slaying, he would be acquitted of murder because of his mental condition and automatically committed to central state hospital, Waupun, until the court believes he is sane and would be unlikely to commit a crime.

Gein, in whose farm home

## Gein

### Gein Found Guilty of Murder

From page 1

Mrs. Worden's headless and mutilated body was found, spent the last 10 years in central state hospital because his mental condition made him unable to stand trial.

Throughout the final arguments Wednesday, Gein sat with his arms folded and his mouth drawn tight — his facial expression more hardened than in earlier portions of the trial.

Sutton relied in his argument on the testimony of a psychiatrist and psychologist that Gein unconsciously forgot unpleasant events in his life, a condition known as hysterical reaction.

### Lesser Charge Suggested

Psychiatrist William Crowley and psychologist John D. Liccione said it would not be inconsistent with a hysterical reaction for Gein to have believed that he accidentally killed Mrs. Worden.

They said Gein was a schizophrenic with a history of hysterical reaction in which he forgot or distorted distasteful things in order to live with himself.

Crowley, clinical director of the Milwaukee county north division mental health center, and Liccione, the center's chief psychologist, were called as prosecution witnesses.

Asked by the judge whether Gein might have committed any lesser offense instead of first degree murder, Frinzi suggested homicide by reckless conduct or second degree murder. Gollmar is hearing the case without a jury.

In another development Wednesday, Sutton was unsuccessful in attempting to prove that Gein killed a Pine Grove woman tavern operator in 1954. Gollmar heard the testimony but refused to admit it as evidence.

Sutton called six investigators to testify Wednesday. Their testimony showed that a .32 caliber cartridge found in Mrs. Hogan's tavern in 1954 was fired from a German automatic pistol recovered from Gein's home in 1957.

Herbert Wansersky, 48, a Stevens Point papermill worker and former Portage county sheriff, testified that he found a head in Gein's home in 1957 that resembled that of Mrs. Hogan.

Frinzi repeatedly objected to introduction of the Hogan case as irrelevant to the Worden death. He accused Sutton of making a "grandstand play."

In refusing to admit the testimony, Gollmar said: "The court cannot feel there is sufficient proof here of a connecting link to a similar crime." He said there was no evidence to show that Gein intended to kill Mrs. Hogan.

Ed Gein

Thurs., Nov. 14, 1968  Daily Northwestern

# Gein Found Guilty Of First Degree Murder

WAUTOMA — Judge Robert Gollmar in circuit court this morning found Ed Gein guilty of murder in the first degree.

In handing down his verdict in a trial without jury, the court ruled that Gein intentionally killed Mrs. Bernice Worden on Nov. 16, 1957 in her Plainfield hardware store.

Judge Gollmar delayed sentencing until after the second half of the trial. Testimony will now begin on Gein's plea of innocent by reason of insanity.

The judge referred to Gein's testimony that the shooting was accidental.

"This court does not accept the defendant's story," the judge said. "It just doesn't ring true to me. The court is satisfied that the defendant formed an intent."

Before announcing his verdict, Judge Gollmar spent half an hour orally reviewing evidence given in the case.

He emphasized during the review that the only issue in the case was that of "intent to kill" on the part of the defendant.

Dr. Edward Schubert, superintendent of Central State Hospital, testified today in the second part of the trial that Gein "could not conform his conduct to the requirements of law."

The witness said he felt society "rationally would not want to punish such a man."

Dr. Schubert testified that at the time of the murder of Mrs. Worden, Gein was schizophrenic with "a strong suggestion of paranoia."

He said Gein had been mentally ill for at least 10 years prior to 1957 and that during the period Gein sometimes had hallucinations in which he heard his mother's voice.

Prosecutor Robert Sutton called a psychologist and a psychiatrist to the witness stand Wednesday afternoon in an effort to refute testimony by Gein on Tuesday. Gein claimed that Mrs. Worden was killed when the rifle he was examining went off accidentally in the Worden store.

Dr. William Crowley, a psychiatrist from Wauwatosa, and Dr. John Liccione, a Milwaukee clinical psychologist, both testified that Gein suffered from hysteroid mental symptoms. They said that a person with a

Continued on Page 16, Column 7

**Local Residents Crowd** the courtroom in Wautoma for Ed Gein's appearances, including an Amish man seated in the front row trying to hide his face with his hat. Gein is in the foreground. (AP Wirephoto)

# Gein Could Be Free Man

With the announcement that Edward Gein, the alleged mutilation slayer of two women and grave robber of Plainfield, is mentally competent to stand trial, comes the realization that under American justice the 61-year-old handyman may once again become a free man.

Gein was adjudged insane in 1958 by Circuit Court Judge Herbert Bunde and sent to the Central State Hospital at Waupun for what could be the rest of his life.

In announcing the 1958 decision, Judge Bunde said, "It is unlikely he will ever be at liberty again." Bunde said he relied on the opinions of experts who without equivocation declared Gein to be legally insane. Testimony about Gein's insanity came from two psychiatrists during a court hearing.

According to Dr. Edward F. Schubert, Central State Hospital superintendent, the hospital "recently found significant changes in the mental status of Ed Gein which meet the criteria for his standing trial in Wisconsin."

Describing Gein as having "kind of mellowed over the years," he explained that Gein had lost most of the paranoid psychosis he had originally.

"Gein is aware of his surroundings," he said, "and of why he was hospitalized and the alleged incidents behind the hospitalization and coherently discusses his case with us which is all that is required to stand trial."

Waushara County Dist. Atty. Howard Dutcher said he was told by Circuit Judge Robert Golmar about information from the state hospital of Gein's current mental condition. Dutcher said a court hearing is scheduled for Monday.

Monday's hearing would consider Gein's mental competency compiled from studies conducted at the state hospital throughout the 10 years he has been confined. If he is found mentally competent a trial date would be set and Gein would be offered the benefit of counsel. He would be offered the same trial procedures he was entitled to 10 years ago had he been capable of facing a judge and jury.

If Gein ever does become a free man it appears unlikely his release would be soon coming about. His only hope for eventual freedom would be a verdict of innocent by reason of insanity at a future court trial. If the court reached such a decision Gein would be sent back to the state hospital and detained for an undetermined length of time.

A separate hearing would consider Gein's future and determine that if he was released there would be no possibility of his sickness returning.

Following Gein's committment to the state hospital ten years ago Plainfield residents felt that the normal path of justice had been detoured in sending him to the mental hospital without a trial. The people felt Gein should have been declared guilty of his crimes before he was committed and then sent to the state hospital for treatment.

In commenting on the legal rights of a prisoner, Judge Arnold J. Cane, Circuit Judge of Winnebago County, said that under the American judicial system a man accused of a crime has to have the intelligence and mental ability to cooperate with his counsel in his defense. It is impossible to offer a person a fair trial unless he is mentally capable of offering assistance to both himself and counsel.

If Gein is found innocent by reason of insnity he would have the right to petition for a hearing one year after the verdict. If he failed to apply to the proper authorities for such a hearing at the end of a five-year period the state would automatically schedule one. It is at such a hearing that Gein could eventually win his freedom or confinement continued for an indefinite period.

Ed Gein, Alleged Plainfield Slayer
—UPI Telephoto

# 10 Years After Slaying, Ed Gein Is Model Patient

Ed Gein, who became internationally notorious when details of his bizarre activities were first revealed 10 years ago Thursday, is now considered a model patient at the central state hospital at Waupun. His name is mentioned only occasionally and with reluctance by his old neighbors at Plainfield (Waushara county). The 100 acres where he lived is a tree farm. The house where he lived alone with grisly trophies of murder and grave robbery has long since burned down.

Gein

The harmless looking little man is now 61. Dr. Richard Pyle, the hospital's clinical director, said Gein seemed content to work in the stone cutting shop of the occupational therapy department and his relations with others there were fairly rational.

### Body Found

Gein had committed one murder and exhumed the bodies of 12 women who reminded him of his dead mother before a second killing focused the nation's horrified attention on him.

It was on Nov. 16, 1957, when the headless body of Mrs. Bernice Worden, a 58 year old widowed grandmother, was found hung by the heels in the summer kitchen of Gein's farmhouse, six miles southwest of here. It was dressed out like a deer carcass.

Investigators found chair seats and lampshades made from human skin. There was a pair of skin puttees. Masks made from human faces were discovered, along with the "shrunken heads" which Gein had shown to children of the community, saying he'd obtained them from the Philippines.

The facts were fantastic enough, but rumors embroidered them. There were unfounded reports of cannibalism and claims that Gein was responsible for numerous deaths.

Sheriff Art Schley, who had been a county highway department truck driver until six weeks before, suddenly found himself in charge of the most notorious episode in Wisconsin's criminal annals. Reporters and cameramen from dozens of American and foreign publications descended on Waushara county.

### Details Withheld

The novice sheriff and other authorities deepened the mystery of Gein's activities by holding back details — at first, so the facts could be given to Mrs. Worden's daughter in Nebraska before she read them in the papers; later, apparently out of resentment at the unwelcome publicity the case was giving Plainfield.

# Judge Grants Motion, Denies 2nd in Gein Case

Circuit court judge Robert Gollmar handed down his dicisions Friday, on the two motions made in behalf of Edward Gein by defense attorneys.

Gein's attorneys, William Belter and Dominic Frinzi, had made a motion to suppress evidence collected in 1957 regarding the murder of Mrs. Bernice Worden on the grounds that it was obtained by unlawful search and seizure due to the fact that law enforcers went into Gein's house without a legal warrant.

They had also entered a motion to suppress statements and admissions, particularly confessions made at Madison by Gein on Nov. 19 and 20, 1957, on the grounds that under the Miranda ruling (retroactive) Gein had not been informed of his rights to have an attorney.

Judge Gollmar denied the motion to suppress evidence in the case. The judge stated that although the fourth amendment makes evidence obtained through unwarranted search and seizure not admissible against an accused criminal, "it is subject to an exclusionary clause based on reasonableness and cannot be stated in rigid and absolute terms, but each case is to be decided on its own facts and circumstances", he said

In the matter of the Gein case, officers were called on the afternoon of Nov. 16, 1957, to the Worden Hardware store in Plainfield where they found Mrs. Worden missing, a pool of blood on the floor and indications of something having been dragged across the floor.

Gein came under suspicion because it was known he had asked Mrs. Worden to go roller skating the day before; he had ascertained that her son would be deer hunting on the date of Nov. 16; indications were that he had purchased anti-freeze at the store; and because he had been observed operating the Worden truck during the afternoon of Nov. 16.

Officers apprehended Gein for questioning at Plainfield about 7:30 at the same time other officers went to the rural home of the suspect.

Judge Gollmar ruled that since officers had reason to suspect that Mrs. Worden was either seriously injured or dead, "It is the opinion of this court that the officers had a right to enter the home of Gein since some suspicion was directed toward him, to search for Mrs. Worden with intent of giving her aid if injured, or finding her body if dead. This clearly comes within the exclusionary rule, as any delay incurred by finding a magistrate for a search warrant would definitely have had life and death significance."

He ruled further that "Any items which were in plain view of the officers during the search are not barred, as a result of unlawful search and seizure, and may be used as evidence in the case."

Regarding the second motion, Gollmar ruled that although he did not feel the Miranda ruling applied (since Gein had obtained counsel, William Belter, before his confession at Madison,) other considerations moved him to grant the motion to suppress Gein's confessions.

He based his decision on:

1. The length of the interrogation: Gein was questioned by local deputies until after 12 midnight on the night of his arrest. Not more than three or four hours later he was subjected to a lie detector test at 4:30 a.m. on Nov. 17. The expert from the state crime laboratory continued to question him intermittently until 6:30 p.m. that evening. On Nov. 18 he appeared in court before Judge Clark and on Nov. 19 was again questioned, this time at Madison, for five or six hours.

2. Third degree methods: Testimony revealed that at midnight when Gein had not confessed to the deputies, the then sheriff, Art Schley, a strong, heavy-set man, physically attacked the small, 51-year-old Gein and continued to abuse him until the deputies intervened and forced him to stop. Gein at that time continued to deny his guilt.

3. Education and background: Gein had only an eighth grade education and had lived for some years as a hermit recluse, which ill fitted him to withstand questioning or understand his rights.

4. Mental conditions: According to testimony given by Dr. E. F. Schubert, Gein was mentally ill with a schizophrenic psychosis at the time of his interrogation. Schubert called Gein a "pitiful individual" who would be inclined to answer "to please",

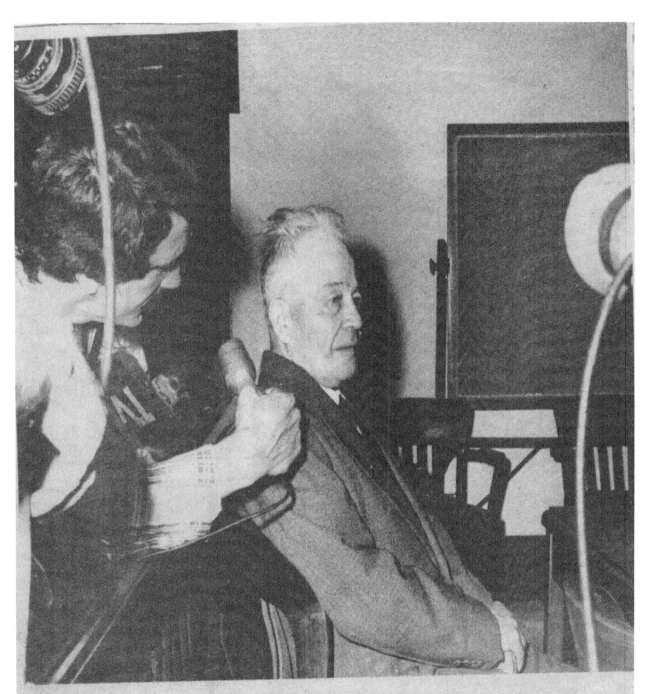

CAMERAS WHIRRING...With bright television lights and numerous microphones surrounding him, Ed Gein chats with Collin Siedor, (left) WLUK-TV 11, Green Bay, prior to Gein's hearing June 27 at the county courthouse. Gein, convicted of first degree murder, had petitioned Judge Robert Gollmar to release him from Central State hospital, Waupun, where Gein had been since 1957. Gollmar denied his petition.

# Gein Seeks Re-examination, Evaluation of Mental Condition

*argus mar 8, 73*

Edward Gein has filed a petition with the Waushara county clerk of courts seeking a re-examination and re-evaluation of his mental state.

Gein, a former rural Plainfield resident, is currently a patient at the Central State hospital in Waupun where he was committed in January, 1958, after he was found unable to stand trial of murder and armed robbery charges.

Gein was brought to trial in Waushara county on the charges 10 years later when the superintendent of the state hospital declared that Gein was "able to understand the charges brought against him, and participate in his own defense."

In the trial before circuit judge Robert Gollmar, Gein was found not guilty by reason of insanity and remanded to the state hospital in November, 1968.

The petition for re-examination, signed by Gein, states, "This patient has now fully recovered his mental health and is fully competent, and that there is no reason why he should be or remain in any hospital."

It further states, "Petitioner (Gein) prays that a re-examination be made of this patient's mental condition, and for a determination that he is now fully recovered, sane and competent."

According to Ina McComb, clerk of courts, who received this petition Feb. 27, Gein will be interviewed by two psychiatrists of his (Gein's) choosing as the next step toward his release.

# Gein Returned To Waupun

Waushara Argus
Wautoma, Wis.
July 4, 1974

Ed Gein, 66, convicted of the 1957 murder of Mrs. Bernice Worden, was returned Friday to Central State hospital, Waupun.

Judge Robert Gollmar, Portage, ruled June 27 that Gein's petition for release from Waupun be denied. Gein had been diagnosed by four psyciatrists as mentally ill.

Newsmen from Green Bay, Milwaukee, LaCrosse, Appleton and Chicago gathered with Wautoma reporters in front of the sheriff's department Thursday morning waiting for Gein to be escorted to the hearing. Gein appeared with Sheriff Vergil Battermann and strolled to the courthouse.

Once seated in the courtroom, Gein told one reporter that the whirring of cameras and flashes of lights reminded him of Castro's Cuba. He did not explain what he meant as his attorney, James Poole, cautioned Gein against talking to newsmen.

Waushara county District Attorney Robert Rudolph, Wautoma, was appointed prosecutor.

Gein took the stand in his own behalf and stated he'd like to travel. If released, however, he would not be eligible for social security benefits. When employed by the town and county, nothing was taken out of his pay checks.

Gein said that in 1970, Dr. Edward F. Schubert, Central State administrator, told his ward that the patients were cured.

"We were told we could be released and make a living on our own," Gein said. "But the only reason were held in the ward was on account of society."

Schubert, testifying later, said Gein was still mentally ill and should remain in Central State.

Dr. Thomas Malueg, Nicolet clinic, Neenah, said that on the basis of his four examinations of Gein, he would recommend that Gein be transferred to a less restricted environment such as at Winnebago State hospital, Oshkosh.

Gein is a schizophrenic and can become actively psychotic again if released, said Ma'eug. Gein's abilities to repress his feelings when confronted with his crimes are not as strong as normal people.

Malueg suggested a gradual integration into society with a minimum of stress.

Testimony from two other psychiatrists was also presented during the one day hearing.

Dr. Lee Roberts, Madison and Dr. George Arndt, Neenah, were appointed by the circuit court to examine Gein and to report their findings. Both concluded Gein should not be released.

Gein is eligible to petition again for release in one year.

## Gein says: 'See you again, lady'

*Sat., June 29, 1974 — Daily Northwestern*

By FRAN HOTVEDT
Northwestern Wautoma Bureau

WAUTOMA — In spite of international attention 17 years ago, centered on perhaps Wisconsin's most famous criminal, Ed Gein, only a handful of people attended a court hearing here Thursday in which he sought to be released from Central State Hospital in Waupun.

There were more members of the news media in the court room than spectators, the majority of those being courthouse employes who kept going in and out of the courtroom, in lieu of the usual coffee breaks. It had been previously conjectured that the hearing before retired Circuit Court Judge Robert Gollmar, would be closed. When it was learned during the noon recess that it was open there were about eight more in attendance than in the morning.

It was this reporter's dubious privilege to attend the trial before Gollmar in 1968 and again this week. It was a sad assignment in both instances. One that caused great difficulty in picturing this man as depraved and violent enough to commit murder and other weird crimes.

Gein, now 66, is a slight man, a little thinner than six years ago, with a typical "prison pallor" and whiter hair. He is soft-spoken, appears to be rather shy and withdrawn, but smiled and conversed more than he did on his last visit.

Some of his replies to direct questioning Thursday by defense attorney James Poole, and prosecutor Robert Rudolph, brought smiles and light laughter from the audience.

When asked by Rudolph if such crimes could ever be committed by him again, Gein said "No one can say that, in this room or anywhere in the United States. I am no mind reader or wizard, and neither are you."

In reply to a question about contact with women at the hospital he said, "When I walk down a hall and accidentally bump into a nurse, that's contact." Several times in his testimony he repeated statements about how many friends he has, how kind they are to him and how really nice people are.

When asked by Poole if he would return to Waushara County if released, he replied, "It's a big county, people here are friendly and some have even wished me luck."

Gein, whose formal education ended with eighth grade, told the court he reads a great deal and especially enjoys books of adventure and National Geographic magazines. He said he would like to travel.

As the day wore on, the courtroom became hotter and stuffier and the testimony of four psychiatrists pointed to the need for continued treatment of the man's sick mind, his smiles, readily exhibited in the morning, decreased. He sat stoically with his hands in his lap during the final two hours and made no outward sign or reaction to Gollmar's closing remarks and his denial of the release.

Leaving the courthouse with a deputy sheriff, Gein chuckled when this reporter remarked about the hardness of the seats in the courtroom. Dressed neatly in a too warm suit, he said, "My seat wasn't too bad, but the heat was terrible." He added he would probably "See you again, lady."

Being of rather heavy stature and past an age that at one time appealed to this man, his final remark did cause just the slightest shudder. It could not help but give an assurance that Gollmar's decision was a very wise one, especially for Ed Gein.

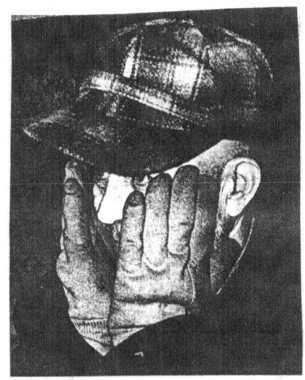

*Photo by Fred L. Tonne*

In the Central Wisconsin farming town of Plainfield, Ed Gein was considered a gentle, timid man — though a bit peculiar, perhaps. He lived alone in a rotting farmhouse that kids liked to call "haunted" and earned his living by babysitting, cutting grass, and doing handiwork. Then, in 1957, shocked sheriff's deputies entered Gein's filthy kitchen and found the body of a middleaged woman dressed out like a deer carcass and strung up by the heels. Elsewhere, deputies discovered death masks made from women's skinned heads, their skulls wrapped in plastic bags, and chairs and lampshades made from their skin. Soon, newspapers throughout the world shocked their readers with Gein's confessions of murder, grave robbing, and body mutilation — always of plump, middleaged women who, psychiatrists thought, somewhat resembled Gein's deceased mother. When deputies later led Gein back to the scene of his butchery, this picture was taken. He was found guilty of first degree murder, and then innocent because of insanity and sent to Central State Hospital at Waupun. Now he is 69 years old, and officials there doubt that he ever will be released.

1975

# Ed Gein's last chance

**BY BERNIE PETERSON**
*Post-Crescent staff writer*

WAUTOMA — There was an air of finality surrounding the Edward Gein case here Thursday.

As the group of some 20 onlookers quietly filed out of the small, second-floor courtroom of the Waushara County courthouse, Gein sat expressionless, erect at the counsel table. Moments before, he had lost his bid for freedom after a five-hour sanity hearing.

Gein gave no hint of his emotions after what must have been a crushing personal defeat. Not only would Gein remain hospitalized, chances appeared excellent that he would spend the rest of his life at Central State Hospital, the maximum security facility at Waupun that has been his home for most of the past 17 years.

Judge Robert Gollmar ruled that putting Gein back into society would be a danger to both society and himself. And the judge pointed out that proposed transfer of Gein from Central State to Winnebago Mental Health Institute, which was being pushed for by Gein's attorney, was an administrative decision, not a matter for a judge to rule on.

Since the superintendent of Central State feels Gein belongs there and has shown little, if any, improvement in his years there, it's likely Gein will remain there.

Gein's expressionless pose was in contrast to his mood before the hearing. He had come here from Central State on Wednesday, staying overnight at the county jail.

Sheriff Virgil Batterman, an eye-witness to the haunting spectacle of human remains at Gein's rural Plainfield farm on Nov. 16, 1957, told of the frail little man's optimistic mood on the ride up from Waupun.

"He seemed like he felt he was really going to get out this time," said Batterman. "He talked about wanting to travel after getting out."

Gein also talked about the nice scenery and about the press, which he felt was responsible for blowing up his case and getting him placed back in Central State after his 1968 trial.

"If it hadn't been for you people, he figures he would have been out," Batterman told a reporter.

Several things had changed from the 1968 trial to Thursday's sanity hearing. For one thing, some of the courtroom figures were new.

Gein's original attorney in the 1957 and 1968 proceedings, William Belter, now is the Waushara County district attorney, so he had to disqualify himself from this hearing.

Two young Wautoma attorneys served as special prosecutor and defense attorney. They were Robert Rudolph and James Poole, respectively.

Some of the psychiatrists who testified were new to the case, but their findings were basically consistent with those testified to in 1968, that Gein was mentally ill, suffering now as then from schizophrenia.

And there was less of an atmosphere of hostility in the community. Last time around, Batterman had to worry about threatening phone calls at the jail. This time there were none.

Little was actually said this time in direct reference to the events of Nov. 16, 1957, when Gein shot and killed Mrs. Bernice Worden, 58, at her Plainfield hardware store, and then transported the body to his farm about seven miles away. There, he decapitated the body and dressed it out like a deer, hanging it by the heels in a shed.

Subsequent investigation turned up other human remains in the farmhouse, such as well-preserved death masks made from the skin of human heads. Those bodies allegedly were taken from graves in the area by Gein.

When the case broke, it became one of the most celebrated criminal cases ever in the state, and at one point the governor ordered the state attorney general to participate in the investigation.

Gollmar didn't think it was necessary to go over all the grisly details of the case Thursday. He had heard them all in 1968, when he found Gein guilty of first-degree murder and then innocent by reason of insanity.

Gollmar was interested in the state of Gein's mental illness, described by several psychiatrists as chronic schizophrenia.

Dr. Leigh Roberts recalled how Gein's troubles started some 13 years before the murder, when his close family ties were broken first by the death of his only brother and the next year by the death of his mother.

The latter death apparently was what set him into abnormally extended grief, as Mrs. Gein had been the dominant figure in the family. Ed had been devoted to her well-being while she was alive, but after her death, he had no family.

Ed Gein, followed by Waushara Sheriff Virgil Batterman, enters the Wautoma courtroom Thursday for a hearing on his release. (Post-Crescent photo)

# Ed Gein's last chance

**BY BERNIE PETERSON**
*Post-Crescent staff writer*

WAUTOMA — There was an air of finality surrounding the Edward Gein case here Thursday.

As the group of some 20 onlookers quietly filed out of the small, second-floor courtroom of the Waushara County courthouse, Gein sat expressionless, erect at the counsel table. Moments before, he had lost his bid for freedom after a five-hour sanity hearing.

Gein gave no hint of his emotions after what must have been a crushing personal defeat. Not only would Gein remain hospitalized, chances appeared excellent that he would spend the rest of his life at Central State Hospital, the maximum security facility at Waupun that has been his home for most of the past 17 years.

Judge Robert Gollmar ruled that putting Gein back into society would be a danger to both society and himself. And the judge pointed out that proposed transfer of Gein from Central State to Winnebago Mental Health Institute, which was being pushed for by Gein's attorney, was an administrative decision, not a matter for a judge to rule on.

Since the superintendent of Central State feels Gein belongs there and has shown little, if any, improvement in his years there, it's likely Gein will remain there.

Gein's expressionless pose was in contrast to his mood before the hearing. He had come here from Central State on Wednesday, staying overnight at the county jail.

Sheriff Virgil Batterman, an eyewitness to the haunting spectacle of human remains at Gein's rural Plainfield farm on Nov. 16, 1957, told of the frail little man's optimistic mood on the ride up from Waupun.

"He seemed like he felt he was really going to get out this time," said Batterman. "He talked about wanting to travel after getting out."

Gein also talked about the nice scenery and about the press, which he felt was responsible for blowing up his case and getting him placed back in Central State after his 1968 trial.

"If it hadn't been for you people, he figures he would have been out," Batterman told a reporter.

Several things had changed from the 1968 trial to Thursday's sanity hearing. For one thing, some of the courtroom figures were new.

Gein's original attorney in the 1957 and 1968 proceedings, William Belter, now is the Waushara County district attorney, so he had to disqualify himself from this hearing.

Two young Wautoma attorneys served as special prosecutor and defense attorney. They were Robert Rudolph and James Poole, respectively.

Some of the psychiatrists who testified were new to the case, but their findings were basically consistent with those testified to in 1968, that Gein was mentally ill, suffering now as then from schizophrenia.

And there was less of an atmosphere of hostility in the community. Last time around, Batterman had to worry about threatening phone calls at the jail. This time there were none.

Little was actually said this time in direct reference to the events of Nov. 16, 1957, when Gein shot and killed Mrs. Bernice Worden, 58, at her Plainfield hardware store, and then transported the body to his farm about seven miles away. There, he decapitated the body and dressed it out like a deer, hanging

*Continued on Page 4*

Ed Gein, followed by Waushara Sheriff Virgil Batterman, enters the Wautoma courtroom Thursday for a hearing on his release. (Post-Crescent photo)

## Murderer Ed Gein dies at 76

Osh.N.W. 7-26-84

MADISON (AP) — Ed Gein, the grisly killer who 27 years ago drew national attention to the tiny Waushara County town of Plainfield, died this morning at the Mendota Mental Institute. He was 76.

Authorities who arrested Gein in November 1957 found such items as preserved human heads and lampshades and chair seats made out of human skin at his farmhouse.

**Gein**

Gein had been at the Mendota institute in Madison since May 1978. He was transferred there after having been almost continually at Central State Hospital at Waupun since his arrest.

His story later served as the model for Alfred Hitchcock's "Psycho." The author of the novel on which the movie was based, Robert Block, lived about 50 miles from Gein's farmhouse.

The story began to unfold on Nov. 16, 1957, when relatives of Bernice Worden, a 58-year-old widow who ran a hardware store at Plainfield, realized she was missing.

Gein's battered pickup truck had been seen near the store twice that day, and a Wood County deputy drove to Gein's farm to ask if he had noticed anything. No one was home.

He returned later and still got no answer. He looked into a lean-to at the side of the house and saw Mrs. Worden's body hanging by the heels, decapitated and "dressed out like a deer."

Gein was found in town. He was declared unfit to stand trial and was sent to Central State.

Gein's farmhouse was all cluttered except for one room that had been boarded off. It was Gein's mother's room. She died in 1945 and he left the room just as she left it.

He began robbing fresh graves of women who, like his mother, were middle aged. The women who he later killed were also believed to resemble his mother, in his view.

In 1968, he was tried in the death of Mrs. Worden. It was ruled that he was insane at the time of the crime and he was returned to the hospital.

In 1974 Gein sought a sanity hearing and asked for his freedom. But Circuit Judge Robert Gollmar sent Gein back to Central State.

Authorites testified at the time that Gein was never a problem in prison, although he reacted rather poorly to other inmates. He worked as a carpenter, mason and hospital attendant while at Central State.

He supposedly was saving his money for a dreamed-of trip around the world.

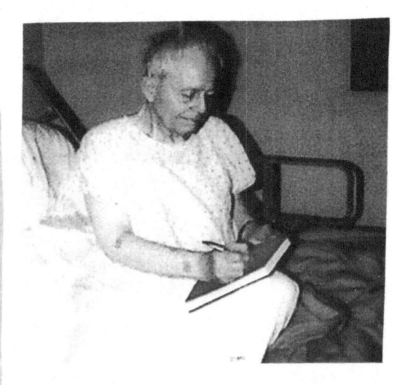

So far as the doctor can recall, no one has ever visited him.

# Obituaries

### Gein burial

Private burial for Ed Gein, 77, a former Plainfield area resident, took place in the Plainfield Village Cemetery. No services were held. Gasperic Funeral Home, Plainfield, handled arrangements.

Mr. Gein died Thursday morning at Mendota Mental Institute, Madison, of respiratory failure, according to institute officials.

[Gein was] born Aug. 26, 1906, in La Crosse, son of the late George and Augusta Gein. He was a farmer. He had been in state mental institutions since his arrest in 1957 for killing a woman.

There are no survivors.

## Circuit Court

A jury of six men and six women found a Round Lake, Ill., man guilty of disorderly conduct following a trial in Circuit Court Friday.

The jury deliberated about 1 1/2 hours before returning the verdict against John J. McGary, Round Lake, Ill., for causing a disturbance in the B.S. Inn in Amherst on March 18 and fighting with deputies who were called to the scene.

Judge Fred Fleishauer, who presided at the trial, withheld sentencing

### Wool price set

The support price for 1984 marketings of wool is $1.65 per pound for shorn wool, according to Robert Granum, Portage County director of the Agriculture Stabilization and Conservation Service.

Pulled wool or wool on unshorn lambs will continue to be supported at a level comparable to the support price for shorn wool, Granum said. Payments will be made on unshorn lambs.

Shorn wool payments will be based on a percentage of each producer's returns from sales. The percentage will be whatever is required to raise the national average price received by all producers for shorn wool in 1984 up to

The following village of Plover meetings will be held next week at the Plover Municipal Center board room:

Finance Committee, 5 p.m. Monday. The agenda includes Gary Pucci, Mabie & Associates to discuss the 19 audit report, class B combination liquor license for Chet Skippy for Ca Extra, bartender licenses for Carolin Wojcik, Janis Jacobson, Nancy Voeler, Julie Sackmann, Joanna Jaquit Richard Kurtzweil, Melanie Adams Cheryl Post and Kevin Chojnack vouchers and assessor's report.

Public Works Committee, 5:30 p.m. Monday. Agenda items include Di Drive street lights, 10-foot turnarou easement at 2307 Gilman Drive, sar tary sewer ordinance and prelimina resolution and reports from the utili and parks and recreation manage and building superintendent.

Public hearing, 6:50 p.m. Wedne day, on zero lot lines for Chet Biga f Oakwood Forest.

Public hearing, 6:55 p.m. Wedne day, on request to rezone 1102 Wisco sin Ave. from R-7 multiple family to 2 general business for a post office a conditional use.

Village Board, 7 p.m. Wednesda The agenda includes bartender censes, class B combination liquor cense for Chet Skippy, Disk Driv

Ed Gein is shown in this 1968 photo as he was transferred from Waupun State Hospital to Waushara County jail. The police officer is not identified. (AP photo)

# Ed Gein story ends with his death at 77

# Gein buried in unmarked grave

PLAINFIELD (AP) — Ed Gein, who served as the model for the character Norman Bates in the Alfred Hitchcock movie "Psycho," has been buried in virtual anonymity.

Gein, who died last Thursday at age 77, was buried in an unmarked grave Saturday in Spiritland Cemetary outside of Plainfield, according to the Wautoma Argus newspaper.

He had spent 27 years in mental hospitals after authorities found preserved human heads and lampshades and chair seats made out of human skin at his farm. Officials alleged that, after his mother died, he began robbing fresh graves of women who, like his mother, were middle aged, and that he also killed several women who resembled his mother.

Don Scherrer, news editor of the Argus, said Gein was buried between the graves of his brother, Henry, and his mother, Augusta.

Waushara Argus, Wednesday, August 1, 1984

# Ed Gein buried quietly at Plainfield

Ed Gein, the man who drew national attention to Plainfield 27 years ago as a result of his grisly crimes, was buried at 3 a.m. Saturday in an unmarked grave at Spiritland Cemetery in rural Plainfield.

Gein, 77, died in his sleep last Thursday morning at Mendota State Hospital, Madison. Joseph Scislowicz of the state Department of Health and Social Services said the cause of death was respiratory failure and indicated that Gein had been in poor health for several years.

The secrecy surrounding the burial indicates authorities were taking extra precautions to keep the media from further coverage. The blue colored coffin was placed between those of Henry and Augusta Gein, Ed's brother and mother. The ground was leveled and the sod replaced so nobody would be able to easily detect the presence of the gravesite.

As word spread Thursday morning of Gein's death, television crews, national media representatives and curiosity seekers descended on Plainfield. People talked in whispers as they recalled the grim details of the 1957 case that received national exposure.

The local people seemed willing to accept Gein's return, at least for burial. They were not willing to speak to the national media writers, but were willing to share their thoughts with local reporters.

"I was about ten when it happened," Stanley Golla, owner of Stosh's Sportsman's Bar in downtown Plainfield, said. "I was friends with the Worden family, referring to Gein's last victim, Bernice Worden.

"I'd like to extend my sympathy, in fact, I think I am conveying the feeling of all Plainfield residents, to the Worden family who are having to go through the trauma of this again.

"I thought it was terrible. I still think what happened back then was terrible. It's been an albatross I've carried with me. No matter where I've been people would bring up Ed Gein when they heard I was from Plainfield, Wi.

"I hope the memory of Gein's atrocity can be buried with him," Golla said. "It'll make it easier on the Wordens, and the town, now that he is gone."

The tragedy of Ed Gein began on Nov. 16, 1957. On the first day of deer hunting season Gein was arrested for the slaying of Bernice Worden, 58, who was missing from the village hardware store which she operated.

A Wood County deputy drove to Gein's farm in rural Plainfield to inquire if he had seen anything. Gein's pickup truck had been seen near the store twice that day.

The deputy found no one at home. He later returned. Looking into a lean-to at the side of the house, the deputy found Mrs. Worden's body. Later that day Gein was found and arrested.

When authorities searched the homestead they found the grisly details and remains of Gein's crimes. The authorities also discovered what they believed to be the remains of Mary Hogen, a rural tavern owner who had been missing for three years.

A room belonging to Gein's mother, Augusta, who died in 1945, was found boarded up and kept the way she apparently left it.

Later, author Robert Bloch, who lived about 50 miles from the farmhouse, used segments of the episode to structure a novel on which the Alfred Hitchcock movie "psycho" was based.

In the movie, the lead actor, Norman Bates, is obsessed by his dead mother and keeps her body in a room.

Declared unfit to stand trial for Mrs. Worden's death, Gein was sent to Central State Hospital at Waupun. In May, 1978, he was transferred to the Mendota Institute.

Authorities alleged that Gein had been robbing graves of middle aged and recently deceased women. He was finally tried for the death of Mrs. Worden in 1968.

Gein was found innocent by reason of insanity and returned to the hospital. In 1974 Gein sought his freedom and a sanity hearing. Circuit Court Judge Robert Gollmar sent Gein back to Central State Hospital.

Judge Gollmar later wrote a book about the case. He believes Gein may have been responsible for several other unexplained disappearances.

"Everybody knows where Plainfield is, but from a bad experience," said village librarian Joan Reid. "Everybody likes to be from someplace known for something good. He made it bad."

Bonnie Foster was a neighbor of Ed Gein. He worked for her father and she often served meals to the man.

"I don't have much of any feeling about it," Mrs. Foster said. "I'm just glad it's over with. Maybe it will put an end to it. This was a bad experience for our community. Hopefully, this is the closing."

Saying she was shocked beyond words when the crime was uncovered, Mrs. Foster said in retrospect she understood some of the funny ways Gein talked. She was subpoenaed to testify at the trial in Wautoma.

**EDWARD GEIN**

Edward Gein, 77, died July 26, 1984 at Mendota State Mental Institute, Madison. He was born Aug. 26, 1906 to George and Augusta Gein at La Crosse, Wisconsin. Gein had been incarcerated since 1958. There are no immediate survivors. Private internment and services were held on Friday, July 27 at 5:30 p.m. at the Plainfield Village Cemetery.

"What made it really horrid was that in a small community like this, everybody knew him," Mrs. Foster said. "He'd been in our homes and was our friend. He was just like any other neighbor or friend. It was a real shocker for us."

She remembers hundreds of cars full of curiosity seekers converging on the area after the 1957 publicity. They tramped over farmland. Media people took pictures and asked obnoxious questions of people while they were still in shock.

Somebody tried to buy the Gein farm and various objects intending to make some kind of grisly museum. The home was burned to the ground shortly before an auction was scheduled to be held. The cause of the fire was never determined.

"I think people are relieved that it's the end of a sad chapter of our history," said Ruth (Mrs. Rex) Humphrey of rural Hancock. Working at the Hancock bank at the time, Mrs. Humphrey recalls the shock and fear that engulfed the area that fall season.

"It was as if suddenly you no longer felt secure. We found ourselves locking our doors and intalling extra bolt locks."

Kathy Mugridge was another neighbor of Gein back in 1957. Although a young girl at the time, she recalled the horror of the days surrounding his arrest.

"His being buried here doesn't matter one way or the other to me. The way I look at it," she said, "there's worse people in the world that are still living and walking around than he was."

Several people discussing the death of Gein in downtown Plainfield indicated they felt the reason it seems so important here is the small rural population.

"In Milwaukee, or someplace else, they've probably got hundreds of murderers, but here it's so unusual. The crime was so heinous. It is blown all out of proportion."

Oshkosh Northwestern
July 26, 1984

## Murderer Ed Gein dies at 76

MADISON (AP) — Ed Gein, the grisly killer who 27 years ago drew national attention to the tiny Waushara County town of Plainfield, died this morning at the Mendota Mental Institute. He was 76.

Authorities who arrested Gein in November 1957 found such items as preserved human heads and lampshades and chair seats made out of human skin at his farmhouse.

Gein

Gein had been at the Mendota institute in Madison since May 1978. He was transferred there after having been almost continually at Central State Hospital at Waupun since his arrest.

His story later served as the model for Alfred Hitchcock's "Psycho." The author of the novel on which the movie was based, Robert Block, lived about 50 miles from Gein's farmhouse.

The story began to unfold on Nov. 16, 1957, when relatives of Bernice Worden, a 58-year-old widow who ran a hardware store at Plainfield, realized she was missing.

Gein's battered pickup truck had been seen near the store twice that day, and a Wood County deputy drove to Gein's farm to ask if he had noticed anything. No one was home.

He returned later and still got no answer. He looked into a lean-to at the side of the house and saw Mrs. Worden's body hanging by the heels, decapitated and "dressed out like a deer."

Gein was found in town. He was declared unfit to stand trial and was sent to Central State.

Gein's farmhouse was all cluttered except for one room that had been boarded off. It was Gein's mother's room. She died in 1945 and he left the room just as she left it.

He began robbing fresh graves of women who, like his mother, were middle aged. The women who he later killed were also believed to resemble his mother, in his view.

In 1968, he was tried in the death of Mrs. Worden. It was ruled that he was insane at the time of the crime and he was returned to the hospital.

In 1974 Gein sought a sanity hearing and asked for his freedom. But Circuit Judge Robert Gollmar sent Gein back to Central State.

Authorites testified at the time that Gein was never a problem in prison, although he reacted rather poorly to other inmates. He worked as a carpenter, mason and hospital attendant while at Central State.

He supposedly was saving his money for a dreamed-of trip around the world.

# Opinion

## The aberration known as Ed Gein

*died July 26-1984*

*Ed Gein died today, or perhaps yesterday; it really doesn't matter.*

Those paraphrased opening words from a book by French novelist Albert Camus are particularly apropos today in the wake of the passing of the man whose life symbolized the macabre, the man whose crimes were so bizarre that they seemingly belonged to another age, another civilization.

Gein died Thursday. But to the people of Wisconsin who remember the case as it developed in the 1950s, he ceased living — if he ever lived at all — when he was packed off to be institutionalized, too sick to be tried, too sick to be returned to the outside world.

In the ensuing years, arguments were made in Gein's behalf that he no longer was criminally insane, that he no longer was a threat to society, that he no longer needed to live behind bars.

But while Gein might have been ready to live with society, a questionable conclusion, it is doubtful that society ever would have been ready to live with Gein.

There were just too many memories.

Gein never earned the privacy which he so zealously sought, but it is ironic nevertheless that he spent the last 27 years of his life in the glare of headlines, in the notoriety which a criminal of his awfulness deserves, so far from the reclusiveness which his Plainfield farm provided.

We would like to think that the headlines will become smaller and even disappear, that the strange case of Ed Gein will be laid to rest along with him. But even that won't happen soon.

Oshkosh Northwestern — July 27, 1984

# Town unable to shake memory of Gein

PLAINFIELD (AP) — The death of the man whose bizarre, bone-chilling story put Plainfield on the map was not an occasion for rejoicing in this small central Wisconsin community.

Like every other bit of news about Ed Gein — who provided the model for the deranged killer of Alfred Hitchcock's film "Psycho" — the death of Gein Thursday after spending the past 27 years in a state mental hospital only revived bad memories.

"Everybody knows where Plainfield is, but from a bad experience," village librarian Joan Reid explained.

"Everybody likes to be from someplace known for something good. He made it bad."

Gein, 77, was found dead in his bed at Mendota Mental Institute in Madison at 7:45 a.m. Thursday, said Joseph Scislowicz of the state Department of Health and Social Services.

He said the cause of death was respiratory failure. Gein had been in poor health for several years, he said.

The story of Gein's escapades began unfolding Nov. 16, 1957 — the first day of deer hunting season — with his arrest for the slaying of Bernice Worden, 58, who had disappeared from the Plainfield hardware store she operated.

Gein's pickup truck had been seen near the store twice that day, and a Wood County deputy drove to Gein's farm to ask if he had noticed anything. Finding no one home, the deputy returned later, looked into a lean-to at the side of the house and found Mrs. Worden's body hanging by the heels, decapitated and "dressed out like a deer."

Authorities searched the home and found preserved human heads, female body parts, a human heart in a coffee can, lampshades fashioned from tanned human skin and a death mask of Mary Hogan, who had operated a rural tavern before disappearing three years earlier.

The room that belonged to Gein's mother before she died in 1945 was found to have been boarded up and left unchanged.

Gein was located in town and taken into custody. Found unfit to stand trial for Mrs. Worden's death, he was sent to Central State Hospital at Waupun.

Robert Bloch, author of the novel on which the 1960 movie by Hitchcock was based, lived about 50 miles from the Gein farmhouse and based his book on the episode. In the movie, the main character, Norman Bates, is obsessed by his dead mother and keeps her body in a room at his motel.

Authorities alleged that Gein had begun robbing graves of recently deceased women who, like his mother, died in middle age. Mrs. Worden and Mrs. Hogan also were believed to resemble his mother, in his view.

Gein was tried in 1968 in the death of Mrs. Worden. Ruled insane at the time of the crime, he was found innocent by reason of insanity and returned to the hospital.

In 1974, he sought a sanity hearing and asked for his freedom, but Circuit Judge Robert Gollmar sent Gein back to Central State Hospital.

He had been at the Mendota institute since May 1978, Scislowicz said.

George W. Arndt, an Appleton psychiatrist who had evaluated Gein in 1974, said the grave-robbing incidents were especially troubling to Plainfield residents, and the graves allegedly robbed by Gein were never reopened.

"It was the grave-robbing that really troubled people far more."

*Appleton Post-Crescent November 15, 1987*

# Sensitive

## Ed Gein remembered as considerate and courteous

PLAINFIELD (AP) — A psychiatrist who examined the killer whose crimes 30 years ago were said to be the inspiration for the Alfred Hitchcock movie "Psycho," remembers Ed Gein as a sensitive man.

Dr. Leonard Ganser said Gein "always acted kind of fuzzy, but was always considerate and courteous and thanked us."

On Nov. 16, 1957, Waushara County Sheriff Art Schley, looking for clues in the disappearance of 58-year-old hardware store operator Bernice Worden, visited Gein's farm home. He turned away after knocking at the back door and nearly ran into a woman's decapitated body hanging in a shed that protected the door from the weather.

Gein, who was charged with first-degree murder, was declared unfit to stand trial and was sent to the Central State Hospital in Waupun. In 1968, he was tried in Worden's death. It was judged that Gein was insane at the time of the crime and he was returned to the mental hospital.

Gein admitted killing Worden and a Portage County tavern owner in 1954. He also admitted that he robbed graves for parts of women's bodies to decorate his home.

In 1984, he died of cancer at age 77 at the Mendota Mental Health Institute in Madison.

Ganser, a retired psychiatrist for the state Department of Health and Social Services, had been asked to sit in on a lie detector test for Gein.

"At that time, they had a number of the items they had found in his home at the (state) Crime Lab," he said. "They were looking into the possibility of his being involved in other crimes."

But Ganser said officials did not detect any evidence from the interview that Gein had committed additional crimes.

"At the time, he did not seem fearful of what was going to happen to him," Ganser said. "He expressed some fear, at times, of other more aggressive patients.

"But he had no particular fear of what would happen to him as a result of his crimes. He was a sensitive man. He did not want to give offense."

*Northwestern Oct. 21, 1987*

# Famous murder trial judge dies

ELKHORN (AP) — The judge who presided over the trial of Edward Gein, one of Wisconsin's most notorious criminals and an inspiration for the Alfred Hitchcock film "Psycho", has died.

Retired Judge Robert H. Gollmar, 84, of Elkhorn, died Monday in Lakeland Hospital. He retired in 1982 as a Walworth County judge.

In 1981, Gollmar wrote a book, "Edward Gein, America's Most Bizarre Murderer," describing the 1957 case.

In the book, Gollmar detailed the death of Gein's last victim, the only one Gein was convicted of killing. Gein also was said to have made furniture from human skin and women's sexual organs.

Robert Bloch, author of the novel "Psycho," upon which the Hitchcock movie was based, has said in interviews that the Gein case was an inspiration for the book

Gein died in 1984 while confined at the Mendota Mental Health Center.

The Gein case began on Nov. 16, 1957, when a sheriff's deputy, looking for a missing Plainfield woman, discovered her decapitated body in a lean-to on Gein's farm near the town.

Inside Gein's house, police said they found death masks and lamp shades made from human skin and several human heads in plastic bags.

**POST-CRESCENT, APPLETON-NEENAH-MENASHA, WIS.** **MONDAY, NOVEMBER 29, 1999**

# PSYCHO: Rural recluse proved to be 'Maddest of the Mad'

*Post-Crescent file photo*

**ED GEIN'S RURAL PLAINFIELD** farmhouse proved to be the site of one of the state's most gruesome murder cases.

County Sheriff's Department and Waushara County Sheriff Art Schley drove to Gein's house. They had no search warrant, just a strong hunch.

Gein did not have electricity. The officers pushed open a door, entered the dark "summer kitchen" and lit a match.

Schley nearly bumped into the headless body of Mrs. Worden, 58, hanging by her ankles from a ceiling rafter. Her body had been cut open and dressed out, much the same as a hunter would field dress a deer.

A subsequent search uncovered a house of horror.

The findings, and Gein's diabolical lifestyle, were the stuff of Alfred Hitchcock's movie, "Psycho" and of the movie, "Deranged."

There were chairs, lampshades, wastebaskets and a belt made of human skin. There were bowls fashioned from human skulls, and there were skulls on bedposts. Female reproductive organs were found in containers.

Mrs. Worden's heart was in a saucepan on the cookstove, leading swiftly to speculation among lawmen that Gein was even a cannibal, something that mortified townspeople who later reported receiving packages of venison as gifts from Gein. During his stay at the asylum, Gein told psychiatrists he had never hunted deer.

Judge Gollmar, in a 1981 book he wrote about Gein, said there was evidence of cannibalism. Gein said he couldn't remember.

One of the death masks found in Gein's home was that of Mary Hogan, a 54-year-old tavern keeper who had been missing since Dec. 8, 1954. Authorities were convinced Gein killed her in the Bancroft tavern, but he was never charged.

While certainly a murderer – authorities never did determine how many times he killed, but Gollmar, in his book, said there was "strong evidence" of several – it was his grave robbing and related taking of body parts that branded Gein as a world-class ghoul and prompted Gollmar to call him "the most notorious character ever to stand before me in court."

From Gein's admissions and from what authorities were able to piece together, Gein's grave-robbing escapades would begin with the newspaper obituaries. He looked only for women. Preferably middle-age women.

He went into a dozen or so graves in at least three cemeteries, beginning shortly after his invalid mother died in 1945 until about 1954. At times, he removed the entire body. Other times, he used hacksaws and a large jackknife to remove body parts that he added to what Gollmar called his "ghoulish collection."

Authorities reopened a few of the graves, just enough to verify that Gein was telling them the truth.

With Gein safely warehoused in the asylum after a judge declared him insane on Jan. 6, 1958, there was the question of what to do with his home.

At first it was a morbid attraction for sight-seers who had to ask directions to Plainfield. Then it was where young people gathered for beer parties.

Then, to the disgust of the community, rumor was the house was going to be bought at an upcoming auction and turned into a museum. On March 20, 1958, a mysterious night time fire destroyed the building.

Gein was able to realize some money from the sale of his property. Someone paid $215 for the 1938 Chev pickup truck he used to carry Mrs. Worden's body from her tavern to his farm.

Someone else paid $760 for the maroon 1949 Ford he used to finish Mrs. Worden's fateful journey. The car was put on display at county fairs.

Until he died in the asylum, Gein talked of using his money for a long trip.

He lies between his brother, Henry, and his mother, Augusta, in an unmarked grave in Spiritland Cemetery, not far from the final resting place of Eleanore Adams, whose body he had stolen and removed to his horror chamber.

# Killer Ed Gein's grave marker stolen in Plainfield

*"Our Father, who art in heaven, hallowed be thy name. Thy Kingdom come, thy will be done on earth as it is in heaven... Amen."* — words of Rev. Desmond Jose at the graveside of Ed Gein in 1984.

**By Patricia Wolff**
OF THE NORTHWESTERN

PLAINFIELD — The most horrible of killers — even a grave robber — deserves to have part of a prayer said at his graveside.

Rev. Desmond Jose acted upon that sentiment when he delivered a shortened prayer during the burial of the man who was perhaps Wisconsin's most loathed criminal of all time: Ed Gein, the man whose fiendish fantasies and actions inspired Alfred Hitchcock's movie, "Psycho."

But Jose's words to bring a sacred ending to Gein's notoriety did little to discourage vandals and curiosity seekers from targeting the grave. Now, in a twist of irony Hitchcock himself may have appreciated, the gravestone of this grave robber has been stolen.

The theft was discovered this past weekend. While authorities have few hard facts to go on, they have some ideas about who would be interested.

Waushara County Sheriff Patrick Fox said his suspicion is that someone intent on selling the marker might have taken the headstone. He also suggested someone with an interest in the occult or Satanism.

Fox said he wouldn't be surprised if someone tried to sell the grave marker on eBay, an Internet auction site. "There are people who would pay big bucks for that."

Gein, described often as a mild-mannered farmhand, murdered women and robbed the graves of others in the Plainfield area in the 1940s and '50s. His ghoulish souvenirs —

Gein

human skulls and other body parts — were found strewn about his farmhouse near Plainfield after he was arrested for murder.

His story, as well as his grave, have attracted a lot of attention.

University of Wisconsin-Oshkosh Professor Patricia Hodgell, who teaches a course on death and strange crimes in Wisconsin, said Gein has a large cult following with a number of Web sites on the Internet. The Gein story is covered in the English course she teaches.

"I'd hate to think it was one of my students," Hodgell said.

Gein was buried in one of the cemeteries he plundered years ago.

A small stone marker, 15 inches high, 12 inches deep, and 24 inches wide, bearing Gein's name, was placed at his grave some

## His body was buried in local cemetery against objections

months after his death from cancer nearly 16 years ago.

Even though some locals, including members of his victims' families, objected, Gein was buried in the local cemetery, close to the final resting place of Bernice Worden, the 58-year-old hardware store owner he killed in 1957. Her headless body was found gutted like a deer and hanging in the old summer kitchen in his home.

Betty Petrusky, caretaker of the Plainfield Cemetery from 1969 to 1996, discovered Gein's stone missing Saturday afternoon when she went to visit her husband's grave. She contacted the sheriff's office.

Petrusky was one of a handful of people who attended Gein's burial. In fact, she and her late husband dug the grave. "We had a little back hoe. We always did an excellent job of grave-digging," she said.

In attendance were the Petruskys; two village authorities; two employees of the company that supplied the bronze-colored plastic casket and unsealed concrete vault in which Gein was buried; Jose, and the late William Belter, Gein's defense attorney.

It was Belter who paid the $75 for perpetual care of Gein's grave.

The former caretaker said that as far as she knew no one ever tried to steal the marker before, though vandalism was a common problem.

Frequently vandals removed flowers from other graves and used them to decorate Gein's grave. Petrusky often found cigarette butts and beer cans at the grave.

About eight or nine years ago, vandals smashed urns from numerous graves against Gein's marker, causing the edges to chip away. Petrusky said she often finds grafitti on the stone and evidence that people have urinated on the grave.

"Just lately I found dirty words and drawings and Satanic signs on the stone that someone did with Magic Marker," Petrusky said.

Some of the writings include "evil never dies," and the numbers "666" along with a pentagram.

Investigators have little information on which to try to recover the marker. The tombstone, which was in a remote section of the cemetery, would have been heavy and difficult to lift, Fox said.

Petrusky said she noticed two, distinct and large footprints in the sandy soil where the marker had rested before being uprooted.

For the soil to have gotten wet, the marker would have to have been removed before the rain came.

Petrusky said she was at the cemetery early last week and everything was in place.

*Oshkosh NorthWestern*
*Tuesday June 20, 2000*

*June 20 2001 paper*

# Gein's headstone makes Seattle rock scene

**By Patricia Wolff**
For The Post-Crescent

PLAINFIELD – The stolen grave marker for Ed Gein, Wisconsin's infamous grave robber and murderer from the 1950s, has been found in Seattle, Wash., but police aren't sure what to do with it.

The grave marker was taken, along with some grave dirt, about a year ago from Gein's grave in Plainfield Cemetery in northwestern Waushara County.

"We could bring it back and put it back in the cemetery, but it would only get stolen again," said Waushara County Sheriff Patrick Fox.

Gein

Members of the Waushara County Historical Society are considering placing it in the old jail museum on S. St. Marie Street near the courthouse in downtown Wautoma. Gein was in the jail briefly in the late 1950s after his grisly crimes came to light.

When Gein's grave marker was stolen last June, Fox and others expected to find it for sale on the online auction site eBay. That never happened. Instead, about a month ago Fox got a phone call from a woman who suggested a connection between the missing marker and the Seattle promoter of the rock band Angry White Males.

Police found the marker when they questioned the promoter. He had been selling rubbings of the stone for $50 each on his Internet site.

He said the marker he had was a reproduction of the original stone. Police did not buy his story, Fox said.

"It was the same granite stone, the graffiti was the same, and it was chipped in the same way," Fox said.

*Patricia Wolff writes for the Oshkosh Northwestern.*

# Notoriety ups ante of Gein property in Plainfield

*mar? 2006*

## Owner of former killer's land wants to get $250,000 for it

**The Associated Press**

WAUSAU — Mike Fisher owns land where one of Wisconsin's most notorious killers was arrested – and where body parts and clothing made from human skin were found – and now it's for sale.

Asking price? $250,000 – probably double what it's worth without its ghoulish past.

"I am just a guy who got stuck with this white elephant," Fisher said Friday about the 40 acres west of Plainfield in central Wisconsin that once contained the ramshackle home of Ed Gein and part of his farm. "I am tired of the frustrations and the headaches. I have a right to ask whatever I want for it."

Gein is the grave robber and murderer whose story inspired the movie "Psycho." He was arrested in 1957.

Fisher, who inherited the land from his grandfather, listed the property on eBay earlier this week under the heading, "Ed Gein's Farm ... The REAL deal!"

The site received more than 1,200 hits by Friday.

Fisher's sales pitch quickly drew the attention of the man leading a national campaign against sales of serial killer memorabilia.

"This is probably the highest ticket item in the murder memorabilia racket that I have seen since I have started watchdogging the industry in 1999," said Andy Kahan of Houston.

Fisher is linking a horrible crime and the notoriety of it to "hook a higher price" and that's wrong, Kahan said.

There's a market for anything linked to Gein but it's unclear whether those kinds of buyers exist when the price is as high as Fisher's land, said Kahan, victim rights director in the Houston mayor's office.

"I have not seen land for sale using a serial killer moniker as the hook," Kahan said. "Without Gein's name on it, it's just another piece of land. And at that price, no one pays attention."

Gein was arrested for murder when the headless body of a hardware store owner was found hanging at his farm. The woman's body was dressed out like a deer carcass. Investigators also found parts of other bodies. They concluded Gein had robbed graves and may have murdered other people.

A fictionalized account of Gein by writer Robert Bloch led to the Norman Bates character in Alfred Hitchcock's 1960 film classic "Psycho."

Gein, eventually ruled guilty but criminally insane, died in a mental hospital in 1984 at the age of 77.

Fisher's grandfather, Emden Schey, bid $3,883 for Gein's farm plus another $775 for the homestead site, outbuildings and 40 acres in 1958. The farmhouse on the property burned down before the auction.

**THIS PROPERTY FOR SALE** in Plainfield is where one of Wisconsin's most notorious killers — Ed Gein — was arrested and where body parts of his victims were found.
*AP photo courtesy of Mike Fisher*

Gein

# CHAPTER 5

## Ed Gein Timeline

# **Gein Family Timeline**

| | |
|---|---|
| 1873 | Ed's father George "Gee" was born. George later changed his last name to "Gein". |
| 1878 | Ed's mother Augusta Wilhelmine was born. |
| 1902 | Ed's brother Henry Gein was born on January 17. |
| 1906 | Ed Gein was born August 27th to George and Augusta Gein at their home at 612 Gould Street in La Crosse, Wisconsin. |
| 1906 | Henry Gein was 5 years old. |
| 1906 | Augusta opens A. Gein Mercantile at 914 Caledonia Street in La Crosse, Wisconsin. |
| 1913 | Ed (age 7) witnesses his parents slaughter a hog in the shed behind the store. |
| 1913 | The Gein's move to Camp Douglas, Wisconsin. |
| 1914 | Augusta moved the family to Plainfield, Wisconsin, to a 195-acre farm because she wanted to move away from the immorality of the city and the sinners that inhabited it. Ed was 8 years old. |
| 1914 | Ed and Henry began school in Roche-a-Cri Grade School. A tiny one-room building with 12 students. Ed was 8 years old. |
| 1920 | Ed graduated from eighth grade and dropped out of school. Ed was 14 years old. |
| 1940 | Ed's father George Gein dies April 1 of pneumonic fluid in the lungs at the age of 66. |
| 1942 | Ed was eligible for the draft and had to travel to Milwaukee, Wisconsin for a physical exam. He was rejected due to a growth on his left eyelid, which slightly impaired his vision. Henry was also rejected because of his age. |
| 1944 | On May 16 Henry died a sudden death under mysterious circumstances, at the age of 43. Ed and Henry were fighting a brushfire on Henry's land. Ed reported that |

|      | he was unable to locate Henry, but then led the police directly to where he lay, dead. The apparent cause of death was not consistent with injuries from the fire. Henry's body was untouched by the fire but had an apparent bump on his head. Ed is 38 years old and had his mother all to himself. |
|------|---|
| 1944 | On May 18 the County Corner listed Henry's cause of death as asphyxiation. The police dismissed the notion of foul play. |
| 1944 | Augusta suffered her first stroke in late 1944. |
| 1945 | On December 29 Augusta died of complications from a second stroke at the age of 67. Ed reacts by boarding up his mother's bedroom and sitting room trying to preserve them as if she were still alive. Ed was 39 years old. |
| 1946 | Ed continues to live on the farm and live off meager earnings from the odd jobs he did around town and babysitting. He rented out sections of land for which people would not pay him. Ed was 40 years old. |
| 1947 | February, eighteen months after Augusta's death, Ed driven by intense loneliness and what he later said to have strange visions, began to think he could raise the dead by his own will. Ed went to Spirit Land Cemetery and dug up his first victim, Grace Beggs. Ed later said he scouted the obituaries for potential bodies that reminded him of his mother. Ed did say he tried to dig up his mother, but the soil was too sandy. Ed was 41 years old. |
| 1947 | On May 1, 8-year-old Georgia Jean Weckler disappeared without a trace, leaving no suspects. The only clue found was a tire track from a Ford. She was taken at the end of her driveway after school in Fort Atkinson, WI. |
| 1950 | Ed goes to Plainfield Cemetery and digs up his second body: Elise Sparks. This would have been at the end of March or the beginning of April. Ed was 43 years old. |

| | |
|---|---|
| 1951 | Ed goes back to Plainfield Cemetery and digs up his third body: Marie Bergstrom. Ed would have taken her after February 6. |
| 1951 | Ed digs up his fourth body from the Plainfield Cemetery sometime after May 15: Mabel Everson. |
| 1951 | Ed digs up his fifth body Eleanor Adams from the Plainfield Cemetery. This would occur after August 26. Ed was 45 years old. |
| 1952 | Victor Travis, age 42, and friend Ray Burgess disappear after spending several hours at a local bar in Plainfield. No trace of them or their car was ever found. |
| 1952 | Ed digs up his sixth body from the Plainfield Cemetery. Ursula Jane Calanan was taken by Ed after November 29. Ed was 46 years old. |
| 1953 | On October 24, Evelyn Hartley age 15 is abducted while babysitting for friends at 2415 Hoeshier Street in La Crosse, Wisconsin. Her body was never found. Ed was 47 years old. |
| 1953 | Ed digs up his seventh body, Lola Foster from Hancock, Wisconsin Cemetery. Ed was 48 years old. |
| 1954 | On December 8, Mary Hogan disappears from her bar in Babcock, The Fox Head Bar. Ed killed her with a .22 caliber pistol. |
| 1955 | In November Ed digs up his eighth body, Harriet Sherman from the Plainfield cemetery. |
| 1956 | In November Ed digs up his ninth body, Alzadia B Abbott from the Spirit Land Cemetery. |
| 1957 | On November 16, Bernice Worden age 58 disappeared from her hardware store. Her son, Deputy Frank Worden returned from deer hunting to find his mother gone. Sheriff Arthur Schley responded to Frank Worden's call. Upon entering the store, he noticed blood on the floor and a .22 caliber rifle that was out of place on its rack at the store. In the receipt book, they noticed that Ed Gein had bought |

antifreeze earlier in the day. Sheriff Schley and a deputy went to Ed Gein's farm and found Bernice Worden's body hung by the rafters, gutted like a deer.

| | |
|---|---|
| 1957 | On November 17, Ed Gein was taken into custody at the home of Lester Hill. |
| 1957 | On November 18th Ed Gein confesses to killing Mary Hogan and Bernice Worden. An autopsy report reveals Mrs. Worden died of a single gunshot wound to the back of the head. Ed was 51 years old. Ed was arrested by Deputy Dan Chase. |
| 1957 | On November 22nd, Ed was taken before Judge Boyd Clark and charged with robbery. The murder charge was held back to determine his sanity. |
| 1957 | On November 23rd, the psychologist and psychiatrist who interviewed Ed asserted that he was schizophrenic. |
| 1957 | On November 24, the graves of Eleanor Adams and Marie Bergstrom were exhumed and found empty. |
| 1957 | On November 29, deputies found more bones buried in a trench on Ed's farm. |
| 1957 | On December 17, the judge received a packet from the Central State Hospital stating that Ed was insane and should be permanently committed to the hospital. |
| 1958 | On January 6, Ed has a sanity hearing in Wisconsin Rapids. He was declared legally insane by Judge Herbert Bunde and he was recommitted to Central State Hospital. |
| 1958 | On January 22 at 1:00 pm Ed's trial begins in Wautoma. |
| 1958 | On March 20, Ed's farm was burned to the ground by a mysterious fire. |
| 1958 | On March 30 anything left after the fire was auctioned off. Ed was 52 years old. |
| 1962 | All body remains found on Ed Gein's property were returned from Madison State Crime Lab to Plainfield to be buried in a mass unmarked grave. |
| 1968 | On January 22, after spending ten years in an institution, Ed was determined to be competent to stand trial and the proceedings began. It took 9 months to pass the preliminary matters such as evidence, filing for briefs and appointment of counsel. |

| | |
|---|---|
| 1968 | On November 7, the actual trial begins. |
| 1968 | On November 14th, Ed Gein was found guilty of first-degree murder for the shooting of Bernice Worden, but the court also found that on the day of the shooting, Ed was not insane. Ed was returned to Central State Hospital. Ed was 62 years old. |
| 1968 | On March 22nd Sheriff Arthur Schley, the arresting officer, died of a heart attack at age 60. |
| 1974 | Ed filed a petition with the Waushara County Clerk of Courts claiming that he has now recovered from his mental illness, is fully competent and wants to be released. |
| 1974 | On June 27, a judge reviewed Ed's petition and ordered a re-examination. The judge rejected Ed's petition and he was returned to the hospital. Ed was 68 years old. |
| 1978 | Ed was moved to the Mendota Mental Institute in Madison. Ed was 72 years old. |
| 1984 | On July 26, Ed was senile and after a long battle with cancer, died of respiratory failure in the geriatric ward at Mendota. Ed was 78 years old. |
| 1984 | On July 27, at 4:00 pm Ed Gein was buried by Bennie P. and Betty J. Petrusky in a blue casket, between his mother and brother. |

# Final Thoughts

The following comments are my own opinions after hours of research into the history of Ed Gein. One of the first questions people have asked me about Ed is, "Was he a cannibal, and did he ever have sex with his victims?" My answer has always been no. After going over all the interviews the police and psychologists had with Ed Gein, I noticed that Ed always seemed to tell the truth. Now, he did admit to trying to have sex with Bernice Worden's body, but he could not achieve an erection. He also admitted that the bodies smelled bad of embalming fluid.

Another question people have asked me about was how Ed Gein got the idea of making things out of human skin and remains. Ed Gein was an avid reader of true crime and World War 2 atrocities that the Germans did to the prisoners in the concentration camps. After the defeat of Nazi Germany, claims circulated that Ilse Koch, wife of the commandant of Buchenwald concentration camp, had possessed lampshades made of human skin and had specifically tattooed prisoners killed to use their skin for this purpose.

Ed's mother, Augusta, always wanted a daughter, and when she decided to have a second child, she was disappointed when her son Ed was born and was not shy about telling him that. Ed always wanted to please his mother and, therefore, wanted to become a girl, so that is why he built the "skin suit," so he could be a girl.

Ed Gein will always be part of history and be linked to the town of Plainfield, Wisconsin. Unfortunately, that will never change for the people of Plainfield.

Made in the USA
Monee, IL
20 August 2025

22633678R00136